D0397619

Fool's Paradise

Stewart Justman

FOOL'S PARADISE

The Unreal World of Pop Psychology

WITHDRAWN
NM STATE LIBRARY
NM STATE LIBRARY
JAN 1 3 2006
SANTA FE, NM

Ivan R. Dee

Chicago 2005

FOOL'S PARADISE. Copyright © 2005 by Stewart Justman. All rights reserved, including the right to reproduce or store this book or portions thereof in any form. For information, address: Ivan R. Dee, Publisher, 1332 North Halsted Street, Chicago 60622. Manufactured in the United States of America and printed on acid-free paper.

www.ivanrdee.com

Library of Congress Cataloging-in-Publication Data:
Justman, Stewart.
  Fool's paradise : the unreal world of pop psychology / Stewart Justman.
    p. cm.
  Includes bibliographical references and index.
  ISBN 1-56663-628-0 (hardcover : alk. paper)
    1. Psychology—United States—History—20th century. 2. Popular culture—United States—History—20th century. 3. Psychological literature—United States—History—20th century. I. Title.
  BF108.U5.J87 2005
  150'.973—dc22   2005005360

To Michael Mayer, historian

Preface

A CELEBRITY PSYCHOLOGIST maintains that society has robbed me of my authentic self; that every standard, precept, and prohibition imposes on my selfhood; that what is inherited from the past is false; that I myself am the only truth in a world of lies; that I must challenge "virtually everything"; that I must "wipe the slate clean and start over." Each of these dicta is a commonplace of pop psychology, and each has almost unimaginably radical implications.

Where did pop psychology come from? What are its promises—and its fallacies?

This book traces the inspiration of the pop psychology movement to the utopianism of the 1960s and argues that it consistently misuses the rhetoric of civil rights. Speaking as it does in the name of my right to happiness, pop psychology promises liberation from all that interferes with my power to create the self I want. In so doing it not only defies reality but corrodes the traditions and attachments that give depth and richness to human life.

I would like to acknowledge the work and the example of Frederick Crews, a keen satirist and a critic of the recovered-memory movement, the ink-blot test, and other impostures and crazes.

Contents

Fool's Paradise

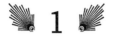

The Golden Path to
Self-realization

"Plagued by anxiety, depression, vague discontents, a sense of inner emptiness, the 'psychological man' of the twentieth century seeks . . . peace of mind under conditions that increasingly militate against it. Therapists . . . become his principal allies in the struggle for composure; he turns to them in the hope of achieving the modern equivalent of salvation, 'mental health.'" Thus Christopher Lasch, writing in 1979 in *The Culture of Narcissism.* By narcissism Lasch meant not conventional self-love but an anxious craving for audience and admiration born of a void within, and maybe it is some such hunger that calls forth the flattering assurances that are pop psychology's note, as when a counselor reminds his unseen reader of "how wondrous and interesting you can be."

The influence of pop psychology now extends from the preschool to the university, from the clinic to the church. Such is the fashion for therapy that it is now offered not only in the psychologist's office—the modern confessional—but on television and radio and, as in the instance just cited, in print. It is the print genre of pop psychology that I explore in this book. Somewhere in this vast field there may be a few who do not subscribe to the dubious doctrines probed here. I am prepared to admit these as honorable exceptions.

Some might ask, Why bother investigating something as vacuous as pop psychology? Its influence is reason enough. Employing the rhetoric of civil rights and drawing on the tradition of dissent even as it celebrates liberation from the past, pop psychology is designed to appeal, and it does. It seems to own a share of the best-seller lists and speaks a language all know by heart. An institution of such magnitude calls for scrutiny. Much as the absurd but academically fashionable doctrine that the laws of science are socially constructed would matter even if it never impeded the activity of science, so I think the theories and precepts of pop psychology would merit inquiry even if they never inspired accusations, on the basis of recovered memories and suspect testimony, of the sexual abuse of children.

Oddly, though, while pop psychology has lent its authority to criminal prosecutions, it has also established the doctrine that blame is destructive—that it warps our humanity. If the historian Gertrude Himmelfarb is right that the aversion to moral judgment "is now so firmly entrenched in the popular vocabulary and sensibility that one can hardly imagine a time without it," it is above all pop psychology, with its pejorative use of the word "judgment," that underwrites this attitude. No other influence, certainly no academic trend, compares. Academic trends are like dry lightning, producing flash, spectacle, and spot fires. Pop psychology is a steady soaking rain that reaches down to the roots of our common life. It not only works itself into general speech but, as I hope to show, alters the uses of words. The dissemination of a language in which it is possible to say, "You 'fall in love' with yourself in much the same way that you fall in love with another," in which the therapist can promise the reader, "Soon you have a whole new history," challenges one's sense of reality.

Like its message that human beings will become moral only if and when they repudiate what the world calls morality, pop psychology's promise of "a whole new history" and its use of a kind of alternative language identify it as a utopian project. In Sir Thomas More's Utopia, all cities are built on the same plan, that of King Utopus himself, the commonwealth's founder. Theory precedes reality. The counselor can assure his reader of "how wondrous and interesting you can be" without ever having laid eyes on this person, because his theory dictates not only that the reader is wondrous and that the reader has lost cognizance of this truth, but that the reader can nevertheless recover the knowledge of his or her own wonder with the proper help—which is a lot of presumption to be packed into a single phrase. (Not only memories but our true selves are forgotten and recovered in the world of pop psychology.) To readers unknown, a psychologist can declare, "You may not know how or why your relationship got into such a mess, but I do know. I know what you're going through, and I know how it all happened." Theory precedes evidence.

The theory that living is a matter of technique, and that techniques are best learned from experts—one of the axioms of pop psychology—has ties to the utopian tradition itself. Charlotte Perkins Gilman's utopia *Herland* (1915) is a fictionalization of theories advanced in her own *Women and Economics* (1898), among them the doctrine that with the evolution of humanity, chores like cooking and cleaning will pass to "the hands of trained experts." The Herlanders are unwilling to entrust child-rearing "to unskilled hands." Pop psychology, in the spirit of Herland, argues that child-rearing ("parenting") must submit to the findings of the appropriate experts if it is to evolve into an enlightened practice—and the writers of advice literature profess to be those experts. The genre thus certifies and advertises its own importance.

There is something self-referential about pop psychology. Authors construct the success stories that verify their doctrines, Stephen Covey cites his own dictates like natural laws (indeed, he insists they *are* natural laws), Melody Beattie in *The Language of Letting Go* quotes Melody Beattie in *Codependent No More* and *Beyond Codependency*, and the entire pop psychology genre seems involved in itself in the same way, as if it really were captivated by its own reflection.

More's Utopia, severed from the mainland by its founder; the island of the rational horses in *Gulliver's Travels*; Herland itself, surrounded by sheer cliffs; Orwell's Oceania—all are more or less closed systems. One of the fathers of humanistic psychology, Abraham Maslow, liked to speculate about an ideal society founded by a thousand self-actualizers on a desert island. Theirs too would be a closed system. Pop psychology, lacking "external validation" of its prescriptions, is a desert island in our midst. Exhorting us to erase the influences that shaped us, to "wipe the slate clean" (a utopian undertaking in itself), pop psychology then addresses our emptiness. The failure of one self-help system sends readers to another, which likewise will not work because, morally speaking, it too defies gravity. You can't write your own life as if you were a character you invented. Surely it is the inefficacy, not the efficacy, of self-help that keeps the genre going. "Perhaps the *next* book will provide the answers, the comfort, the cure, the secrets being sought." The single-minded search for happiness is liable to be self-defeating. Life's enjoyments, John Stuart Mill discovered,

> are sufficient to make it a pleasant thing, when they are taken *en passant*, without being made a principal object. Once make them so, and they are immediately felt to be insufficient. They will not bear a scrutinising examination. Ask yourself whether you are happy, and you cease to be so.

Readers of self-help prescriptions are drawn into an incessant scrutiny of their own happiness or lack of it. The rhetoric of self-help—its promises, declarations of emergency, urgings and warnings, commands, prayers, assurances—summons one into an endless maze.

Like a closed system, self-help manuals virtually quote one another, urging readers to live in the moment and accept no precepts but their own. The genre gives every appearance of feeding on itself. Can it be that instead of curing ailments it promotes an ailment—inflames an obsession with the recovery of one's true self which, both because of the irrational nature of obsession and the imaginary nature of one's true self, cannot possibly be satisfied? Self-help books generate more of the same because a quest for the true self is a quest without an object.

Although I don't believe in the supremacy of therapeutic categories, one aim of this book is indeed the curative one of exposing fallacy and pretense. If now and then the tone turns satiric, satire itself undertook to cure illusion long before psychiatrists, counselors, personal coaches, therapists, and bibliotherapists ever did. In the self-help manual *Excess Baggage: Getting Out of Your Own Way*, the particular need that dominates one's personality is designated a ruling passion. "Ruling passion" was once a term of moral, and satiric, psychology.

Swift would have been at home with it. Dickens's characters seem ruled by their passions, stuck like jammed mechanisms. Among the targets of Dickensian satire is the kind of success story told in Samuel Smiles's *Self-Help* (1859), which today's self-help authors do not recognize as a prototype of their stories of psychological success.

Why does pop psychology flourish? The boldness of its promises would be one reason. The author of *You Can Negotiate Anything* (a best-seller twenty-five years ago) probably didn't believe you can negotiate a new existence, but a new existence is just what the self-help genre promises, at times in so many words. That promise in turn would find few takers if not for a widely held belief that within us, at our core, there exists the potential of another life and another self—our true self. But if the governing trope of the pop psychology movement is that we have become estranged from this true self (or lost the well-being that is our birthright and our natural state), that belief was identified by the scholar of romanticism M. H. Abrams as enjoying "wide currency" on the other side of the Atlantic some two hundred years ago. In the age of Wordsworth and Coleridge, and under the double impact of the French and Industrial Revolutions, the belief arose that "man, who was once well, is now ill, and that at the core of the modern malaise lies his fragmentation, dissociation, estrangement, or (in the most highly charged of these parallel terms), 'alienation.'" Writing in 1971, Abrams remarked,

> These ideas are shared in our time by theologians, philosophers, economists, sociologists, psychologists, artists, writers, critics, and readers of *Life* magazine and *The Reader's Digest*, and the copious writings on this theme have been assembled into widely-read anthologies.

Evidently a belief that we have been separated from our true selves accompanies the formation and haunts the success of a modern commercial society governed largely by impersonal mechanisms.

Although pop psychology is hostile to tradition, which it envisions as threatening to the self, its theme of the loss and recovery of authenticity is itself, by now, traditional, even generic. The experiments of the romantics have become the conventions and dogmas of the therapists. When Wordsworth wrote, "The Child is the father of the Man," could he have envisioned Inner Child exercises? When he and others dreamed of humanity's recovery from alienation, could they have imagined the recovery movement? In any case, maladies of the spirit that in one form or another have existed for some two centuries are not about to be cured by workbooks and exercises. Acceptance of our own condition, with all of its fragmentation, seems wiser at this point than the pursuit of panaceas.

☞ In making the now-celebrated argument in the Preface to the *Lyrical Ballads* (1800) that nothing distinguishes good poetry from good prose except meter, Wordsworth transposed the criticism of "artificial distinctions," and the leveling impulse, from politics to poetry. Pop psychology transposes utopianism from the political register of the 1960s to a therapeutic one. But the spark was already there. In 1961, a few years before the outbreak of the social revolt, Maslow was asked how we can work toward a healthy society. He replied,

> The primary tool we now have for doing this, and I suppose the best way for doing it, is by psychoanalysis or some other form of depth analysis with the help of a skilled person. However,

since this is not a very practical suggestion for most of us, certainly not for most of mankind, we must turn our attention to more and more mass techniques of helping the person to discover this precious human nature deep within himself—this nature that he is afraid of expressing.

Those mass techniques became pop psychology—its most cherished doctrine that within us we bear an undiscovered self—but not before an upheaval set events in motion. If humanistic psychology was a spark, the social revolt of the 1960s, with its indictment of an inauthentic society, was the wind that set the fire racing.

In turn, the utopianism of the 1960s, codified in Charles Reich's *The Greening of America* (1970), settled into the institution of pop psychology. Where the counterculture celebrated by Reich sought "to disavow the very idea of the past," the therapists have made that wish into a program and an industry, admonishing us even now to start living "instead of continuing in the old direction that is grounded in a tired, outdated, and irrelevant history." Those who tell us to turn off the past have at this point several decades, and an infinity of repetition, behind their exhortations. The very word "irrelevant" echoes the cry of "relevance" raised in the 1960s. Likewise, the counterculture's aim of "displacing Dick-Jane-Spot-Baby" grew into the standard exercises of the self-help genre, where readers learn to liberate themselves, one little step at a time, from their own upbringing. At the beginning of *Self Matters*, Phil McGraw, the influential psychologist, confesses that his own life reached an impasse some years before. It is the same impasse reached by Reich's Consciousness II:

Consciousness II is the victim of a cruel deception. It has been persuaded that the richness, the satisfactions, the joy of life are to be found in power, success, status, acceptance, popularity, achievements, rewards, excellence.

According to Reich, those of insufficiently advanced consciousness "wear themselves out in pursuit of a self that is not their own"—which has become the story line of pop psychology as well as the story Phil McGraw tells of himself. For that matter, the countercultural refrain "Do your own thing" was an invention of Dr. Fritz Perls, originally a psychoanalyst, later the father of Gestalt Therapy.

As its name suggests, the counterculture opposed the mainstream. Pop psychology is a counterculture so fully institutionalized that it *belongs* to the mainstream. Where the dissident psychiatry of the 1960s held that "madness is health," pop psychology markets the paradox that blame is blameworthy and morality immoral. It preaches against preaching and instructs you to unlearn. "Thou shalt not" it replaces with "Do it." Objecting to what it calls the programming of the self, pop psychology undertakes to reprogram it with its own formulas, instructions, and exercises. To a culture that values achievement, it replies that the self cannot be measured by achievement. Dedication to a high standard it labels perfectionism; obligation it redefines as obligation to self. As in the story of Phil McGraw, success in pop psychology often spells failure; failure on the other hand is the seed of enlightenment. In stark contrast to our legal customs, those accused in the pages of self-help books are always presumed guilty and never allowed to speak for themselves. In one notable work of the self-help school, the Golden Rule itself is inverted. In pop psychology the oppositional spirit of the counterculture has become a reflex, a doctrine, a program.

By the end of the sixties, countercultural activism was already shading into therapy, as psychodrama, encounter groups, and the like became the new idiom of revolt. Esalen Institute at Big Sur, a sort of laboratory of countercultural theory and practice, became a hub for psychiatrists and psychologists, one of whom, William Schutz (inventor of the encounter group) wrote in the 1967 best-seller *Joy*, "The time is now. We'd better hurry. The culture is already getting to [the author's infant son]—Ethan looks as if he is beginning to feel frightened and guilty." The declaration of a state of emergency; the indictment of "the culture" as an all-enveloping menace; the myth that we come into the world filled with joy and authenticity, which we are then deprived of; the portrayal of guilt as a force destroying our well-being from within—these are the buds and shoots of pop psychology as we know it today.

The student revolt for its part, driven as it was by the assumption that American society was sick, felt an attraction to the language of therapy from the beginning. With its affirmation of the human "potential for self-cultivation, self-direction, self-understanding, and creativity," the 1962 Port Huron Statement of the Students for a Democratic Society—the manifesto of the student revolt—was already spinning potentially endless compounds of the word "self," just as the therapists and counselors of the next generation would do. Offering readers the means to cure themselves without submitting to psychiatric authority, and without spending a lot of money in a lengthy analysis, the genre of self-help might be construed as a version of the SDS ideal of participatory democracy. Patients become their own doctor. An SDS statement like "The goal of man and society should be human independence: a concern not with image or popularity but with finding a meaning in life that is personally authentic" is pop psychology in the making. To this day it is the text of innumerable psychological sermons.

But so too is the indictment of society in the broadest terms being reproduced over and over to this day. The preferred psychiatrist of the counterculture of the 1960s, R. D. Laing, maintained not only that madness is health, but that "from the moment of birth you are programmed to become a human being, but always as defined by your culture and your parents and your educators," a theme repeated ever since in the self-help genre like a program in its own right. Pop psychology doesn't just deliver the comforting—and many would say innocuous—message that you the unseen reader are a person of worth; it alleges that your knowledge of your own worth has been blocked by a hostile force, identified by Phil McGraw as a "devastating conspiracy" encompassing not only "your parents, teachers, friends, spouse, employers" but "the whole of society."

To the spirit of positive thinking that once ruled advice literature, the pop psychology movement adds a tone of accusation and a rhetoric of rights that grow out of the era of the student revolt and the civil rights revolution. As I will argue, pop claims like "You have the right to be who you are and how you are" usurp and trivialize the language of civil rights. I concentrate on works of the self-help genre that date from the 1960s and later, seeking to identify and evaluate their utopian features. (The same SDS statement quoted above also notes with regret "the pervading feeling that . . . our times have witnessed the exhaustion of Utopias.") The utopianism of pop psychology consists of more than a leaven of innocent fantasy. A discussion of utopianism in Karl Popper's *The Open Society and Its Enemies* is prefaced with a comment from a novel by one Roger Martin du Gard: "Our whole damned civilization has got to go before we can bring any decency into the world."

Pop psychology doesn't say this but sometimes implies it, replete as the genre is with denunciations of "our culture," "our society," "the Western model."

Pop psychology is especially hostile to the family, frequently spoken of as the seedbed of human affliction and the primary threat to selfhood, and in this too it recalls not just the countercultural animus against Dick-Jane-Spot-Baby but the utopian tradition. From the guardians of Plato's republic, who hold wives and children in common, to the rational horses of *Gulliver's Travels*, who have no special feeling for their mates and simply apply to the island council for a replacement if one of their foals should die, the family in many utopias (and many communes inspired by utopian literature and lore) either doesn't exist or is subordinated to the one big happy family of the community. With all its citizens theoretical siblings of Big Brother, Orwell's Oceania turns children against their actual parents. According to the psychiatrist and popular authority M. Scott Peck, therapy often begins with "putting . . . parents on trial"—in absentia.

A master of literary criticism and a reader of Orwell, Lionel Trilling observed in one of his final essays that "virtually all novels used to be about" how a life was constructed: "how you were born, reared, and shaped, and then how you took over and managed for yourself as best you could." In outline, this is just how pop psychology conceives the course of a human life, except that "taking over" now means uprooting the influences that shaped you, and "managing" doesn't mean getting by but engineering the self you desire. The fantastic quality of this fable of self-authorship, repeated over and over in the pages of advice literature, generates strange precepts—for example, the duty to "challenge everything in your life that you can identify . . . as having been adopted out of history or tradition." Inasmuch as the English language comes to us through history and tradition, pop psychology must therefore challenge the very tongue it is written in. (Maslow once said, "I have had to make up . . . words because the English language is rotten for good people.") Only in the alternative language of pop psychology is it possible to say that "the best we do . . . is whatever we do."

In another of his late essays, this one expressing powerfully, though by implication, his disagreement with the utopian movements of the 1960s, Trilling discusses the expurgation of human life in a utopian romance by William Morris. Life, writes Trilling (citing William James), "feels like a fight," and literature too has its share of rivalry, showmanship, "competitive aggressivity." I refer to works of literature in this study not only because pop psychology itself does, but because literature gives rich expression to ridicule, parody, contest, and other modes of action that pop psychology prohibits. The energy of satire flows through literature like an animating principle, making itself felt not just as scorn and indignation but in modes as diverse as genius. Satirists appearing in these pages range from Chaucer to our contemporary David Lodge, from Swift to Dostoevsky, from Erasmus to the competitive Dickens, all of whom say things that cannot be said and do things that cannot be done within the confines of pop psychological doctrine. Doctors, system builders, buyers and sellers of delusion (at times the same person), speakers of jargon—for centuries these have been the special objects of satire. The Friar of the *Canterbury Tales*, hearing confession sweetly, soothing the spiritually uneasy, anticipates today's therapist offering the balm of enlightened counsel.

"Watch out for shame. Many systems and people reek of shame. They are controlled by shame and may want us to play their game with them. They may be hoping to hook us and control us through shame. We don't have to fall into their shame. Instead, we'll take the good feelings—self-acceptance, love, and nurturing." Perhaps because pop psychology can offer little support for its theories and assurances, it makes the questioning of them seem like attacks on love. As in the instance just cited, the advice author poses as a true friend—indeed, one's only true friend—whose counsels spring from the benevolence not to be found in the outside world. To any potential critic, the advice-giver seems to say, "To dispute me is to assault those in suffering." Surrounding itself with heavy rhetorical fortifications of this kind, pop psychology seeks to block, and by and large *has* blocked, the thoughtful scrutiny that such expansive claims about the world and the self might be expected to receive. Its heightened rhetoric, its pathos and prayers and promises, its direct address of the reader (as if transcending all that usually alienates people from one another), its posture of selfless devotion to the reader (in high contrast to everyone else's indifference and cruelty), its proclamations of its own truth—all serve to cloak the poverty of a genre of secondhand theories.

While utopian literature at its most interesting, like More's *Utopia*, cannot be taken at face value, pop psychology's every word is supposed to be a word to live by, quite as if irony of any kind would disrupt the confidential bond between writer and reader. In accordance with this sort of literal-mindedness, the self-help genre speaks of the ideal self as something that actually exists and can actually be reclaimed. "There is a whole other level of existence, distinct from what you do, that is the real, true, genuine sum and substance of who you are." If a doctrine were designed to promote evasion, could it do so more effectively? For if I have a real self quite distinct from my daily self, then I can say that any act of deceit or cruelty I may commit from day to day doesn't really tell against me—all the more because pop psychology recognizes no obligation beyond that to my own happiness anyway. The real, true, genuine Platonic self clears the deeds of its empirical counterpart.

It is ironic that this familiar and potent technique of moral dissociation should be authorized, wittingly or not, by those who profess to be expert in the ways of the human mind. Writing in 1992, Wendy Kaminer paraphrased the message of the self-help movement:

> No matter how bad you've been in the narcissistic 1970s and the acquisitive 1980s, no matter how many drugs you've ingested, or sex acts performed, or how much corruption enjoyed, you're still essentially innocent: the divine child inside you is always untouched by the worst of your sins.

By the same token, pop psychology promises that no matter what you continue to do, you are still in the clear. Pop psychologists are indeed successors of the enterprising clerics of the Canterbury pilgrimage, dispensing indulgences and absolution.

If advice authors agree that an authentic self, quite distinct from the everyday self, actually exists, this doesn't mean that all of them have arrived through investigation at the same finding. It simply signifies that all adhere to the same doctrine. On less doctrinal matters, the consensus breaks down. One classic of the genre, written by a psychiatrist, features a section entitled "The Healthiness of Depression"; another, also by a psychiatrist, maintains that

> However mild and chronic, or severe and acute, depression never fails to hurt, scare, destroy function and happiness, and to kill part of the limited time a human being has to feel happy on this earth of ours. Many people have been depressed for so

long that they no longer know they are depressed. . . . In speaking to very depressed people I have often had the feeling that they have been living in closest concert with a deadly enemy who has never let up in torturous occupation and castigation for even a moment.

For his part, Wayne Dyer, uninterested in "deep-rooted psychological explanations," takes the view that depression is caused by inaction and cured by action. The absence of such disagreements over the core doctrines of pop psychology (such as the existence of the authentic self and the threat posed to this self by blame and guilt) signifies only that these doctrines have been elevated beyond the possibility of disagreement, to the status of principles. In utopia all think fundamentally alike.

I have mentioned the therapists' campaign against "our society" and "the Western model." In 1965, Abraham Maslow, addressing a community of former drug addicts that seemed to him "a little Utopia," portrayed the outside world as dishonest, friendless, and insane. With the ascent of pop psychology, judgments like this began to be made as if they were scarcely controversial findings of professional expertise. Portraying the United States as a virtual concentration camp, an author just cited, a medical doctor, asserts that "our culture dictates extreme harshness and punitive measures when violation of any of its dictates and standards are revealed [sic]." He likens a strong conscience to a Nazi guard. "We live in a state of inner terror." (This sort of rhetoric becomes more comprehensible when one remembers how loosely charges of fascism were thrown around only a few years before.) Declares a psychiatrist, "We live in a cowardly, death-denying culture." Announces a therapist, "Sexism, racism, ageism, and homophobia are outgrowths of an addictive society," that is, American society. According to another therapist, ours is a "culture that is rife with girl-hurting 'isms,' such as sexism, capitalism, and lookism." Self-help writers make sweeping accusations as health propositions. A genre that disparages judgment, turning the very word into an epithet, makes the most venomous judgments freely. A genre that intones the beauty of growth retails juvenile views and resentments. And these too mirror the utopianism of an earlier decade. A survey and celebration of social experiments of the day, compiled in 1972 under the title of *Utopia, U.S.A.*, concludes by exposing the "conditioning" that adapts us one and all to "a basically possessive, competitive, acquisitive, sexist, self-emasculating, and unsharing social order." "It takes time to change ingrained habits and defensive behaviors," the author continues. "It takes time to overcome our conditioned authoritarianism, paternalism, and self-deprecation. . . . Where [the utopian movement] will lead is not known, but a new and self-aware beginning is now being made." The utopian movement led to the pop psychology movement. Indeed, *Utopia, U.S.A.*'s last word to the reader is a call to join "encounter and sensory awareness groups" and to "remember you are not what you want to be but still mostly the product of the old ways." The drive to overcome the ingrained habit of self-deprecation and make yourself, at last, what you want to be—this became the program of pop psychology. From the revolt against the establishment came the established clichés of our era.

Before the 1960s the self-help genre of the twentieth century was fueled largely by the spirit of positive thinking, the same spirit that made the Little Engine That Could say, "I think I can, I think I can"—which in turn is but a simplified way of saying what the practitioners of "autosuggestion" repeated to themselves: "Day by day, in every way, I am getting better and better." (The 1980s version of this mantra: "Today I like myself more than yesterday. Tomorrow I will like myself even more.") Let this correspondence index some of the parallels between popular culture and popular psychology. The chain of stores named The Gap advertises the legendary generation gap of the 1960s, incorporated into pop psychology at every turn. *The Aquarian Conspiracy* proclaims the advent of the age of Aquarius, just as the song says. *Looking Out for #1*, the title of a bestseller of the 1970s, became a Toyota slogan. A few years after the movie *The Exorcist* came Scott Peck's justification of exorcism in *People of the Lie*. A few years after the sensational story of "Sybil" and her multiple personalities came the multiple-personality revolution. The 1980s crusade against the sexual abuse, real and imagined, of children coincided with Alice Walker's *The Color Purple* (whose heroine endures such abuse), the movie version of which featured Oprah Winfrey. The recovery movement fed off television talk shows, and vice versa.

If psychologists can sound like advertisers (as when Carl Rogers acclaimed the encounter group as "the most rapidly spreading social invention of the century, and probably the most potent"), so too does advertising echo pop psychology. "Be all you can be," the Army slogan, has the ring of something from the human potential movement. Nike's slogan, "Just do it," reiterates the self-help theme "Try changing 'Do your best' to simply 'Do.'" "Challenge everything," the slogan of a computer game, is the message of Phil McGraw in two words. Like the repetitions so frequent in the self-help world—a nonconforming sect now become an established church—popular culture accustoms us to doctrines and dogmas that might otherwise appear strange and presumptuous.

2

Pop Psychology as a Utopian Enterprise

A century ago the identification of morality as an institution at once odious and unhealthy was already taking shape in the minds of many Americans. With the magical vitriol of his pen, H. L. Mencken fixed the image of the new puritan as a moral killjoy. "In the same way that birth-control champions succeeded in joining their cause with the cherished liberal values of progress and freedom," a scholar has written,

> Mencken joined his with the winning modern values of sophistication and urbanity. And the distinguishing mark of the modern sophisticate was the hard-won ability to detach aesthetic from moral judgment—the capacity to regard *all* aspects of the human condition without blanching or passing moral judgment.

It was in the spirit of the modern sophisticate that Freud's nephew Edward Bernays launched his career around the same time by stirring up public discussion of venereal disease. The virtual inventor of public relations as we know it, and perhaps the closest thing to a stage manager of the public realm the United States has ever had, Bernays went on to promote clients, crazes, and causes from Lucky Strikes to racial equality. But if public relations has to do with the planting of certain impressions in people's minds, the triumph of the art may be the popularization, by now, of the image of morality itself as a dark and indeed immoral institution, and the corresponding celebration of therapy as an emancipation from all such backwardness. That morality is a repressive force and a shackle on human progress now is a first principle in the pop psychology that fills sections of bookstores, pours forth from the television and radio, and has somehow established itself even in the classroom. Such a saturation of our common space with a single reductive message was beyond the abilities of even Edward Bernays.

☞ "You are sold 'self-improvement' the same way you're sold everything else: it's easy, five simple steps; you can't help succeeding, because you're so wonderful; your results will be fast, fast, fast. But we are paying dearly—in more ways than one—for this polluting flood of psychobabble." "It is amazing to me how this country is overflowing with marital therapies, psychiatrists and psychologists, counselors, healers, advice columnists, and self-help authors, yet their approach to relationships is usually so embarrassing that I want to turn my head in shame."

This from the well-known psychologist and self-help author Phil McGraw, associate of Oprah Winfrey. Evidently the writer exempts his own book from his indictment of the self-help genre. And just as his counsel represents a saving exception in a world of lies, so the message beamed from every page is that you—for the author, like so many others in the genre, writes in the second person—represent a saving spark of possibility in a false world.

> The world is not devoted to your nurturance. It is devoted to your *conformity* and *compliance*, independent of how that dovetails with your gifts, skills, abilities, wants, and visions. . . . The marketing machines, your parents, employers, friends, all have needs for you to be a certain way. And in all likelihood, you have complied with and conformed to those expectancies, at the expense of your own gifts, abilities, and dreams.

Statements like this run like a refrain through the self-help genre. They filled the pages of Wayne Dyer before they filled the pages of Phil McGraw. In one of his books, identifying him on the cover and on the top of every other page as Dr., Dyer admonishes the reader that "By conceding special titles like 'doctor' [to various professionals] you are constantly putting yourself in inferior positions." Evidently because of his uniquely good intentions, Dyer like McGraw is able to make an exception in his own favor. In the imagination of McGraw and Dyer among others, parents, society, even the world—everyone but the therapist—is in league against the reader. So it is that each and every reader receives the assurance that he or she is free of the hypocrisy and cruelty that blight every other reader. "This is a book about you—no one else, just you," says Mc-Graw in the first chapter of a book identified on its cover as "the #1 *New York Times* Bestseller," read by a multitude.

About the sheer volume of psychological counsel on the market Phil McGraw seems to me quite right. To the naked eye, the multitude of competing self-help books, with their inspirational systems and alluring promises, resemble so many diet plans—plans that notoriously do not work, as McGraw says of all therapies not his own. (McGraw himself has published a diet.) Pop psychology speaks a babel of dialects. Jerry Rubin, the renowned radical of the 1960s, records that from 1971 to 1975 he "directly experienced est [Erhard Seminars Training], gestalt therapy, bioenergetics, rolfing [therapeutic massage], massage, jogging, health foods, tai chi, Esalen, hypnotism, modern dance, meditation, Silva Mind Control, Arica [a salad of mystical notions], acupuncture, sex therapy, Reichian therapy, and More House—a smorgasbord course in New Consciousness." To this day pop psychology remains a smorgasbord—not of philosophies but of programs and styles. McGraw uses a slangy Texas style, sounding a certain populist note of "They're robbing you blind"; John Gray, best known for *Men Are from Mars, Women Are from Venus*, is more Californian. Both seem to prefer the decimal system to the recovery movement's twelves and sevens: McGraw refers us to the Ten Laws of Life, Gray to the Ten Love Tanks responsible for emotional health. The robust McGraw offers one diet, the astral Gray another, and so on down the self-help aisle. Some pop psychology is politically driven, some indifferent to politics altogether. Nevertheless, underlying the genre is a constant: the repudiation of everything traditionally known as, or associated with, morality.

In *On Being a Real Person* (1943), the minister and counselor Harry Emerson Fosdick declared that "Moral ideals, stiff, rigid, and promiscuously applied, can do incalculable harm." The pop psychology movement maintains that morality *does* do incalculable harm. Where morality speaks of obligation, pop psychology asserts my supreme obligation to myself—the obligation, that is, to confront and overcome all that stands between me and happiness. If, as Phil McGraw says, the world is devoted not to my happiness but to my unhappiness, then by internalizing morality I have simply bought into what the world says—consumed the poison. Pop psychology views guilt, therefore, as a curse cast on the self, a toxic delusion. Through all the trends and changes of the genre over the past quarter-century, these messages have persisted. Wrote Wayne Dye in 1976, "The world is full of 'shoulds' that people apply to their behavior without evaluation, and the total of these shoulds makes up a very large erroneous zone"—erroneous in that such imaginary obligations simply confuse the issue and generate unhappiness. The argument has since been repeated too many times to count. Indeed, in the parlance of self-help literature, "should" is still being used as a noun in place of "morality." The word "morality" itself, as used in pop psychology, flies like a black flag.

☞ Interspersed through self-help literature are life-stories that tend to follow a rigid pattern: under the guidance of a therapist, an unhappy person uncovers the source of his or her unhappiness, typically the oppressive influence of a parent. With the way to happiness now clear, the story ends. Because the theory underwriting such stories dictates that happiness will follow, it simply goes without saying that happiness *does* follow. Self-help uses the rhetoric of liberation, telling of emancipation from oppression, not the details of freedom. It echoes the Declaration of Independence, not the Constitution.

Although pop psychology's animus against morality is new to the world, ours is not the first generation to view morality with suspicion and to question its efficacy in the ordering of human affairs. The most celebrated of the Federalist Papers arguing for adoption of the Constitution—the tenth, Madison's argument for an extensive republic as the best security against the dangers of faction—rests on the stated principle that "moral motives" cannot be relied on to tame factious passions, if only because men dignify their worst passions, even their acts of "injustice and violence," with the name of morality. This doesn't mean that Madison was ready to do away with morality; it does suggest that skepticism toward its power, and disapproval of those who abuse its name for their own ends, are built into our political order and way of life. Today's campaigners against morality might find their work harder if not for the rich tradition of questioning the efficacy of moral sanctions, a tradition of which Madison is part. It is interesting that Madison uses the language of "disease" and "cure" throughout the paper.

To some degree, the current revolt against moral precepts and prohibitions in the name of health reflects a dislike of sheer coercion that most of us moderns share, no matter what our leanings or beliefs. But to the same degree, that position is an inherited one, despite all talk of wiping the slate clean and liberating the self from the shadow of history and the forces of acculturation. While the self-help genre is filled with compounds of the word "self," it was in the age of Shakespeare that terms like "self-praise," "self-love," "self-regard," and "self-knowledge" began to appear in our language. Around the same time, one of the masters of self-reflection took issue with the brutal methods of education then prevailing—the practice of beating learners into submission, perhaps under the moral pretext of correcting their unruliness and inattention.

> Instead of children being invited to letters as guests, all they are shown in truth are horror and cruelty. Get rid of violence and force: as I see it, nothing so fundamentally stultifies and bastardizes a well-born nature. . . . [During lessons] you will hear nothing but the screaming of tortured children and of masters drunk with rage. What a way to awaken a taste for learning in

those tender timorous souls, driving them to it with terrifying scowls and fists armed with canes!

Thanks to the liberal-mindedness of his father, Montaigne himself was educated quite differently.

> As for Greek (which I scarcely understood at all), my father planned to have it taught to me methodically, but in a new way, as a sort of game or sport. We would bounce declensions about, rather like those who use certain board-games as a means of learning arithmetic and geometry. For among other things he had been counselled to bring me to love knowledge and duty by my own choice, without forcing my will, and to educate my soul entirely through gentleness and freedom.

If the depiction of a school as a madhouse anticipates Dickens, the educational experiments in which the young Montaigne's powers were engaged instead of crushed prefigure the methods recommended by Locke a century later in his influential *Thoughts Concerning Education*. In a piece of advice characteristic of his subtle pedagogical method, Locke cautions the concerned father to "keep [children] to the practice, of what you would have grow into a Habit in them, by kind Words and gentle Admonitions, rather as minding them of what they forget, than by harsh Rebukes and Chiding, as if they were wilfully guilty." The dislike of repression and brute force, and the preference for calling human desires into play that animate Locke's discussion of education as well as Montaigne's, also led to new thinking about the way the passions of adults could best be civilized. As education, properly conceived and practiced, calls forth and develops the powers of the child, so would the activities of a commercial society engage and refine the passions of men. Madison's argument that moral motives could not tame dangerous passions belongs to a tradition of thinking about what *could* tame them.

"A feeling in the Renaissance became firm conviction during the seventeenth century that moralizing philosophy and religious precept could no longer be trusted with restraining the destructive passions of men," writes Albert Hirschman. In a sense, morality had therefore already acquired a bad name among some thinkers hundreds of years ago. In the judgment of these men, the great merit of the pursuit of gain was that owing to the unusually steady, predictable, and benign nature of the *passion* for gain, economic acquisition could stabilize human affairs far better than moral coercion and brute force could ever hope to do. If pop psychology today decries society and its indifference to the self, it was theorists of commerce and its civilizing effects who introduced the idea of society as a self-regulating system—though their aim, far from defending repression, was to liberalize the field of human affairs. Speaking of the psychological discoveries of the theorists of commerce, Hirschman emphasizes their rehabilitation of what was once condemned as avarice and their belief that this passion could neutralize more aggressive ones and thus contribute to the civilizing of men.

If ours is not the first generation skeptical of coercion and prohibition, neither are we the first to question belligerent ideals of masculinity. So too, long before pop psychology campaigned against guilt as such, theorists of commerce sought to lift the shadow of guilt that hung over the pursuit of economic ends—a more qualified and restricted goal, just as the tonality of their analysis is more skeptical than utopian. That Adam Smith (whose skepticism approximates Hume's) sought the preservation and not the dissolution of morality is established by the title of his *Theory of Moral Sentiments* (1759), a work reprinted many times during his life.

Over the world of Adam Smith presides an Invisible Hand that steers the actions of men toward ends they never intended and out of their shortsighted motives brings forth a greater good. Over the world of self-help presides an occult Hand that guarantees that others will benefit from our refusal of their claims on us and somehow preserves morality after it has been rejected outright—after the very word "morality" has been stigmatized. Even the cynical Robert Ringer contends that by looking out for Number One we "bring happiness to others." Dedicating his book to "the hope that somewhere in our universe there exists a civilization . . . where governments as we know them do not exist," Ringer writes as one who does not really believe in the utopianism of the 1960s but does find existing arrangements completely absurd. So it is with many others in the self-help movement. In any case, it was the indictment of society in the 1960s that launched pop psychology as we know it, just as the utopianism of that decade laid to rest the philosophy of limited goals that underwrote more traditional advice. While self-improvement goes far back in our culture—at least to Benjamin Franklin, who took the liberal view of the passion for gain and its civilizing potential—not until the 1960s did self-help catch the spirit of utopia, and examples of the genre cited in these pages accordingly date from that time and later.

Some trace pop psychology to the humanistic psychology movement associated with Abraham Maslow, among others. In the second issue of the *Journal of Humanistic Psychology* (1961), Maslow dreams of an ideal society of the psychologically healthy, named Eupsychia—an unwitting parody of Rousseau's ideal of a small, closed community of noble souls. Later in the decade, of course, utopian sentiment and speculation became more general; and these in turn inspired Charles

Reich's millennial polemic, *The Greening of America*, with its argument that the transformation of consciousness already in progress "confronts us with a personal and individual choice: are we satisfied with how we have lived; how would we live differently? It offers us a recovery of self." Seeking to transform consciousness, pop psychology poses this choice and promises this recovery, just as it builds on the distinction "between those needs which are a product of a person's authentic self, and those which are imposed from the outside by society," albeit without citing the authority of Marx and Marcuse as Reich does. Used in combination, "choice," "recovery," "self," "authentic," and "society" have become the very passwords of the pop psychology movement. Advanced consciousness, according to Reich, "says, 'I'm glad I'm me.'" In four words, this is the message of pop psychology.

The difference between nonutopian and utopian thinking is the difference between a right to pursue happiness and a right to happiness itself. The Declaration of Independence affirms the former: "We hold these truths to be self-evident, that all men are created equal, that they are endowed by their Creator with certain unalienable Rights, that among these are Life, Liberty, and the pursuit of Happiness." Yet a long tradition, and a robust tradition of Enlightenment skepticism in particular, warns of the elusive nature of happiness. In the July 3, 1753, number of *The Adventurer*, Samuel Johnson wrote in a characteristic tone of disillusion,

> Whatever any man ardently desires, he very readily believes that he shall some time attain: he whose intemperance has overwhelmed him with diseases, while he languishes in the spring, expects vigour and recovery from the summer sun; and while he melts away with the summer, transfers his hopes to the frosts of winter: he that gazes upon elegance or pleasure, which

want of money hinders him from imitating or partaking, comforts himself that the time of distress will soon be at an end, and that every day brings him nearer to a state of happiness. . . . Such is the general dream in which we all slumber out our time; every man thinks the day is coming, in which he shall be gratified with all his wishes. . . . The day is always coming to the servile in which they shall be powerful, to the obscure in which they shall be eminent, and to the deformed in which they shall be beautiful.

This sort of disenchantment, seconded by Adam Smith in his own way in the *Theory of Moral Sentiments*, finds no reception in the world of pop psychology. It is ironic that pop psychology uses the idiom of nonconformism whose highest expression is John Stuart Mill's *On Liberty*, inasmuch as Mill came to believe (as his autobiography records) that those who chase after happiness will never find it.

In the rhetoric of pop psychology, happiness is there for the seizing, and it is also a right, a sovereign entitlement, of every reader. Some are prepared to argue that it is, in addition, our true, natural, and original state:

Mornings when we greet the world with weariness and worry are a poignant reminder of what most of us lose as we grow older—the natural state of curiosity, wonder, gratitude, and enthusiasm that makes children so delightful. . . . As we grow older, our duties, responsibilities, and roles too often assume control of us. . . . Our natural moods and impulses seem shameful, and we gradually learn to block them out, resigned to live in a state of unhealthy guilt.

On this showing, responsibility oppresses the self and saps authenticity. Another counselor, also concerned with the loss of happiness, affirms that "because our true being is based on an inherent and universal wellspring of confidence, even the most self-doubting among us have known the splendor of inner harmony at one time or another, even in our adult lives." If we were born for happiness but find ourselves unhappy, if indeed happiness was once ours but is ours no longer, some cause of loss and ruin must be responsible. Pop psychology calls that cause morality, or judgment, or blame. The genre prosecutes a ceaseless attack on blame—or rather, on all blame except the blame of one's parents, society, culture, and world.

The strain of accusation and resentment running through much of pop psychology is especially interesting, conflicting as it does with the spirit of positive thinking that once dominated advice books, zealous exhortations, children's stories. ("I think I can, I think I can.") A century ago William James took interest in New Thought with its faith in "the conquering efficacy of courage, hope, and trust, and a correlative contempt for doubt, fear, worry, and all nervously precautionary states of mind." In the judgment of the self-help world, the way to overcome fear, worry, and self-doubt is to identify, and rise up against, those who planted such noxious weeds in our minds to begin with. The tone has turned adversarial, with the therapist now indicting a society so cruel that it attacks the very springs of selfhood. The turning point, again, was the 1960s, when the British psychiatrist R. D. Laing portrayed the family as a machine "to promote respect, conformity, obedience . . . to induce a fear of failure; to promote a respect for work; to promote a respect for 'respectability'"—a polemic which has since become an axiom of the self-help movement. The strange marriage of prosecutorial animus and positive thinking (the latter still coming through in the message that you can have and indeed be whatever you want) contributes to the sometimes contradictory tone of pop psychology. In the voice of Phil McGraw, *The Power of*

Positive Thinking meets up with the rhetoric of indictment, producing the message, "I accuse you, reader, of the crime of neglecting your own happiness."

☞ It is from the past that pop psychology derives many of its fantasies of closing the book *of* the past and authoring a new world. If, as I suggest, pop psychology is utopian in spirit, even its much-repeated theme of living in the moment has roots of a kind in the utopian tradition. "One must live completely at each moment," proclaimed Charles Reich, the apostle of Consciousness III. And so it is in William Morris's utopian romance *News from Nowhere*, where, as Lionel Trilling once noted,

> Life is lived without urgency and without anxiety. It is lived for itself alone, for its own delight in itself. In the life of each individual, the past now exercises no tyranny and the future is not exigent. The present is all, and it is all-satisfying.

As pop psychology would say, these happy souls live in the moment. In More's Utopia everyone lives in the moment in the sense that the island seems to have no past. "Like Tolstoy's happy family," writes Robert M. Adams, Utopian society "is a family without a history. A simple verbal device for abolishing time is to narrate everything about Utopia in the present tense." In the world as we know it, the idealization of the present moment translates into an urge to keep current, that is, to keep up with trends. Pop psychology moves with trends—encounter groups, primal screams, and multiple personalities, for example, being no longer in vogue—and we can expect new themes in the genre to follow new ideological waves, new clinical diagnoses, and new drugs as they come onto the scene.

So trend-sensitive is pop psychology that commentators on the movement sometimes assign each decade from the 1960s forward its own theme and rubric. Not that trends necessarily have a ten-year life span. The prosecutorial tone of the self-help genre as an indictment of society reflects a trend that set in with the 1960s, just as the language of rights now used in pop psychology rides the trend of the rights revolution initiated by the civil rights movement of the same era.

As an example of the accusatory mode, consider a typical statement by Phil McGraw regarding the dignity, pride, passion, and independence presumed missing from the reader's life: "I'm going to show you exactly, precisely why and how they have been robbed from you, and exactly, precisely how to restore them to your life." How can Phil McGraw know these good things have been stolen from me when he doesn't even know me? ("I do think I know a lot about what may be going on in your life," he says a few pages before.) Only by assuming that I am a generic person, the person his theory requires me to be, can he know. The inhabitants of literary utopias do seem to be generic, that is, indistinguishable. More just speaks of "the Utopians," using the plural. Then too, in utopias people are known through and through, whether because their nature is fully expressed and thus stands revealed or because they are under surveillance at every moment, as in Utopia or Oceania. Only if the reader were an open book could Phil McGraw presume to know what the reader lost and exactly how it was lost. Like many others both inside and outside the world of pop psychology, McGraw has too little respect for human opacity and too great a belief in theory as the revealer of all things. Equipped as he is with such a theory, he finds it simply self-evident that the happiness which is my right has been taken from me, and that it is up to me to reclaim it. "If now is not the time to reconnect with your authentic self, when will there be a better time?" A question not to be answered.

In the self-help genre, the doctrine that I have a categorical right to happiness occupies a position analogous to the self-evident truths proclaimed near the beginning of the Declaration of Independence: it is an axiom, a principle, an almost sacred point of origin. Pop psychology exhorts me to declare my own independence of rules, roles, society, the world. (A chapter in Wayne Dyer's *Your Erroneous Zones* is entitled, "Declare Your Independence," while *Pulling Your Own Strings* posts a sentence from the Declaration as its epigraph.) On page after page, Phil McGraw tells me that I am indeed entitled to happiness but that I have allowed this birthright to be taken from me and I will never reclaim it unless and until I heed the practical counsels of Phil McGraw—with the implication that everything else that has been written or taught up to this point in human history is worthless. In one version or another, this is the fable pop psychology tells. Even as it proclaims the power of choice, the genre presents me with a false choice: either I liberate myself completely from the rules imposed by morality or society, or I remain hopelessly enslaved to these hostile forces. That the prescriptions of pop psychology might themselves count as an imposition on the reader never occurs to the authors.

Along with the rhetoric of rights goes the rhetoric of complaint against all that obstructs or frustrates those rights (as indeed the Declaration of Independence is dominated by a catalogue of abuses). So it is with the right to happiness. Once having affirmed a right to happiness, pop psychology blames our lack of actual happiness on morality above all. In other words, beginning with a utopian postulate, it leaps to the conclusion that somehow we would be better off if notions like responsibility were abolished (for such notions "too often assume

control of us" and deprive us of happiness)—and more im-
probably still, that with the abolition of all received thinking
about morality we will finally actually *become* moral. The ag-
grieved tone of much pop psychology bespeaks resentment; but
in contrast to traditional resentment of wealth or privilege, or
even power, pop psychology often breathes a resentment of all
existing institutions inasmuch as they stand in the way of our
power to invent ourselves—utopian resentment, one might call
it. I would argue that existing institutions and received traditions are not, generally, shackles on potential but the enabling
conditions of human life, enabling even pop psychology, which
has after all become an institution in its own right.

Among those in the world of fiction engaged in self-help in
their own manner are the orphans and orphan figures in Dickens, struggling through life as best they can. (The term "self-
help" was itself a Victorianism.) When a psychiatrist observes
in *Compassion and Self-Hate* that as children "we are extremely sensitive, vulnerable and impressionable," he states abstractly what Dickens renders as drama. For Dickens, alive to
his language, compassion means pity pure and simple—pity for
others, not self—and it must have been, in some degree, his
power of eliciting pity that made him in the eyes of Tolstoy the
greatest novelist of his century. Dickens can't be imagined saying with the author of *Compassion and Self-Hate* that "compassion is any and all thoughts, feelings, moods, insights and
actions that serve the interest of actual self." But something
more divides the novelist and the psychiatrist. Regarding the
world as a menace to the self, and the self as the source and
bearer of all value whatever, the psychiatrist has no place in his
thought for tradition. The fiction of Dickens is filled with the
shades of his predecessors (Fielding, Shakespeare, Cervantes,
even Chaucer), the wealth of satire (a word that originally

meant "full"), the ancient conventions of romance. When Pip remarks on the first page of *Great Expectations* that he has no idea of his parents, he brings to mind the anguished remark of Telemachus to Athena in the first book of the first romance, the *Odyssey*, that "Nobody really knows his own father."

☞ Erasing traditional usage, counselors and therapists redefine responsibility as obligation to self—an obligation with the status, once again, of a first principle. If pop psychology refers to treachery, in all probability it is talking about treachery to oneself; if to honor, honoring one's own needs and desires. ("A higher order takes over to support us when we make the choice to honor ourselves in spite of our fear or discomfort.") The received meaning of such terms is simply abolished, with the suggestion that no conventional act of, say, treachery could compare with the betrayal of one's own self by buying into the judgments of others. Convinced that we have all been programmed by external agencies, pop psychology concludes that we need to be deprogrammed (hence its emphasis on wiping the slate clean) and reprogrammed (hence its repetitions and exercises). The language of pop psychology follows the same logic, first systematically emptying words of their historical meaning and then legislating a new meaning for them. Thus one counselor deletes the pejorative content of "selfish," noting that people who think this word disreputable have difficulty "putting [their] needs before others." Such people need to learn to "honor their extreme self-care." *The Portable Therapist*, concurring, notes that "our western model has taught us that selfish is a terrible concept." In *You Own the Power*, the word "selfish" is listed as a Positive Trait along with the words "caring," "kind," "generous," "sensitive," "patient," and "tolerant." The very term "self-help" as used in self-help deletes nineteenth-century connotations of individualism and installs a new meaning in which following twelve steps, reciting seven principles, and saying "I love you" into the mirror as a directed exercise constitute acts of Emersonian self-reliance.

According to *The Portable Therapist*, "our conscience can be thought of as a gentle teacher, instructing us in the moment how things are progressing and what we need to change." Surely this vague guidance counselor bears no relation to anything formerly known as conscience. Similarly, when pop psychology speaks of courage, it means your courage to embrace the prescriptions of pop psychology, or your "courage to heal," but in any case a courage alien to all received usages of the word. "I think the bravest thing most of us do is to get up each morning and to face whatever life has in store for us." To learn that "compassion is any and all thoughts, feelings, moods, insights, and actions that serve the interest of actual self" is to unlearn the dictionary. "Slaves" in pop psychological parlance are those who allow themselves to be "owned" by their family. Even a word like "murder" is redefined in the genre. "We 'murder' ourselves when we invoke self-hating devices and when we annihilate our potential for enjoying life's realistic good offerings." Similarly, in this alternate language to say "I felt hurt" is to "take responsibility for your emotions." "Obligation" becomes a pejorative, as when a therapist condemns parents who plant "seeds of fear, obligation, or guilt."

Pop psychology exhorts us to abandon the past, and the genre itself certainly makes rubble of the language of the past; or when it cites works of literature, takes a line or two for use as an epigraph, shearing away the context. Removed from its speaker and context, the aphorism of Milton's Satan, "The mind is its own place, and in itself / Can make a Heaven of Hell, a Hell of Heaven," is cited in pop psychology as an inspirational proof of our power to create ourselves. In context it is a boast and a falsehood, coming true perhaps only in the ironic sense that Satan carries his private hell of malice and envy into the Garden of Eden. A manual on spiritual healing, auric energy, and communication with the dead features epigraphs from Alexander Pope and Edmund Spenser. Advice authors read literature with scissors, just as the stories they themselves tell seem trimmed and expurgated. When Isaiah Berlin, the historian of ideas, warned against the elimination of moral terms from ordinary language in the name of science, when Iris Murdoch, philosopher and novelist, urged us to "preserve and cherish a strong truth-bearing language, not marred or corrupted by technical discourse or scientific codes," each overlooked the injurious potential of a source neither technical nor scientific, though at times masquerading as both. We may hope that enough common sense, resistance to legislated definitions, and memory of established usages remains to counteract these effects.

The once moral terms used in the self-help genre remind me of some Persian carpet unwoven for the sake of its wool. Consider the word "integrity." As traditionally understood, integrity refers to moral strengths like trustworthiness. In a characteristic work of the self-help genre (strewn with compounds of the word "self," in keeping with the master principle that the only true obligation is to self), integrity means being all there, which is also to say that it loses meaning altogether. To the self-doubting, confident people "had a certain presence about them. They conveyed a sense of *integrity* because they were willing to be all there [emphasis in the original]." Similarly,

Beth's presence emanates from deep within, reflecting the deep confidence that comes with self-acceptance. And because of that self-acceptance, Beth is "all there." She has the personal integrity to know that she is far from perfect and that life is good anyway.

Again:

PERSONAL INTEGRITY: This term has two closely related meanings, both associated with a "unified wholeness." First, there is the *fact* of our integrity. *Each of us is a whole person.* The second meaning refers to our *sense* of integrity. This is the *sense of wholeness* that results from self-acceptance. It is a satisfying feeling of being unified within, of being all there, fully present.

The newspeak of pop psychology so distorts meaning that integrity comes to signify a vague emanation. Characteristic therapeutic locutions like "Practice being spontaneous" have the ring of Newspeak itself; and much as the language of the past would become a foreign tongue to one habituated to Newspeak, so I believe the literature of the past would be lost to one who adopted the altered definitions of words like "integrity." Like Newspeak—the official language of a theoretical utopia—the language of pop psychology is a utopian construct.

Isaiah Berlin once observed that the thoughts and feelings of human beings are so permeated with moral evaluations that "to think them away" is a project as bizarre as "to pretend that we live in a world in which space, time, or number in the normal sense no longer exist." Many a pop psychologist is in open revolt against the tyranny of the normal, and the genre exhorts us to think away moral categories and evaluations as if conducting us to its own land of nowhere. By thinking them away, we deprogram ourselves and open ourselves to the prescriptions of pop psychology. If "utopian" meant merely "fantastic," the utopian character of this exercise might be cause for interest and amusement, nothing more. But the conclusion that morality is an oppressive fiction is an inapt one to draw from a century in which millions perished at the hands of the Nazis, tens of millions were murdered at the altar of communism, and a shocking percentage of the entire population of Cambodia was slaughtered in the effort to establish a utopia. I do not mean to imply that pop psychology lends itself to crimes of this order; I mean to impugn the authority of a school of thought that simply closes its eyes to history. If, as the authors of *Self-Esteem* maintain, it is only because of "the tyranny of shoulds" that people are "willing to die in wars," then fighting the Nazis made no sense. Indeed, when pop psychology mentions Nazism, it is to dramatize the horror of *American* life. To Robert Ringer, the Securities and Exchange Commission is "gestapo-like." Theodore Rubin speaks not only of "countless people" in this country whose "actual selves have been reduced to ashes" but of the "tyrannical concentration-camp form of living" that prevails here, as if the United States were Auschwitz. In the Nowhere of pop psychology, space and time (and indeed number) in the normal sense cease to exist.

It is from literature that the word "utopia" derives. From More's *Utopia* to Charlotte Perkins Gilman's *Herland* (whose Aryan residents have all the individuality of blades of grass or columns of ants, filled as they are with the one thought of "building up a great race"), from Plato to *1984*, utopias are separated from dystopias by a fine line, if that. The phrase "With total discipline we can solve all problems," from the first pages of *The Road Less Traveled*, the most popular self-help work ever written, sounds like a prescription for dystopia. While most self-help authors campaign against morality (a term of odium in the genre), the elimination of morality could not possibly take place without heavy costs. Is it conceivable that the true meaning of integrity will reveal itself once the inherited usage of the term is abolished—that with human history zeroed out, people will finally begin to show what good really is? In *1984* the past is abolished too; and in works of the recovered memory movement, such as *The Courage to Heal*, we seem at times to pass through a totalitarian warp and enter a world where unreality governs, children denounce parents, rules of evidence are inverted, drugs elicit truth, questioning is heretical, people are convicted in absentia, and the ruling myth makes thought on any terms but its own impossible.

If parents are attractive targets in pop psychology, so too, however, does the genre liberate parents from children. "Psychological independence means total freedom from all obligatory relationships," writes Wayne Dyer, offering as exemplary the story of a mother bear who one day simply deserts her young forever. In another volume the same author celebrates those who

> enjoy freedom from role definitions in which they must behave in certain ways because they are parents, employees, Americans, or even adults; they enjoy freedom to breathe whatever air they choose, in whatever location, without worrying about how everyone else feels about their choices . . .

—which can only mean that parents have a perfect right to desert their children if and when they so choose (as Jack Rosenberg did when he reinvented himself as Werner Erhard and began offering self-realization seminars). In the world of pop psychology, one's very children are foreigners. "*I am*, not because of books I write, money I earn, degrees conferred, children I have—*I am* with or without these accoutrements. These *things* and *people* are not *me!*" writes Theodore Rubin. A psychiatrist puts children in the category of accoutrements.

Of parents who "refuse to accept responsibility for the world into which they have brought the children," Hannah Arendt once wrote that they tell those children, in effect:

> "In this world even we are not very securely at home; how to move about in it, what to know, what skills to master, are mysteries to us too. You must try to make out as best you can; in any case you are not entitled to call us to account. We are innocent, we wash our hands of you."

It seems to me that a genre that makes words like "responsibility" odious and recognizes no responsibility except to self is likelier to produce this sort of nonchalance than to make people at long last caring and morally attentive. To be sure, nowhere does pop psychology argue in detail that with the death of morality human beings will finally become moral (though *The Greening of America*, precursor of the pop psychology movement, asserts just that). But the entire genre is built on this presumption, and the implied promise of such a rebirth radiates from every line. And the inability of pop psychology to make its utopian dreams convincing parallels in its own way the inability of utopian fabulists to bring their earthly paradise to life. In the work that coined the word, we learn that the Utopians

> in general are easygoing, cheerful, clever, and fond of leisure. When they must, they can stand heavy labor, but otherwise they are not very fond of it. In intellectual pursuits they are tireless. When they heard from us about the literature and learning of the Greeks . . . it was wonderful to behold how eagerly they sought to be instructed in Greek.

And so it continues: generic description of a way of life.

In the way More describes the Utopians in general, *The Greening of America* describes "the new generation." Almost nowhere in the nearly four hundred pages of Reich's book will you find an actual person. The pages are packed with types, personifications, and abstractions like Consciousness III that govern verbs as if they enjoyed the power of persons ("Consciousness III rejects many of the laws, forms of authority, and assumptions that underlie our present political State"), but persons themselves are absent. In the tradition of Reich, Wayne Dyer's "Portrait of a Person Who Has Eliminated All Erroneous Zones" depicts a category of people, not an individual at all:

> First and most obviously, you see people who like virtually everything about life—people who are comfortable doing just about anything, and who waste no time in complaining, or wishing that things were otherwise. . . . There is no pretending to enjoy, but a sensible acceptance of what is, and an outlandish ability to delight in that reality. [Etc.]

To my mind, such people are no less generic and no more convincing than the also outlandish Utopians. Pop psychology abounds with life-stories that have the life edited out of them as decisively as More's account of Utopia. If a utopia represents the happy ending of history, the stories in a work like Stephen Covey's *Living the 7 Habits: The Courage to Change* march toward their happy ending as inexorably as history itself was said by some, not that long ago, to be approaching its consummation.

☞ The archetype of the happy ending is that of the *Odyssey* (ancestor of the utopian tradition, as I will suggest). One of the more influential works of didactic fiction ever composed,

Fénelon's *Telemachus* (1699), reportedly the most widely read and reprinted book of its age, recasts the meaning of the *Odyssey*. Interpolated between the books of the original, *Telemachus* omits Odysseus's revenge and has this archetypal liar say, "He that can lie is unworthy to be called a man." Instead of a Ulysses who, like Dante's, pursues forbidden experience, Fénelon presents a Telemachus carefully shepherded through his adventures by Minerva, in the guise of Mentor, "for the purpose of gaining experience." Embedded in the work are two utopias, each with the quality of a still life, one natural and one minutely designed by Mentor. The goal of a sovereign, says Mentor, must be "to make men good and happy." The reading of *Telemachus* was to be a transforming event in the life of Jeremy Bentham (1748–1832), who held precisely that goal, aspired to reform the criminal and the idle as Mentor did the city of Salente, and dreamed of running a clean, healthful, glass-paned prison as minutely regulated as Salente. Today of course it is the therapists who mentor us, who seek to make us both happy and good—happy by the abolition of blame and judgment, and good as a result—and whose stories and promises are as unreal as a scrupulously honest Odysseus, an idyllic city, a prison of glass.

The prison Bentham dreamed of was inspired by the principle of transparency. The revolutionaries of France were possessed by the will to transparency. To these men who set out to wipe the slate clean and start over, and to fashion a people in accordance with Fénelon's understanding of government as an instrument for making citizens both happy and good, Rousseau was a "spiritual guide." (So close are the sentiments of Rousseau and Fénelon, as well as their modes of reasoning, that in reading *Telemachus* we seem to be reading Rousseau before the fact. Rousseau's *Emile* is also a treatise in which a candidate for manhood is prepared for that estate by a tutor who super-vises his very thoughts. Within *Emile* itself, Sophie reads *Telemachus* and falls in love with the hero before falling in love with Emile, "the new Telemachus," who for his part thanks the tutor who has "made me free.") In a sense, the shade of Rousseau continues to serves as a spiritual guide or mentor to the pop psychology movement. Most of us, wrote Northrop Frye in 1963, have been brought up in a "half-baked Rousseauism." When we read that children who are insuffi-ciently loved "disconnect from their natural state of inner love, joy, peace, and confidence" (John Gray); or that

> we came as infants "trailing clouds of glory," arriving from the farthest reaches of the universe . . . and we offered this gift to our parents. They didn't want it. They wanted a nice girl or a nice boy; (Robert Bly)

or that infants are

> authentically human and free to express themselves in a way that adults often cannot. As we grow older . . . our natural moods and impulses feel shameful, and we gradually learn to block them out, resigned to live in a state of unhealthy guilt where the futile effort to please everyone, do good, be "per-fect," and keep ourselves safe and secure in the process keeps us prisoners of the urge to do what we "should" do; (Joan Borysenko)

or that

> a newborn infant has no hangups. He is open and honest in stating who he is and what he wants moment by moment. He has not yet learned the façades, roles and inhibitions with which he will later distort his naturalness . . . (Jerry Greenwald)

. . . when we read these orthodox expressions of the master myth of the therapeutic movement, we know exactly what Frye meant. It is as if we encountered a faded translation of Rousseau's argument, in the *Discourse on Inequality*, that humanity has fallen "from the natural state to the civil state"; that "original man has disappeared by degrees" and left in his place only "artificial men and factitious passions which . . . have no foundation in nature." Rousseau in fact recognized not only that modern people no longer lose themselves in "the sense of existing here and now," like their primordial ancestors, but that they—we—cannot recover such innocence. Pop psychology, practically from the time Frye wrote, has been insisting that people live in the here and now.

Inasmuch as self-help borrows from Rousseau with a kind of blind zeal, it is all the more significant that Rousseau came to believe himself the object of a vast, sinister conspiracy.

In the abyss of evil in which I am sunk I feel the weight of blows struck at me; I perceive the immediate instrument; but I can neither see the hand which directs it nor the means by which it works. Disgrace and misfortune fall upon me as if of themselves and unseen. When my grief-stricken heart utters groans, I seem like a man complaining for no reason. The authors of my ruin have discovered the unimaginable art of turning the public into the unsuspecting accomplice of their plot.

In the therapeutic version of the conspiracy against Rousseau, a reader filled with worth is surrounded by uncaring others and enmeshed in a world interested only in his defeat. "To be victimized, as I use the word here," writes Wayne Dyer in *Pulling Your Own Strings*, "means to be governed and checked by forces outside yourself; and . . . these forces are unquestionably ubiquitous in our culture." Because every reader is deserted and betrayed like a Rousseau (even if this means that every other reader is against him), the therapist can present himself as the reader's one true friend in this world—the sole exception to the reigning falsehood. Throughout the self-help genre, that is the pose the therapist strikes. The world, says the reader, does not know my inner wisdom: only the therapist knows it. It may be that not even I know it.

Perhaps just as improbable as the notion that we are wise without knowing it (quite in contrast to a Socrates who knows that he doesn't know) is the belief that we will become moral only if and when we discard all received concepts of morality, or that we can in fact wipe the slate clean and return to nature. In the name of Rousseau, the revolutionaries of France proclaimed the Year One; readers of pop psychology are to create their personal Year One. "I am asking you to hit the erase button on ideas that you may have been holding for ten, twenty, thirty, or forty years. I am asking you to wipe the slate clean and start over in your thinking," writes Phil McGraw. But so too have any number of other psychological visionaries and evangelists over the past twenty, thirty, or forty years. Maybe it is only to be expected that those bent on erasing our programming should seek to replace the old program with another—and a program, in this sense, is not just a set of instructions but a set of instructions repeated ad infinitum, a ceaseless mental drill, a constant catechism. The works of pop psychology that call on us to break with all precepts but their own are so repetitive of one another, so formulaic and unoriginal, as to mock their own authority.

Twenty-five years before Phil McGraw urged his readers to wipe the slate clean and start over in their thinking, Wayne

Dyer offered "some beginning strategies for wiping your guilt slate clean," and Robert Ringer, on the first page of *Looking Out for #1*, advised the reader to proceed with "a clean slate." In *Self-Esteem* (1987), Matthew McKay and Patrick Fanning advise readers to place themselves in a hypnotic state and then erase demeaning labels from their mental blackboard. "See those labels on the blackboard and now see an eraser in your hand." For all its rhetoric of starting anew, pop psychology is actually a vast echo chamber of reproduced ideas. "It's as if we're waiting for permission to start living fully. But the only person who can give us that permission is ourselves. We are accountable only to ourselves for what happens to us in our lives. We must realize that we have a choice: we are responsible for our own good time." So says Phil McGraw; but these words are actually from a best-seller of 1971, *How to Be Your Own Best Friend*.

Why is pop psychology so repetitive? In part because that is how it drives its doctrines home. Pop psychology speaks of the tape or script playing in one's head, and the genre might be likened to a tape in its own right, played over and over in an effort to reprogram the listener. "Day by day, in every way, I am getting better and better." Then too, while many of the doctrines, even the core doctrines, of pop psychology may well seem fantastic to a reader encountering them for the first time, by the *n*th time they may seem familiar and somehow established. Even as they purport to say things that have never been said before, pop psychologists therefore rely heavily on their peers and predecessors. "I believe that one of the greatest gifts you can offer the other people in your life is your authentic self, rather than your fictional self," writes Phil McGraw, echoing Cheryl Richardson's proclamation, "Honoring yourself is the greatest gift you can give to someone else," which echoes Charles Reich's proclamation some thirty years before: "by being one's true self, one offers others the most." These authors, and no doubt many others, say the same thing in the same way because all want to show that people who learn to love themselves will become the opposite of narcissists, and that people who defy the world's precepts and prohibitions will behave better and not worse than before. They offer a Disney version of Rousseau's argument in favor of an innocent *amour de soi* as distinguished from a sense of self geared to the judgments and opinions of others.

Contrary to the fantasy of self-creation, pop psychology cannot invent its own foundations, and so it is condemned to borrow again and again from what already exists. Borrowed is the very posture of the straight talker affected by Phil McGraw: "Warning: This is an extremely direct, plain-talking, tell-you-the-unvarnished-truth, common-sense book about how to take control of your entire life. The control I'm talking about is a control that comes from reconnecting with what I call your *authentic self*." Using a passage from *The Catcher in the Rye* as an example, the novelist and critic David Lodge identifies

> a type of first-person narration that has the characteristics of the spoken rather than the written word. In this kind of novel or story, the narrator is a character who refers to himself (or herself) as "I," and addresses the reader as "you." He or she uses vocabulary and syntax characteristic of colloquial speech, and appears to be relating the story spontaneously rather than delivering a carefully constructed and polished written account. . . . It is an illusion that can create a powerful effect of authenticity and sincerity, of truth-telling.

Except for the references to fiction, every word of this, right down to the emphasis on the carefully constructed impression of authenticity and truth-telling, applies to the style (which is also a selling point) of Phil McGraw. Indeed, authenticity is McGraw's most cherished value, as phoniness is Holden Caulfield's detestation. We are to recover the authentic self we have forgotten and betrayed. So said Reich in 1970, citing Holden Caulfield as the first prophet of Consciousness III. What is original in Huck Finn is less original in Holden Caulfield, and still less so in Phil McGraw.

The very language of iconoclasm, the modes and poses of rebellion now so much in fashion inside and outside the self-help world, are in the highest degree derivative. As Michael André Bernstein has argued, society's accuser, while claiming to represent something defiantly original, and while exercising a strange authority, derives that authority from sources long established, and practically plagiarizes his own originals. One of his sources is "the archetypal 'wild man in the desert' whose imprecations and prophecies proved true when all the philosophies professed by the officially sanctioned sages were revealed as hollow," as in the biblical voice crying in the wilderness. Phil McGraw and all the others who cry, "Don't listen to the world; listen to me!" play on this tradition even as they exclaim against tradition. "Doctors, lawyers, professors, executives, show-business and sports personalities, etc., have achieved far too inflated a status in our culture," writes Wayne Dyer, conspicuously omitting those like himself, counselors. Bernstein also notes that society's accusers now seem to enjoy the esteem of society. One form taken by that esteem is the title, income, quasi-medical status, and mystique of knowledge conferred on the practitioners of psychology.

☞ The mystique that I refer to gives generic statements of doctrine and belief an appearance of enlightened knowledge. Consider statements like these, common in the genre:

> (1) As long as we're prisoners of guilt, we cannot discover who we are, because the Natural Child is asleep, and our vitality is low.

> (2) Typically, perpetrators get protection and people who are victimized get blamed.

> (3) You will soon see that everything you have and have not become is no accident. It is no accident, because there are no accidents.

The author of each of these statements seems to have a Ph.D. and expects to be taken on trust. But what sort of statements are they? In appearance they are statements of fact, but a moment's thought dispels that impression. The Natural Child is a myth; the typical perpetrator and typical victim, respectively coddled and persecuted, are political cartoons; the nonexistence of accidents is a dogma. These statements and countless others like them—the substance of the genre—resemble nothing so much as reports from a utopia (or dystopia), like Herland:

> For five or ten years they worked together, growing stronger and wiser and more and more mutually attached, and then the miracle happened—one of these young women bore a child.

Years compressed into phrases, facile judgments expressed in a way that places them beyond dispute, mind-over-matter miracles—all have become features of the self-help genre. (Severed from the outside world and reproducing without the assistance of men, the Herlanders practice self-help indeed.) And just as Herland simply illustrates doctrines already expounded by Gilman in *Women and Economics*, so each of the three statements cited above simply restates doctrines presumed true and placed beyond dispute—in the first case the doctrine of the inner child, in the second that of the evils of patriarchy, in the third the doctrine of authenticity. Like Herland itself, each of the statements of "fact" is really a doctrinal fantasy; and so I believe is the self-help genre as a whole. Pop psychology speaks of the recovery of our inner child; a resident of the new England in Morris's *News from Nowhere* says, "Let us rejoice that we have got back to our childhood again." Phil McGraw proclaims that there are no accidents. In the Soviet Union industrial accidents were so embarrassing to the official utopian myth that they were treated as official secrets.

Some would say that pop psychology, with its doctrine of the supremacy of the self, is an expression of American individualism, but I hesitate to apply that term to a genre that prescribes exercises, assignments, and step-by-step procedures without end. No individualist would submit to such dictations. To my mind there is a lot more of the pedagogue than of Emerson in pop psychology, as indeed utopias from Plato forward have tended toward authoritarianism (Morris's being an exception). The theorist of humanistic psychology Abraham Maslow, who once confessed that he lived in a "private world of Platonic essences," worried over the authoritarian potential of utopia even as he pondered exactly how to set up and manage Eupsychia, or the Good Society. Maslow posed the same sorts of questions about the regulation of private behavior and the regimentation of taste, among other issues, as John Stuart Mill did in his essay *On Liberty*. But where Mill asked them about an existing society (his own), Maslow had in mind a community that he and similarly enlightened minds were somehow to construct from scratch, designing every feature to promote a given psychological ideal of the good life. The very ambition is an authoritarian fantasy. "My opinion," wrote Maslow, "is that any group trying to be Utopian or Eupsychian must also be able to expel dystopian individuals who slip by the selection techniques."

The inhabitants of More's Utopia can proselytize for their religion, provided they are not too strenuous or divisive. The website of a popular psychologist invites the public to contribute stories and comments, stipulating however that "no religious, political or other potentially divisive subjects" are to be discussed. Nothing but "empathetic expressions and solutions" are to be offered in reply to other postings, and no humor "at the expense of others" is to be used. Pop psychology is not only a utopian but in some sense an authoritarian kingdom. "Surrendering to a Power greater than ourselves is how we become empowered," writes one recovery author in an example of the new newspeak; her language finds its own power in that of Alcoholics Anonymous. To Wayne Dyer, as we have seen, it is unquestionably the case that victimizing forces are everywhere in our culture. In the life-stories that are a staple of the genre, readers are told how to interpret and define everything and everyone, and denied any information that would allow them to reach an independent conclusion—like visitors to a closed society who can't go anywhere without a minder, as in Herland. In *Living the 7 Habits*, Stephen Covey not only prints stories illustrating the power of his principles but specifically tells the reader how to understand each story. The principles themselves he deems "permanent, natural laws, like gravity." They admit no argument. To Phil McGraw, however, it is his own Ten Life Laws that admit no argument. "Like the laws of gravity, they simply are. You don't get a vote. . . . If you violate these Life Laws, you are likely to suffer severe penalties." There is an authoritarian in Phil McGraw; he acts almost like a higher power to which we surrender in order to find power. You need to, You must, You have to, he tells the reader. He uses imperatives frequently. The exercises in advice literature are often framed in the imperative as well, as when the author of *Ending the Struggle Against Yourself* tells the reader, "When you come to the end of this sentence, put down this book," or the author of *Authentic Happiness* says, "If you have been skimming this section, I want you to stop right here; in fact I **insist** on it," or when McGraw gives the reader the following assignment: "Adopt the attitude of questioning and challenging everything in your life that you can identify as having been accepted on blind faith or as having been adopted out of history or tradition." The double use of the word "adopt" in the latter command seems to say, "Adopt nothing except what I tell you to adopt; challenge everything but what I say." The deprogram/reprogram model employed by McGraw and many others in the genre seems inherently authoritarian, implying as it does that we live and act according to sets of instructions.

Some in the self-help school go even further than McGraw, not just demanding that we question (that is, dismiss) tradition but excoriating it. According to Theodore Rubin, for one, tradition is "an impossible cultural value system of which both we and our parents are victims"—a curse on us all. The extremism of this author's argument terminates in the conclusion that without compassion (by which he means self-acceptance)

the ruthlessness of self-hate is such that it reduces the individual to the level of a nonhuman automaton. Driven by self-hate, we have no opportunity to feel, to evaluate, to make choices or decision or to grow. We are reduced to a slavelike status and must obey the commands of an implacable slave master.

While like others in the genre the author uses liberation rhetoric, his language, here and throughout, is itself dogmatic, distorted, overcharged, repetitive, and anti-rational—authoritarian. That consumers freely buy into, or at least buy, such advice doesn't mean that its rhetoric isn't coercive. In the 1970s people paid good money to attend est training sessions that have been likened to boot camp.

In the days of the Chinese Cultural Revolution, when utopianism went mad, the party proclaimed the "one-two-three system," the "one good leading four good/four good leading one good," "the three red flags," and so on. Self-help proclaims Twelve Steps, Seven Principles, Ten Laws. The more political of the self-help authors actually do seek to foment a cultural revolution—hence, for example, the vilification of our "dangerous, sexualized and media-saturated culture," our "girl-poisoning culture," our "junk culture," our "dysfunctional culture" to cite a few of the epithets brandished in *Reviving Ophelia*. ("The revolution must be cultural," wrote Charles Reich.) It was said that the Chinese propaganda system "illustrates, explains, organizes, warms up and serves over again and again the same ideological stew"; so does self-help literature its own theories and doctrines. Where the Red Guards reversed traffic lights, the self-help movement reverses valences, declaring blame blameworthy, devaluing achievement. During the Cultural Revolution all traditional opera was banned and replaced by six Revolutionary Model operas; the generic success stories of pop psychology represent, if not model operas, inspirational fables. Pop psychologists talk of wiping the slate clean; an infamous adage of Mao's states, "It is on a blank page that the most beautiful poems are written."

That our cultural value system is impossible, as Theodore Rubin maintains, is a dogma and an absurdity. Our culture is not only possible but actual. What *is* impossible is utopia. If the tradition or culture we inherit carries prejudice and error, it also enriches and educates, enabling us, for example, to resist coercive rhetoric, to discern impostures and fallacies, to hold things at their worth. As I hope to show, pop psychology itself borrows freely from the tradition it deprecates. Despite itself, it attests to the richness of the past and its continuing presence.

3

Blame

With a power that no one who encounters it is likely to forget, Dostoevsky's Grand Inquisitor makes the argument to the face of Christ that if there is one thing human beings crave above all, it is to have the burden of freedom lifted from their shoulders. "I tell Thee that man is tormented by no greater anxiety than to find some one quickly to whom he can hand over that gift of freedom with which the ill-fated creature is born," and by freedom the Grand Inquisitor means acting on one's own responsibility. Perhaps all who have commented on the Grand Inquisitor's diatribe on the childlike nature of the human race have felt its dire force and recognized its black implications. To the self-help movement, however, human beings *are* childlike; hence its rhetoric of the Inner Child, the Adult Child of Alcoholics, the authentic infant; hence the exercises, workbooks, fables, and elementary tone of the self-help genre, as if we had gone back to a primary school of the soul. The movement further depicts human beings (again in accordance with the Grand Inquisitor) as beset with anxiety and fear. Most threatening of

all, in the eyes of pop psychology, are the very institutions associated with responsibility—conscience, morality, blame. This
is the threat that it undertakes to lift.

☞ If one thing is sure to be condemned in a self-help manual
no matter what its slant, it is condemnation—blame, or as the
literature calls it, judgment. Some years ago the way of acceptance was proclaimed in *I'm OK—You're OK*. Interpreting
Christianity as a precursor of the revelations of transactional
analysis, the work describes grace as but "a theological way of
saying I'M OK—YOU'RE OK. It is not YOU CAN BE OKAY, IF, or
YOU WILL BE ACCEPTED, IF, but rather YOU ARE ACCEPTED,
unconditionally"—without a hint of blame. It is as if Christianity had found its true explication only with the arrival of the
gospel of transactional analysis, as if the past had been waiting
for the present. The tale told in this influential work dating
from the 1960s is the now-prevailing fable of authenticity lost
to outside influences and authenticity regained by overcoming
such influences and "turn[ing] off the past." Like the more political utopianism of its day, the doctrine of I'm OK—You're
OK presented itself as the solution to the riddle of things and
promised the power to overcome the past, take charge of one's
destiny, and enter upon a new existence.

What makes blame especially noxious in the eyes of pop
psychology is that the receiver of blame tends to internalize it in
the form of self-blame or guilt, which is the blight of human life
precisely because it works on us from within. According to
Theodore Rubin, a psychiatrist, the worst things done by human beings are "always outgrowths of self-hating, overwhelming, castigating consciences." John Gray, a psychologist, lists
twelve blocks to personal success, beginning with blame and

ending with guilt: "blame, depression, anxiety, indifference, judgment, indecision, procrastination, perfectionism, resentment, self-pity, confusion, and guilt." The undesirables here grouped with blame give a good idea of its reputation in the genre. Like the author of *I'm OK—You're OK*, Gray makes it known that all of human thought has been but a preparation for his own system. "Right now mankind is taking part in another leap forward to understand the secrets of personal success. All the great teachings and religions have led mankind to this point." Now that we possess the secrets of success, in other words, there is no further need for the great teachings and religions. I leave it to others to discuss the stripping of transcendence and sublimity from religion, as when Gray proclaims, "God wants you to have it all."

Prominent among the secrets of success, according to Gray, is the destructiveness—the blameworthiness—of blame. Robert "had to move through many blocks. He had to let go of his blame, judgments, and indifference toward his ex-wives." When George and Rose "stopped blaming each other for their unhappiness, they began to realize that they could have a good time." "Whenever you are caught up in the grip of blaming others, you get sidetracked from believing you can have what you want," and when you believe that, you get it, because "If you have strong desire, you get what you want."

Although, as noted, the television psychologist Phil McGraw inflects his message differently, he too censures blame. "The problem is that it is at the very core of human nature to blame other people; it is fundamental self-preservation to try to escape accountability." But

while you're passionately blaming someone else, your self-diagnostic skills simply fall apart. Your best chance to get real control of your life is to stop that thinking right now. . . . You will never, ever fix your problems blaming someone else. That is for losers. Don't be a sucker just because it hurts to admit the truth. You're the one screwing up, if anybody is. The sooner you accept that, the sooner your life gets better. Let's face it. No matter who you might want to blame.

Not that McGraw blames the reader. "I didn't say you are to blame. I said you are accountable, as in 'responsible.' There's a huge difference between blame and responsibility." (The responsibility referred to is responsibility for one's own happiness.) Unless and until we get out of the habit of blame, we will never enter the promised land of happiness. "Can you stop playing the blame game and recognize that it is a new day?"

So widely held, by now, is the view that the assignment of fault is a pointless fixation that a new cliché has been born: "blame game." But blame does more than repress our own possibilities. The most pernicious form of blame, in the eyes of the self-help movement, isn't the blame we level at others for our own miseries and mistakes but blame leveled at others for the misery we inflict on them. We blame the victim. The familiarity of this claim, the rhetorical power that resides in the role of one unjustly accused, and the theory circulating through self-help literature, and beyond, that one suffering a painful sense of shame must have been the victim of abuse as a child—all suggest the resonance now possessed by the therapeutic prejudice against blame.

Aside from the special case of presumed victims of abuse who learn to put blame where it belongs, that is, on the abuser, blame in self-help literature is simply no good. It always seems to point the wrong way—to others when I am at fault, to myself when I am innocent. Blame is a noxious fallacy strongly associated with cruelty, futility, deception, self-deception, and unhappiness. What good could blame possibly serve? What could be said in praise of blame?

☞ For one thing, without blame, praise loses meaning. Traditionally, the terms "blame" and "praise" are coupled inseparably, as if one entailed the other. To praise generosity is to dispraise meanness; to praise loyalty is to censure disloyalty and betrayal. The world of pop psychology, where everyone is wonderful but somehow loses sight of that fact—"Even today in my own life, sometimes I forget what a wonderful person I am," writes John Gray—is a world where no one is anything.

The fact is, human beings do things worthy of condemnation. The counselors themselves condemn many things, most vocally the abuse of children. It is also a fact that a vocabulary invalidating praise and blame, indeed a utopian vocabulary, has already been tried out. The historian of ideas Isaiah Berlin has written at length, with learning and power, of totalitarian thought systems where moral evaluations vanish and the real actors are vast impersonal forces, like the Class Struggle, not mere human beings subject to praise and blame. Confronting the purportedly scientific Marxist claim that history is made not by responsible moral agents but by superhuman laws that cannot be evaded, Berlin saw praise and blame not as archaisms or hang-ups obstructing human progress but as the indispensable preconditions of human dignity and political sanity. The importance attached by Berlin to sheer blame bears particular emphasis. He did not consider blame an error that human beings need to be cured of; on the contrary, he brought out eloquently the inhuman nature of an ideology that portrays moral categories and evaluations as delusions to be cured. Note, in the

following representative passages from a single Berlin essay, the
importance borne by the word "blame":

> [Given the belief in historical inevitability], to *blame* and
> praise, consider possible courses of action, accuse or defend
> historical figures for acting as they did, becomes an absurd
> activity.

> What are we to make of . . . the perpetual pleas to use our
> imagination or our powers of sympathy or of understanding in
> order to avoid the injustice that springs from an insufficient
> grasp of the aims and codes and customs of cultures distant
> from us in time and space? What meaning has this, save on the
> assumption that to give moral praise and *blame*, to seek to be
> just, is not totally irrational, that human beings deserve justice
> as stocks and stones do not, and that therefore we must seek to
> be fair, and not praise and *blame* arbitrarily, or mistakenly,
> through ignorance, or prejudice, or lack of imagination?

> [We complain of propaganda, but] to speak of propaganda at
> all, let alone assume that it can be dangerously effective, is to
> imply that the notion of injustice is not inoperative, that
> marks for conduct are, and can properly be, awarded; it is in
> effect to say that I must either seek not to praise or *blame* at
> all, or, if I cannot avoid doing so because I am a human be-
> ing and my views are inevitably shot through with moral as-
> sessments, I should seek to do so justly, with detachment, on
> the evidence. . . .

> [Moral] categories permeate all that we think and feel so per-
> vasively and universally that to think them away, and conceive
> what and how we should be thinking, feeling, and talking with-
> out them . . . psychologically greatly strains our capacity—is
> nearly, if not quite, as impracticable as, let us say, to pretend

that we live in a world in which space, time, or number in the normal sense no longer exist.

When everything has been said in favour of attributing responsibility for character and action to natural and institutional causes . . . we continue to praise and *blame*. We *blame* others as we *blame* ourselves; and the more we know, the more, it may be, we are disposed to *blame*. Certainly it will surprise us to be told that the better we understand our own actions—our own motives and the circumstances surrounding them—the freer from self-blame we shall inevitably feel. The contrary is surely often true. . . . We ourselves may be accused unjustly, and so become acutely sensitive to the dangers of unjustly *blaming* others. But because *blame* can be unjust and the temptation to utter it too strong, it does not follow that it is never just.

According to Berlin, to think away moral categories and evaluations amounts to a bizarre act of pretending and a flight from our own humanity. Yet this is just what the help manuals tell me to do. They speak of letting go of blame; of receiving each moment "without criticism, blame, guilt, or judgment"; of abandoning "fixed beliefs [that] express themselves through concepts like 'should' and 'must'"; and so on through countless iterations. They liken self-blame to a reign of terror, a concentration camp in our own minds. What to the historian of ideas, informed by the record of terror in the twentieth century, constitutes the safeguard of our common humanity is to the therapists a poison to be gotten out of our system. To Berlin it is factually absurd to claim that the better we understand our actions, the less we blame ourselves; the help manuals promise on every page to acquaint me with my true self and to release me from guilt, quite as if these two ends were one and the same. "Our ordinary speech would become fantastically distorted," writes Berlin, "by a conscious effort to eliminate from it some basic ingredient—say, everything remotely liable to convey value judgments, our normal, scarcely noticed moral . . . attitudes." "Fantastically distorted" well describes the utopian idiom of pop psychology, with its transvaluation of all moral terms and its attempt to rewrite the human constitution to do away with our capacity for evaluation.

People do things worthy of condemnation. Can anyone say with certainty to the nearest ten million how many perished at the hands of the state in the Soviet Union? In practice, the inhuman ideology exposed by Berlin—the dogma that human agency and thus human beings count for nothing, that history is a battleground of abstract forces, that moral categories are illusions—translated into criminality on a scale never seen before on earth. Pop psychology, with its insistence that morality is the great impediment to human progress and happiness, does not lend itself to crimes of apocalyptic magnitude. What it does lend itself to, it seems to me, are crimes of prosaic magnitude— little acts of treachery, desertion, indifference. What reader of pop psychology, warned a thousand times over with a kind of evangelical fervor that no betrayal compares with the betrayal of our own selves, that no neglect compares with our neglect of our own happiness—what reader can fail to draw the conclusion that betrayal and neglect as commonly understood simply count as nothing? At times pop psychology comes close to saying that the *real* totalitarianism, the very source and origin of all that is worst in the world, is self-hatred. "There is no question that the self-hating autonomy [that is, self-hatred that has become automatic] is a totalitarian slave master."

I have suggested that the right to pursue happiness enshrined in the Declaration of Independence is raised by pop psychology into a right to happiness (as the catalogue of abuses and injuries in the Declaration broadens into the victim rhetoric of the therapeutic movement, and independence itself becomes independence of society). But the Declaration also speaks of "a decent respect to the opinions of mankind," and some of those opinions are unfavorable. Mankind blames; the Declaration blames. Respect for the opinions of humanity includes— presupposes—respect for blame. The argument that blame as such is destructive—and moreover, that when Jill's mother says, "Don't be a selfish girl. Leave some cherries for your brother and sister" she is in actual fact setting up a police-state in Jill's mind—this is so contrary to common sentiment and practice as to express contempt for the opinions of humanity.

☞ The bedrock defense of blame is that as human beings, and therefore moral beings, we are *going* to blame, and this being so, we might as well blame well.

Everyone blames. The self-help genre blames guilt, the instillers of guilt, parents, "the demands and expectations of others," labels, perfectionism, society, the world. Conspiracy theorists blame cabals or the CIA. Many otherwise intelligent persons portray political opponents as virtual conspirators against the common good, staging an elaborate deception. Jews are blamed for poisoning values and killing Christ. In the case of resentment ("*ressentiment*," as it is sometimes called), detraction itself becomes a way of life. The resentful direct their blame at anything that may call forth the malice of a rancorous mind. "It is peculiar to '*ressentiment* criticism' that it does not seriously desire that its demands be fulfilled," Max Scheler wrote. "It does not want to cure the evil: the evil is merely a pretext for the criticism." The envious blame those who enjoy what they do not. The fox blames the grapes. Our trouble is not that we blame but that we misdirect blame, and blame wildly. "Because I am a human being and my views are inevitably shot through with moral assessments, I should seek to [praise and blame] justly, with detachment, on the evidence," insisted Isaiah Berlin.

Blame being a mode of human expression, even poems blame.

As Helen Vendler explains, poems perform speech acts—they boast, banish, protest, vow, supplicate, command. A partial list of such actions provided by the author begins with "Apology" and ends with "Reproach." A poem may reproach because reproach is a mode or idiom of human expression; that is, it may reproach because—the human constitution being what it is—we ourselves do. We can no more remove blame from human life than we can remove the other speech acts, from the celebration to the plea, from questioning to prayer, named by Helen Vendler.

It is utopian to believe that blame either could or should be eliminated from human life, as utopian as the wish to delete the past and rewrite one's own birth (a thought experiment actually suggested by a therapist). We do not and cannot choose our own constitution, and neither is it possible to expunge blame from the human constitution. All we can hope for is to blame justly—to elevate blame from a habit or mentality to a discriminating act.

4

Guilt

If in the eyes of pop psychology blame is destructive, the most concentrated form of blame, and thus the nemesis of human life, is self-blame: guilt. Some thirty years ago the convention of questioning guilt was well enough established to be parodied by Woody Allen: "Good Lord, why am I so guilty? Is it because I hated my father? Probably it was the veal parmigian incident. Well, what *was* it doing in his wallet?" Readers of pop psychology are also to ask themselves, "Why am I so guilty?" No matter what differences tint their pages, practically all works of pop psychology agree that guilt is a poison injected into our minds to make us feel bad about ourselves. Even Norman Vincent Peale, writing in 1952, advised readers to empty their minds of "guilt feelings."

From *Compassion and Self-Hate* (1975): "Guilt and continuing self-denigration are a way of reminding oneself of low worth and insuring the continuation of the self-hating process." From *Your Erroneous Zones* (1976): "If you have large worry and guilt zones, they must be exterminated, spray-cleaned and sterilized forever." From *Looking Out for #1* (1977): "Guilt is a state of mind you needn't endure. . . . Most important, don't feel guilty about looking out for Number One." From *Toxic Parents* (1989):

> When Fred decided to go skiing instead of spending Christmas with his family, he was trying to be an individual, trying to free himself from the family system. Instead, all hell broke loose. His mother and his siblings treated him like the Grinch who stole Christmas, shoveling guilt by the trainload.

From *The Language of Letting Go* (1990): "It's imperative that we stop feeling so guilty. . . . Guilt can stop us from taking healthy care of ourselves." From the back cover of GUILT *is the Teacher;* LOVE *is the Lesson* (1990):

> GUILT. It is the self-defeating inner voice that calls forth the lost, fearful child within each of us. And it is the relentless, accusing voice of blame with which we punish our most childlike selves . . . for our failed relationships, our disappointing careers, and even our illnesses. Still, although guilt has become a profoundly destructive part of the "human condition," it need not become a part of yours.

Step seven of the "Sixteen Steps for Discovery and Empowerment" in *Many Roads, One Journey* (1992): Women must "become willing to let go of guilt, shame, and any behavior that keeps us from loving ourselves and others." From *The Portable Therapist* (1994):

> Guilt can be thought of as a malevolent dictator. Guilt tells us that we are bad, that the sum of ourselves is inappropriate or evil or uncaring. Guilt takes one action or thought of feeling

and generalizes it to the total person. Guilt allows us to feel overwhelmed with negativity and leaves us feeling powerless and helpless. . . . Guilt is also insidious in that it perpetuates the continuation of the "bad" behavior.

From *You Can't Afford the Luxury of a Negative Thought* (1995):

[Guilt] poisons relationships, inhibits growth, stifles expansion. And it hurts. It can become self-hatred. It puts enormous stress on the mind, emotions, and body.

Over time, it can kill.

Perhaps the most tragic part about guilt is that it is thoroughly unnecessary.

That's the bad news. Now, let's lighten up a bit and discuss the good news: after reading this chapter you'll never have to feel guilty again.

From John Gray's *How to Get What You Want and Want What You Have* (1995):

When we absorb negativity, we may try to feel good about ourselves, but we still feel the occasional grip of guilt and unworthiness. We are unable to feel the purity of our innate goodness and innocence and the peace of mind that it affords. We feel tainted or stained by our past mistakes and are unable to forgive ourselves. As a result we experience being overly responsible for others. If as children we were punished for our mistakes, we will continue to punish ourselves.

You become stuck in guilt when you have disconnected from your innate ability to love yourself and forgive your mistakes. . . . Lingering guilt robs you of your natural state of innocence and keeps you from feeling a healthy sense of worthiness and entitlement.

From Phil McGraw's *Life Strategies* (1999):

> Guilt is a powerful and destructive weapon in relationships, and you must steel yourself against being manipulated by it. Guilt paralyzes you and shuts you down. No progress is made if you are whipping yourself with shame. The healthy alternative is to acknowledge any problem behavior; figure out why the problem behavior happens; and make a plan for change. The universe rewards action; guilt is paralysis.
>
> There's nothing wrong with who you are.

From McGraw's *Self Matters* (2001):

> The authentic self is based in accurate knowledge of who and what you are and are capable of controlling. It is the fictional self that is grounded in guilt.
>
> I recall a man who constantly judged himself as irresponsible, never trusting himself for any event or cause, all as the result of the accidental drowning of his little brother. Although he had been in school at the time of the accident, one day he overheard his mother say that if he had been home, the tragedy would not have happened. The result was that, throughout his life, at some level he had been carrying the guilt of his brother's death.
>
> Starting at the tender age of twelve, [Rhonda] had been beaten, raped, and sexually exploited by her biological father. . . . Instead of adopting the belief that she is "damaged goods," Rhonda will have to adopt the new view that she should be looking at herself as important and respected. She might need to consider the alternative belief that she is not guilty of one single thing and that no one is entitled to judge her. She must also generate an AAA [Authentically Accurate Alternative] that says: "I have to stop judging myself."

Like the whole that exceeds the sum of its parts, the self-help genre exceeds any single manual, and the cumulative message of pop psychology is that guilt is simply fallacious—not remorse for things done, but remorse for things *not* done, a delusion that holds the psyche captive. Guilt is the internal enemy. If the master myth of the psychology movement is that I was born to be happy but have had this birthright taken from me, or let it be taken, by a false world, guilt is the last cruel means by which that falsehood maintains its empire over the self. Guilt is false. It should not exist. As in the extreme cases of the boy who blames himself for his brother's accidental drowning, or the girl who blames herself for being raped, guilt is a stubborn, pernicious error that eats away at the possibility of happiness. So guilt-averse is pop psychology that some practitioners worry that its own doctrine of self-creation may be causing guilt, implying as it does that whatever befalls us, from colds to cancer, is our own doing.

Even in the rare case when guilt is earned, pop psychology seems to say it shouldn't exist. In Stephen Covey's anthology of stories illustrating his own seven principles, we meet a man who drives drunk and gets into an accident that kills his friend Frank. Although the story occupies a number of pages, after a few lines Frank virtually disappears, and the word "guilt" occurs but once. The reason is clear: in the Covey system, as elsewhere in the world of pop psychology, there is no point, no gain, in dwelling on the past. You can't do anything about the past, only about the present and the future, so put the past out of your mind and fix your vision straight ahead as in a military drill. "You can sit there forever, lamenting about how bad you've been, feeling guilt until your death, and not one tiny slice of that guilt will do anything to rectify past behavior," declares the author of *Your Erroneous Zones*. "No matter how great your error, simple logic tells you that a guilty state of mind will do nothing whatsoever to help the situation," warns the author of *Looking Out for #1*. "When guilt is legitimate, it acts as a warning light, signaling that we're off course. Then its purpose is finished," states the author of *The Language of Letting Go*, as if the drunk driver did right to put remorse out of his mind once he got his life in order.

Like the other tenets of pop psychology, the doctrine of the falsity of guilt has countercultural sources that today's psychological professionals seem reluctant to acknowledge. In the chronicle of his adventures at Esalen in the 1960s, Stuart Miller learns of a woman who (as a friend tells him)

> "had a husband. He died in an automobile accident about three years ago, and she's hung up about it. We've got to make her realize she's all right. That she needn't feel guilt and that she should start life over, enjoy herself."
>
> "But Herbert," I answer, "you constantly say there are no accidents. She must have had something to do with the death. She must be responsible, in part."
>
> HERBERT: "Of course; she killed him; she drove him to it. But that's over. We can't let her feel guilty, it might make her kill other men. We should tell her she is truly good, truly existent."

Within a few pages both Herbert and the author bed the woman.

That we are each truly good; that we should erase the past and start life over; that guilt is not only a nuisance but a danger—these principles, here associated with the encounter groups and bed-hopping of Esalen, have since been enshrined in pop psychology.

☞ In exposing guilt as a senseless habit that needs to be broken, pop psychology does battle with a way of thinking it calls puritanism. Thus Wayne Dyer: "Our culture has many strains of puritanical thinking which send out messages like, 'If it's fun, you're supposed to feel guilty about it.'" But if our guilt flows from puritanism, it is a good while since puritanism was at full strength. Indeed, unless a certain relaxation of guilt had already taken place—unless it had already lost some of its terror—guilt probably wouldn't have been such an easy target of ridicule and refutation at the hands of pop psychology in the first place. If the impossibility of changing the past were enough to make guilt over misdeeds pointless, such guilt would have been deemed pointless centuries ago, as people knew then quite as well as we do now that the past is past. "What's done cannot be undone," says the sleepwalking Lady Macbeth. It is exactly the temptation of saying, "That was then but this is now" that makes the acceptance of responsibility for the deeds of one's past what Leslie Fiedler once called "the qualifying act of moral adulthood." Pop psychology disdains terms like "moral adulthood." The genre's insistence on the perfectly obvious fact that what's done is done, as if this were a powerful discovery, only means that guilt was already vulnerable to criticism. One reason Freud's thought never really caught on in the United States may be that, whatever the talk associating his name with a loosening of sexual customs, Freud thought too highly of guilt as a civilizing force. His favorite poet was a Puritan, Milton.

Commenting recently on E. B. White and James Thurber's spoof of advice literature of the 1920s, John Updike noted that both authors "were raised as Christians early in the last century, when the Puritan heritage was *still* vitally felt in the respectable middle class." Pretending to be at war with a foe at full strength, the advice authors of today write as if nothing happened to that heritage in the intervening decades. Plainly, something did happen. In 1977 a psychiatrist, Herbert Adler, was quoted in a pamphlet published by the National Institute of Mental Health as saying, "Most of us have been brought up to believe that all guilt is harmful, unnecessary, and should be eradicated." Even reducing "most" to "some," this is a remarkable statement, doubly so in a publication of the Department of Health, Education and Welfare, an agency of the United States government. Such a statement could not have been made fifty years earlier. (Not surprisingly, the same pamphlet makes the "no amount of guilt can ever change history" argument. "If you have done something morally or ethically wrong, accept it—and forget it," we are counseled.)

But how is it possible to establish that acts that once excited much guilt now excite less?

In *The Wealth of Nations*, published in the year of the Declaration of Independence, Adam Smith observes that in advanced societies

> There have been always two different schemes or systems of morality current at the same time; of which the one may be called the strict or austere; the other the liberal, or if you will, the loose system. The former is generally admired and revered by the common people: the latter is commonly more esteemed by and adopted by what are called people of fashion.

A point of distinction between the two systems, according to Smith, is their attitude toward sexual license, the common people viewing it with "the utmost abhorrence and detestation" because they can easily be ruined by the same sort of loose conduct practiced by the privileged. Abhorrence and detestation are blood relatives of guilt. Few today, I imagine, would speak of the austerity of the average American. But let us descend to numbers.

Consider the question of illegitimacy, so close to the heart of Victorian fiction. Gertrude Himmelfarb reports that "Starting at 3 percent in 1920 (the first year for which there are national statistics), the illegitimacy rate [in the United States] rose gradually to slightly over 5 percent by 1960, after which it grew rapidly: to almost 11 percent in 1970, over 18 percent in 1980, and 30 percent by 1991—a tenfold increase from 1920, and a sixfold increase from 1960." Other statistics are equally eloquent. The therapists and counselors who inveigh against guilt as though dismantling an iron curtain of silence not only repeat one another but follow a trend that has been in place for decades. The curtain is already down.

☞ If it is associated with cruelty, repression, and futility, what can be said on behalf of blame? If guilt is blame in its most acute and intimate form, if it is so potent a cause of unhappiness, poisoning us from within, what can be said in defense of guilt?

For one thing, people do things for which they perhaps ought to feel deeply and abidingly guilty. Consider "Rhonda's" father, of whom we are told (though we have no means of verifying any of this) that he was "a sick drunk with a terrible psychopathic mean streak" who not only raped his daughter but gave her to his customers to be raped while he "sat by watching" and drinking himself into oblivion. Here surely is a case of someone who deserves to feel guilt. Or should we suggest, in the favored language of pop psychology, that the man should have admitted his mistake, forgiven himself, attended to his alcohol problem, and put the past behind him?

Assuming the accuracy of the report, this father committed an atrocity. But there exist realms of wrongdoing well short of atrocity. Self-help literature so concentrates attention on the sensational, such as the sexual abuse of children, that one may go blind to lesser acts of betrayal and somehow surrender *to* the sensational. When pop psychologists argue that no act of negligence can possibly compare with our neglect of our own happiness, they trivialize real negligence. In the same way, when they magnify the lurid, especially sexual abuse, they reduce all other wrongdoing to the trivial level of mistakes. "You become stuck in guilt when you have disconnected from your innate ability to love yourself and forgive your mistakes." Mistakes refer to innocent errors. "Problem behaviors," one of the genre's terms of art, is a virtually pediatric euphemism. It is a peculiarity of the genre that it can speak of acts of the utmost depravity but not of ordinary moral life.

Under the influence of pop psychology, we speak of putting the past behind us and moving on with our life. This is exactly what Hamlet is instructed to do by Claudius in Act 1, Scene 2 of *Hamlet*—bury his grief, cease dwelling on the bygone, return to the light of day, and make over his love and loyalty to Claudius himself, King Hamlet's assassin. Over the entirety of *Hamlet* hangs the shadow of Claudius's great crime—fratricide and regicide in one. But this doesn't mean that Gertrude suffers no remorse, even if she had no part in that crime and doesn't know her husband to be an assassin, or that Rosencrantz and Guildenstern are innocent even if they don't know they are bearing Hamlet's death warrant, or that Polonius is not guilty of spying, obsequiousness, voluntary bondage to a fixed idea, disloyalty to the memory of King Hamlet, and the prostitution of his position as the new king's senior counselor. In a play that uses all degrees of illumination from full light to shadow and darkness, we confront many shades of crime, from the great primal crime of Claudius to the banal treachery of false friends. The crime of Claudius does not cancel all other crimes, like the sun canceling the stars in the day sky. If anything, it brings other crimes out. Everyday wrongs still matter. In the fantasy world of pop psychology, everyday wrongs matter little, constituting as they do mere mistakes or behavioral problems. Only the deeds of the Claudiuses, the moral monsters, matter. If everyday wrongs really mattered, they might raise guilt, and pop psychology is concerned above all to preserve me from this ruinous force that estranges me from my true self.

☞ But while books in the self-help section nullify guilt, those perhaps one aisle over that give political expression to the therapeutic or caring ethos presume a reader with a lively sense of guilt over oppression, injustice, and social irresponsibility in all their forms. If therapists seek to break the power of guilt by raising our consciousness of its sources, others—advocates, accusers—seek to induce guilt by heightening our awareness of human suffering. In Wayne Booth's *The Company We Keep*, a study of the ethics of fiction, we learn of a student who confesses in tears that reading Toni Morrison's *Song of Solomon* "made me feel really guilty about how I had been thinking about blacks these days—you know, with all the headlines about crime—and I've really acted different toward them." Many would say a liberal education should have just this effect. Is it possible that the same student who learns to profess guilt in certain politically approved ways also learns, in the course of the same education, that guilt is a baseless fiction instilled into the self to keep us miserable? Pop psychology and humanitarianism agree this far: each trains attention on some single concern before which everything else dwindles into insignificance (in the case of the former, my right to happiness; in the case of the latter, human rights).

Where the self-help literature implies that no obligation can possibly rival my obligation to myself, and no honor means as much as my honoring my own needs, appeals to the social conscience imply that no ordinary act of mendacity or failure of obligation is of any significance next to issues of such moment and magnitude as AIDS in Africa or world hunger. Before an emergency, everything gives way. All traffic yields to the fire truck. But if the therapists want to expose guilt as a fiction, a guilt that I profess over, say, the institution of slavery—which in the United States was abolished a century before my birth—such a guilt is more or less fictitious already. Certainly it bears little resemblance to the guilt that singles me out and tracks me to my hiding place, that bears down on me with a force impossible to deny or evade, as guilt was once envisioned. When, after his years in Burma, Orwell became "conscious of an immense weight of guilt that I had got to expiate," he was thinking not of the crimes of the British Empire but of his own crimes— "subordinates I had bullied and aged peasants I had snubbed, . . . servants and coolies I had hit with my fist in moments of rage." Guilt I profess over the history of slavery attaches to no such actions of my own, quite as if guilt itself had been refashioned in conformity with the therapeutic myth of our own natural innocence—"our innate goodness and innocence and the peace of mind that it affords." Even the guilty student professes guilt not for anything she did but for her thoughts.

It is clear, anyway, that guilt over the extinct institution of slavery differs from a criminal's guilt over his crime. In the former case the guilty one has not committed a crime but grieves the crimes of others, and in part for that reason the profession of guilt is not shameful at all, but honorable. Humanitarian guilt is guilt worn with pride. Unlike the guilt that preys on me, humanitarian guilt is a sentiment I choose to suffer and display;

far from being a penalty to which I am condemned, its moral pain is a purely elective experience, and in some sense a gratifying one, as it proves my own generosity. And precisely as a sentiment I choose, such guilt is consistent with pop psychology's portrayal of guilt as "a choice, something that you exercise control over."

The therapy myth tells of brave and sensitive individuals who ultimately overcome habits of feeling and behavior they had no choice but to acquire when young. From subjection arises freedom; from the deprivation of choice, choice itself. The humanitarian guilt so widely professed and promoted today (and the promotion of this sentiment is itself the sort of act that you exercise control over) tells of politically brave and sensitive individuals who abandon the dark guilt that keeps us in subjection in favor of an enlightened guilt freely chosen. At some level, guilt-inducing programs and guilt-reducing programs are telling the same story. The notion that we should be able to lower and raise our guilt level at our own will and pleasure—lower it in order to overcome any corrosive sense of unworthiness and to cancel the commands and prohibitions once imprinted into us; raise it at the behest of the social conscience and in response to the moral urgency of human suffering—this in itself reflects the pop psychological ideal of an agent able to pull his own strings. Both the guilt reducers of the therapeutic movement and the guilt producers of the humanitarian camp would make me, in effect, the manager and operator of my own self. Those who argue that the exaltation of self in pop psychology fosters social irresponsibility may miss the point. With its disapproval of our culture and its idealization of the act of choice, pop psychology is quite consistent with the sort of social conscience that chooses to grieve the sins of others.

Telling as it does of the passage from subjection to freedom of choice, pop psychology is so choice-obsessed that some of its practitioners are willing to say that we choose our very thoughts—and not only this but the bodily reactions that accompany thoughts: "When you choose the behavior, you choose the consequences. When you choose the thoughts, you choose the consequences. When you choose the thoughts, you choose the physiology." The new modeling of guilt as a humanitarian experience—the conversion of a terrible force into an enlightened option, a choice—provokes at least two questions. At what point does a guilt not personal but vicarious, not shameful but honorable, not a preying force but an embraced possibility, lose its nature and cease to be guilt in anything but name? And how can I choose everything about myself as I might choose what to wear in the morning? Both the exaggeration of choice in pop psychology and the nature and origin of humanitarian or liberal guilt will be taken up in later chapters.

☞ If certain influences in our world arouse the social conscience while others (closely related) discredit guilt, the theory of addiction generates dissonance in its own right. The twelve-step program of Alcoholics Anonymous—perhaps the original model of addiction treatment—calls for the individual to confess his helplessness before alcohol with a guilt-filled heart. After having "made a searching and fearless moral inventory of ourselves" (Step 4), alcoholics are to admit "to God, to ourselves, and to another human being the exact nature of our wrongs" (Step 5). But some would say that the overmastering force of an addiction erases guilt, and the prospect of such absolution has no doubt contributed in recent years to the identification of new modes of addiction, from gambling to food to sex. Addiction itself, it seems, is being liberalized. Luther grounded Christian liberty in the inability to keep the law; Alcoholics Anonymous, in a similar spirit, grounds hope in the confession of powerlessness. In contrast to Alcoholics Anonymous, the self-help movement declares guilt an addiction—a poison to which sufferers subject themselves. It too promises salvation by faith, but faith in the power of therapy to reform human life.

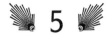

5

Obligation

One of the peaks of the satiric tradition and a work of Shake-spearean richness and ambiguity, Erasmus's *Praise of Folly* describes medicine as practiced by most doctors as "nothing but a branch of flattery, like rhetoric itself." Ingratiation flows like honey through the works of the self-help genre, many of them written by authors advertising doctorates.

As clients need someone "who will remind them of their greatness," the author of *Take Time for Your Life* obliges. Most pop psychologists scale ingratiation down to more modest levels. "Trust me when I tell you . . . you are worth it." "You're a person with a rich array of thoughts, feelings, and desires that are all worthy of being known and accepted." Many self-help authors claim acquaintance with the secret selves of readers who are perfect strangers. Most address the reader directly, in the second person, like rhetoric itself.

The message of self-help is that you the reader are so undervalued, not only by others but even by yourself, that henceforth your mission must be the rebuilding of your psyche and

the reclamation of your well-being. Indeed, the only duty recognized by the genre is this one. Instead of proclaiming the end
of obligation as such, pop psychology concentrates all obligations into the supreme imperative to realize one's right to happiness, quite as if all other concerns of human life will look after
themselves if only we ignore them in favor of this paramount
interest. Thus we read in *Codependent No More*: "This book is
about your most important and probably most neglected responsibility: taking care of yourself." The implication is, first,
that everything the world has known as obligation counts as
nothing compared with this urgent necessity; second, that more
or less everyone but the author has an interest in persuading
you to neglect yourself (or else you wouldn't have overlooked
something so obvious); and third, that a sense of responsibility
to others signifies a lack of self-esteem and is itself, therefore, a
great cause of human misery, a threat to the integrity of the self,
and a factor in "codependency." In *Take Time for Your Life* as
in other works of this kind, you are advised to "put your self-
care above anything else." Advertisements declare that I owe it
to myself to try a cologne, to experience a car's ride: pop psychology declares that I owe it to myself to rise up against all
that has been forced upon me, and to taste happiness.

As we might expect, Phil McGraw orates in this vein:
"What I'm telling you here is that you don't just have a right to
find your way back to the authentic and true you; you have a
responsibility to do it," and a corresponding responsibility to
remove yourself from "the bottom of the priority list." (Hence
the note of the victim's revenge.) When McGraw preaches,
characteristically, that

> to redefine your life and your self-concept, you must do two
> things. First, you must acquire some very specific tools. Second,

> you must commit to being totally and courageously honest. . . .
> You must be accountable and action-oriented. . . . You're going
> to have to find the courage to continue to be real. . . . You must
> decide which elements of your self-concept you value,

his refrain of "must" makes it plain that the obligation to self
is the supreme obligation, next to which any other is not just a
distraction but a betrayal. Responsibility, then, continues to exist, but in transmuted form: I am responsible to myself for my
own well-being, or in Marilyn Ferguson's version of the theme,
"our highest responsibility, finally, unavoidably, is the stewardship of our own potential."

In a genre where the subject of the book is the reader, where
people grieve for themselves, honor themselves, give gifts to
themselves, heal themselves, become their own best friend, hug
themselves, terrorize themselves, even give birth to themselves—
where a book may be dedicated to its own author—compounds
of the word "self" proliferate. Within a few inches of text in
Ending the Struggle Against Yourself, one finds "self-doubt,"
"self-monitoring," "self-deprecation," "self-affirmation," "self-
awareness," and "self-actualization." The index of *Compassion
and Self-Hate* lists fourteen such hybrids. A revealing measure of
the solipsistic character of the genre appears in John Gray's *How
to Get What You Want and Want What You Have*. At a certain
stage in life we feel a need for children, writes the psychologist,
"but if we don't have children, then a pet will work as well." In
any case we need some living thing to feel responsible for.

> If you are without children at this time, it is not enough to be
> spending time with nieces and nephews. It takes really being re-
> sponsible. Every pet owner knows pets are a real responsibility.
> They have to be fed and walked regularly. They get sick, and
> you have to care for them. There are times of great sacrifice,

just as in parenting, but it is all worth it. If owning a pet doesn't fit your lifestyle, then caring for a plant or garden can also be a way to express your nurturing instincts.

If not a child then a pet; if not a pet then a plant. Clearly the object of my concern doesn't matter as long as it serves to bring my nurturing instincts into play. In my responsible relation to another living thing, it is the therapeutic benefits to *myself* that count. Similarly, according to the ethos of self-help, I forgive another person not for that person's sake but for my own sake—to release myself from the bondage of resentment. "Forgiveness of those who have transgressed against you, or those you love, is not about *them*; it is about *you*. . . . You have the ability to forgive those people—not as a gift to them, but as a gift to yourself." I owe it to myself to forgive those who wrong me.

Where self is the only reality, how could any obligation other than to self survive? A manual cited above, *Ending the Struggle Against Yourself*, actually offers sample contract-with-self forms, reading in part:

> I'll set aside at least four hours every Saturday morning, beginning at about 8:00, for Integrity Time. I'll start this coming Saturday morning and continue for at least three months. I commit myself to use that time for solitude, self-reflection, and self-nurturing. I won't plan anything that would require concentrated attention. If a scheduling conflict arises I will make up the time on either the following Sunday morning at 8:00 or the following Monday night at 6:00.
>
> Signature   Date

Like the primer language widely used in the genre, building-block methods like this one seem regressive.

To be sure, the contract holds a place of importance in post-Renaissance political thought. Among the limitations of liberty, John Stuart Mill in his essay *On Liberty* notes that "in this and most other civilised countries, an engagement by which a person should sell himself, or allow himself to be sold, as a slave, would be null and void; neither enforced by law nor by opinion." (Running with this principle, pop psychology argues that we enslave ourselves to society or some other external thing, and that this transaction is invalid, that is, contrary to the interests of the authentic self.) It may be that the inalienable rights invoked in the Declaration of Independence refer not, or not only, to rights that cannot be taken away, but rights that cannot even be given away, just as we cannot alienate our own freedom by entering into slavery. Locke, whose political writings were of course well known to the Americans, made the argument that just as a man cannot enslave himself to another, so the subjects of an absolute ruler cannot be presumed to have consented to their own subjection. It is Locke's intent to define the polity as a contractual community, one where the citizens owe the sovereign not an unconditional obedience but an obedience contingent on the fulfillment of certain well-understood conditions, chief among them the protection of their lives, liberties, and property. The citizens contract with the sovereign. Contract is contract with *another*.

Although Locke justifies revolution (and his *Second Treatise of Government* has been read as the philosophical writ of the Glorious Revolution of 1688), under normal conditions Lockean citizens will look after their lives and property peaceably. Much as the presumption of liberty theory is in favor of liberty (so that the nullity of a contract to make myself a slave is just an exception to the principle that I can do as I like provided I harm no one else), so contract theory presumes as its

norm citizens who follow the law, if only because they consented to the law in the first place. Even the most resounding
defense of lawbreaking in our own time, Martin Luther King's
protest of segregation in the "Letter from Birmingham Jail"
(where segregation is understood as a kind of afterlife of the
institution of slavery)—even this expresses a high respect for
law in general. From Locke's "long train of abuses, prevarications, and artifices, all tending the same way," to the also long
train of abuses listed one by one in the Declaration of Independence, to the powerful catalogue of abuses cited, along
with the name of Jefferson, in King's Letter, there runs a long
if broken line. As befits someone in this tradition, King esteems
the law enough to require of his followers that they accept, in
fact embrace, the penalty imposed by the law for civil disobedience. Citing King's statement

> I submit that an individual who breaks the law that conscience
> tells him is unjust, and willingly accepts the penalty by staying
> in jail to arouse the conscience of the community over its in-
> justice, is in reality expressing the very highest respect for law,

Roger Shattuck remarks that "These words deserve a place
alongside the most valued documents of our founding fathers."
   Shattuck censures the antinomian, "a person who believes
he or she has a claim to be above the law." Antinomianism
originally refers to the doctrine of salvation by faith, not works
and a secular version of this mode of belief, long powerful in
the United States, persists in the tenets of pop psychology.
"There is a whole other level of existence, distinct from what
you do, that is the real, true, genuine sum and substance of
who you are," so that no matter what deeds you commit, they
do not really implicate you. The therapist has faith in you, and
you are to have faith in yourself. But so too does antinomian-

ism in Shattuck's sense—the conviction that one is simply not bound by the world's laws—permeate the self-help movement. According to Charles Reich, advanced consciousness (Consciousness III) "rejects many of the laws, forms of authority, and assumptions that underlie our present political State." In M. Scott Peck's *The Road Less Traveled*, readers learn that if they are sufficiently psychologically advanced, they are exempted from all rules and restrictions.

> Saint Augustine wrote, "*Dilige et quod vis fac*," meaning "If you are loving and diligent, you may do whatever you want." If people progress far enough in psychotherapy they will . . . one day suddenly realize that they have it in their power to do whatever they want. The realization of this freedom is frightening. "If I can do whatever I want," they will think, "what is to prevent me from making gross mistakes, from committing crimes, from being immoral, from abusing my freedom and power?"

These scruples should not, according to the author, a psychiatrist, stand in the way of one's assuming "peership with God." (Perhaps it is a sense of being one of the enlightened that emboldens psychological experimenters to do things that would be abhorrent if performed by anyone else, such as shocking dogs into helplessness, passing off T-shirts as Hitler's, adding time to a colonoscopy, and getting people to submerge their hands in ice water, to cite some exercises mentioned incidentally in Seligman's *Authentic Happiness*. In his now-legendary experiment on obedience to authority, Stanley Milgram racked subjects into administering high levels of [fictitious] electric shock to a confederate. For some, peership with God seems to come down to playing God.) The sort of antinomianism preached in *The Road Less Traveled* and elsewhere in the genre may inspire transcendent intuitions, but it also inspires gross mistakes and abuses of freedom.

And all the more because of the resentment the genre excites toward existing rules and institutions, now portrayed as cruel traps. In the eyes of much pop psychology, the entire world is what Martin Luther King called an unjust law. Simply by virtue of being initiated into society and subjected to its cruelty and falsehood, each and every one of us suffers an oppression comparable to the experiences memorably documented by King. If the soldier's post-traumatic stress disorder was made over to the presumed victims of sexual abuse, the psychological devastation wrought by the system of segregation has been made over to simply everybody. For example,

> When a child is not taken seriously by her parents, whenever her creative efforts or feelings are belittled or discounted, shame occurs as the little shock of nonrecognition and nonacceptance reverberates through the nervous system.

> Every human being encounters traumas, losses, and disappointments in life that leave us feeling bad—sad, angry, hurt, vulnerable, betrayed, or frightened.

The victims of segregation, as Martin Luther King portrays them, indeed suffer nonrecognition and nonacceptance, and know well what it is to be vulnerable, betrayed, and frightened. The Everyman or Everywoman of pop psychology is thrust into a similar position. In making the argument that people either pull their own strings or are slaves of others, Wayne Dyer actually cites King. Reminded time and again that the world is unjust and spurious, that what it calls morality is an instrument of domination, that "the most important person in the world, to whom you should be unswervingly loyal, is yourself," readers of pop psychology might well conclude that they have the right, even the duty, to violate the world's morality and the world's laws.

"The marketing machines, your parents, employers, friends, all have needs for you to be a certain way. And in all likelihood, you have complied with and conformed to those expectancies, at the expense of your own gifts, abilities, and dreams. When those needs are at odds with your being your authentic self, *you must prevail.*" In other words, "You Shall Overcome." What does this mean but that the world is an unjust institution whose ways you have a duty to defy? What is this but antinomianism?

"Musts and shoulds are a great way to motivate yourself as a human *doing,* but they block the joy of human *being.*" What does this say but that conventional precepts and prohibitions are not binding on the self?

Again:

> Have you ever been attacked or threatened with a stick, knife, gun, or any other kind of weapon? Have you ever been forcefully shoved, punched, slapped, kicked, thrown against a wall, or knocked to the ground? Have you ever been coerced into taking drugs or alcohol when you didn't really want to? Have you ever been forced or tricked into having unwanted sexual contact? . . . Has anyone ever lied to you in order to trick you into giving away money or property? Has your house or car ever been burglarized or vandalized?
>
> If any one of these events has happened to you, do you remember feeling frightened? embarrassed or ashamed? confused? guilty?

It is as though the author had set out to replicate the catalogue of cruelties in King's letter, now implying that everyone is subject to the police dogs. There for the gleaning is the further implication that the world is an unjust institution by which we are not bound.

Perhaps it is a measure of the territory already won by the therapeutic movement that the Supreme Court's *Brown* decision of 1954 (invoked by King as an example of just law) emphasizes the psychological damage wrought by segregation, even citing academic studies of the effects of prejudice. But so too is the "Letter from Birmingham Jail" stamped with the language of mental health. Segregation is termed a disease, oppression is said to be psychologically costly, authenticity compromised by conformism, rebellion healthy, and King himself is likened to a doctor—we might say, a therapist—treating root causes and not just symptoms. Recall if you will the observation of M. H. Abrams that by the 1960s, the belief that modern man has fallen ill had taken root among not only psychologists but sociologists and theologians. As the language of the "Letter from Birmingham Jail" makes plain, King writes as theologian, psychologist, and sociologist all at once. Just as the feelings of inferiority cited by the Court in 1954 as an insidious effect of segregation have been generalized into the "low self-esteem" of pop psychology, so the argument and in a sense the language of King's Letter have since been appropriated by those in the therapeutic movement who exhort each and every one of us to reclaim our long-denied rights.

The universalization of the rhetoric of civil rights was already in progress in the 1970s when a self-identified "activist in the civil rights movement" proposed the following exercise: Let all members of the family pin a paper with the letters IALAC (for "I Am Lovable and Capable") on their chest. When someone says something cruel, the recipient of the remark tears off a bit of the sign, and when something complimentary is said, the receiver of the compliment tapes on an extra bit. "After a couple of hours or more, the family comes together and looks at each other's signs." Over time such therapeutic exercises would become a trait of the self-help genre—readers being instructed, for example, to look into the mirror and pronounce the words "I love you." It was the usurpation of civil rights rhetoric by those who deemed morality itself oppressive, as King did not, that produced this embarrassment.

"You can apply the lessons of effective liberation of groups to your own life," writes Wayne Dyer, citing King. "Anyone who attempts to force you in a direction you don't choose for yourself is no less irresponsible or out of line than a slaveowner, a Tory or a dictator." Thus does the reader of *Pulling Your Own Strings* become the heir of the civil rights revolution.

☞ As if the line running from the Declaration of Independence to King's letter (citing Jefferson) had been extended to its own declaration of independence from society, the self-help movement affirms a God-given right to happiness and an obligation, reducing all other obligations to insignificance, to the cause of one's own happiness. In the words of Theodore Rubin, "loyalty to self, in all circumstances whatsoever, is of prime importance in the human hierarchy of values. Being responsible for ourselves and taking good care of ourselves without guilt or other forms of self-hate take precedence over all other human activities." This sentiment echoes like an anthem through the entire genre. Obligation to self is the one absolute.

It is obvious that a profession of love made to the mirror means little. What of a contract with oneself? Just how does an obligation to no one but oneself oblige?

Here I would like to turn from the arid and abstract world of theory to the richly realized world of a Shakespeare play already briefly mentioned. *Hamlet* is indeed a play of mirrors—not the mirror of self-love but the satiric mirror of indignation and disgust, the mirror the prince compels his mother to peer into, the mirror of forms reversed ("Hamlet, thou hast thy father much offended"; "Mother, you have my father much offended"), the mirror of his own reflections, the doubles in whom he confronts figures of himself, the mirror held up to Nature by drama itself, the "glassy" stream in which Ophelia drowns. In the world of pop psychology, *Hamlet* figures mainly as the source of Ophelia, a young woman always under the shadow of others, denied the possibility of self-determination. While there is some truth to this characterization, it does not take account of Ophelia's first speech of any length in the play—a spirited and richly figured reply to her brother's exhortation to chastity.

> I shall the effect of this good lesson keep
> As watchman to my heart. But, good my brother,
> Do not, as some ungracious pastors do,
> Show me the steep and thorny way to heaven
> Whiles like a puffed and reckless libertine
> Himself the primrose path of dalliance treads
> And recks not his own rede [does not follow his own counsel].

Not reduced to wordless submission (as with her father) but addressing Laertes as an equal, and using bold, rich, highly expressive diction, Ophelia here shows powers of speech stifled elsewhere in the play. Her point is that Laertes too must be chaste—that an obligation he imposed on her but failed to honor himself would be a mockery. The world of *Hamlet* is full of mockeries, however; and later in the play we learn of another obligation that has been reduced to nothingness, in this case because the holder of the bond of obligation has died.

No one really knows what speech delivered in the play-within-the-play was slipped into the script by Hamlet. But perhaps it is one, spoken by the Player King, whose greatness seems to lift it out of its immediate context, and whose broad and deep reflections begin with a topic bitterly pertinent to Hamlet himself: the loss of resolution with the passage of time.

> Purpose is but the slave to memory,
> Of violent birth but poor validity,
> Which now, like fruit unripe, sticks on the tree,
> But fall unshaken when they mellow be.
> Most necessary 'tis that we forget
> To pay ourselves what to ourselves is debt.
> What to ourselves in passion we propose,
> The passion ending, doth the purpose lose.

The speech broadens into a vision of human life as a spectacle of opportunism, shifting loyalties, desertion, and betrayal (a world that might include Ophelia's hypocritical pastors and preceptors). In the first instance, the cited passage refers to the Player Queen's overstated vow never to remarry following the death of her now frail husband: a vow that will be reduced to an obligation ("debt") to herself once the king, the holder of the bond of obligation, should die. The point of the first part of the speech, seemingly informed by Hamlet's observation of his mother's infidelity to the memory of King Hamlet and perhaps his own still unfulfilled vow to a questionable second party, is that an obligation to oneself and no one else proves no obligation at all. As Ophelia might say, it is as hollow and untrue as an obligation I lay on someone else but do not keep myself. In a play of incomplete actions, an obligation to oneself is another incomplete action. When time has eroded the Player Queen's passionate resolution, when the receiver of her vow has died and a possible second husband appears, the Player Queen will release herself from a vow that no longer has any force and proceed to a new husband as readily as, it seems, Gertrude passed to Claudius.

Within the surrounding text and context, the "Purpose is but the slave to memory" speech has great resonance. "Purpose" anticipates the Ghost's announcement to Hamlet later in the same act, "This visitation / Is but to whet thy almost blunted purpose" (the last two words brilliantly summarizing the Player King's disquisition on the rusting of resolution over time). "Memory" looks back to the first words spoken by Claudius, "Though yet of Hamlet our dear brother's death, / The memory be green"; back to the Ghost's parting admonition to Hamlet in Act I, "Remember me"; and forward to Fortinbras's opportunistic invocation of certain obscure "rights of memory" at the very end of the play, as he takes possession of the Danish throne. The treachery and degenerating effects of custom, the human capacity to habituate oneself to the inconceivable, hinted at in "slave to memory"—all becomes "That monster custom" in the scene in Gertrude's chamber shortly to follow, and later Horatio's offhanded profundity, spoken of the gravedigger, "Custom hath made it in him a property of easiness." Even the word "slave," the last insult, connects with Hamlet's soliloquy on his own failure of obligation beginning, "O, what a rogue and peasant slave am I!" But if the "Purpose is but the slave to memory" speech broadens as it goes, so does its application broaden to encompass in effect the whole of *Hamlet,* where treachery has been normalized and, in keeping with the speech's theme of forgotten debt, King Hamlet, for all the godlike language attached to him in the play, appears to have passed into oblivion.

Somehow containing within itself the play as a whole, the Player King's speech seems to say that an obligation to oneself

and no one else counts for nothing. In graveyard terms, it is like one row of teeth without the other, or one half of a bond of indenture without the other half; in Ophelia's terms, it is like a duty imposed on another but not oneself. But in view of the sympathy for Ophelia in pop psychology, is it not ironic that the genre as a whole should take as its motto the words of her tyrannical father? "To thine own self be true," says Polonius—*Polonius*, obsequious to the king, a despot to his daughter, the fool of his own theory of Hamlet's madness, wise only in his own opinion.

To pop psychology the words of Polonius are sacred. Quoting the last three lines of the old counselor's farewell to his son (but rendering them as prose and attributing them to "William Shakespeare"), *The Language of Letting Go* comments,

> To thine own self be true. A grounding statement for those of us who get caught up in the storm of needs and feelings of others. . . . *Today, I will honor, cherish, and love myself. When confused about what to do, I will be true to myself. I will break free of the hold others, and their expectations, have on me.*

We are back to a profession of love made to the mirror.

☞ The "Purpose is but the slave to memory" speech considers the erosion of will and shifting of loyalties with the passage of time—the word "passion" itself, twice used in the speech, perhaps connoting something that passes. The first chapter of Gail Sheehy's influential *Passages* alludes to *Hamlet* via its title, "Madness and Method," the meaning of which seems to be that the method of the author's investigation grew out of the crisis of her own mid-thirties, so severe that it took her close to madness. But the helping literature, with its programs and exercises, its forms and formulas, conveys an impression of method gone absurd. And those programs and directions are all powered by a single fictitious imperative, the imperative that gives them their prescriptive force: the neglected duty to myself.

I have suggested that pop psychology so aggrandizes the obligation to self, and so focuses our indignation on the abuse of the innocent, that all else sinks into insignificance. But in fact other things, and dealings with others, continue to matter, and perhaps only because of obligations to others can we be true to self in the first place. Without others I could not even *be* a self. Just as, when I speak, my utterance "is preceded by the utterances of others, and its end is followed by the responsive utterances of others," so too does my existence presuppose the existence of others and indeed address others. The attempt to supplant others by contracting with myself, giving gifts to myself, grieving for myself, honoring myself, forgiving myself, even (as one therapist has it) falling in love with myself—such a project is an exercise in futility. If self-help books really are like so many diet plans that people try one after another as each seems to fail, one reason they fail is clear: unlike an obligation to others, the supreme obligation to self does not really oblige. It is an obligation in name only. "Most necessary 'tis that we forget / To pay ourselves what to ourselves is debt."

The inability to recognize others may help account for a strange but conspicuous feature of pop psychology: its clippings from authors as unlike as Alexander Pope and Kahlil Gibran, Ben Jonson and Erica Jong, to say nothing of Shakespeare, and its use of fables from anywhere and everywhere, as though all of this signified the same thing and all of it mirrored the psyche of the reader. A work of the genre lays down as its first principle, "The universal consciousness, or lifeforce, is present within each human being as the Self," and the genre as a whole treats traditions and disciplines, works of literature and religious parables as if they were all indeed identical with myself. They are not identical with myself. Iris Murdoch finds that what makes great novelists as great as they are is precisely the recognition of others, "a real apprehension of persons other than the author as having a right to exist and to have a separate mode of being which is important and interesting to themselves." She also suggests that imagination at its best resists "the facile merging tendencies of the obsessive ego. . . . Obsession shrinks reality to a single pattern." Melting down the differences between poets, mystics, and thinkers from diverse and conflicting traditions, reducing all literature and all religion to a mirror of the self, portraying people indistinguishably, equating an ordinary upbringing with grievous injustice, condensing all obligations into one—the self-help genre is obsession in action.

 6

Patience

"All experience hath shown that mankind are more disposed to suffer, while evils are sufferable, than to right themselves by abolishing the forms to which they are accustomed." So reads the epigraph to Wayne Dyer's *Pulling Your Own Strings*. As the argument of *Pulling Your Own Strings* is that people betray their own right to happiness by allowing themselves to be victimized, it appears that Dyer thinks Jefferson's words are an indictment of human passivity. In context they are no such thing. Immediately preceding them appears the statement, "Prudence, indeed, will dictate that Governments long established should not be changed for light and transient causes," meaning precisely that mankind *should* bear with evils as long as they are endurable. Even in the Declaration of Independence, that great manifesto of revolt, there remains some feeling for patience.

Traditionally patience is a virtue, but its reputation has dwindled in recent years as the word "virtue" has itself dwindled to an archaism. The pursuit of happiness is an impatient activity, after all (you don't just wait for happiness to come to

you), while radicalism regards patience as a sedative administered to the oppressed to keep them oppressed. Some pop psychology still professes respect for patience; but by and large its
rhetoric not only promises a much quicker fix than anything to
be expected from old-style psychoanalysis, and not only plays
on and inflames impatience as radical rhetoric might do, but
thoroughly discredits patience by suggesting that it is just
that—patience, the endurance of injuries over time—that has
got you, the reader, to the state you are in.

The disqualification of patience, a virtue so fundamental
that it belongs to no single religion or moral system, certainly
has the effect of estranging us from the past and the wealth of
the past. It would be difficult to enter into *King Lear* without
some feeling for patience in the sense of enduring things one can
do nothing but endure. In the great sonnet on his blindness,
Milton is visited by dread and anguish until the voice of Patience makes itself heard at the exact turning point of the poem,
and the turmoil in the mind of the stricken poet is stilled, the
strength scattered in the anxieties of the opening lines collected.

"Applying one or two insights to your life can literally
change everything overnight," states John Gray. "By changing
the beliefs that were formed early in life, you make everything
better right away. . . . The ideas of personal success are simple
and easy to understand, and can be put into practice immediately." If, as I will argue, the theory that we can transform ourselves completely—the animating promise of the self-help
movement—is questionable, still more so is the notion that we
can transform ourselves overnight, as if our own Year One had
been instantly realized or a switch were thrown and a current
of healing energy flowed. The projected reader of *How to Get
What You Want* has little use for patience. How to Get What
You Want means how to get it Now. Even guilt can be cured

instantly. "After reading this chapter you'll never have to feel guilty again," vows Peter McWilliams. Perhaps it is because the reader is presumed to have no patience that the stories contained in self-help manuals usually run to no more than a paragraph or two, as if it were possible to capture the truth of a life in so small a space—a river in a thimble. Many tones and dialects of impatience are heard in the schools of self-help. Some seem to say to the reader, "You have suffered long enough. The time for healing has come." Such is the message sounded in titles like *Codependent No More* and *Victims No Longer*.

Some *have* suffered too much. It is precisely Martin Luther King's argument in the "Letter from Birmingham Jail" that his people have suffered too much, too long, and that the time for patience is therefore past.

> For years now I have heard the word "Wait!" It rings in the ear of every Negro with piercing familiarity. This "Wait" has almost always meant "Never." We must come to see, with one of our distinguished jurists, that "justice too long delayed is justice denied."
>
> We have waited more than 340 years for our constitutional and God-given rights. The nations of Asia and Africa are moving with jetlike speed toward gaining political independence, but we still creep at horse-and-buggy pace toward gaining a cup of coffee at a lunch counter. Perhaps it is easy for those who have never felt the stinging darts of segregation to say, "Wait." But when you have seen vicious mobs lynch your fathers and mothers at will and drown your sisters and brother at whim; when you have seen hate-filled policemen curse, kick, and even kill your black brothers and sisters . . . [there follows a long and unforgettable train of abuses]; when you are plagued with inner fears and outer resentments; when you are

forever fighting a degenerating sense of "nobodiness"—then you will understand why we find it difficult to wait. There comes a time when the cup of endurance runs over.

The Letter appears in a collection of King's writings entitled *Why We Can't Wait.*

It is as though King's rhetoric were used without attribution by crusaders of the self-help movement whose message is that you have suffered enough, that the time for transformation has arrived ("She had decided it was time to be there for herself," says Phil McGraw of one of his success stories), that you deserve to be freed of your fears and self-doubt. The rhetoricians of therapy often imply that every reader has undergone an oppression somehow comparable to the historical subjugation of the black race. Wayne Dyer orates against "slavery." "I cannot be owned by anyone else," he proclaims. King's attack on discrimination gives way to the undiscriminating use of victim rhetoric. Thus too a "feminist, Quaker, psychologist, healer, peace and social activist, and . . . woman on my own spiritual journey" cites racism as just one of the evils arising from "hierarchy and patriarchy," others being sexism, poverty, and addiction in all its forms. Another theorist-practitioner identifies racism as one of many "outgrowths of an addictive society." For these authors and, it must be said, many others in the helping movement, therapy is politics by other means. Yet exaggeration, caricature, unreality, and overheated passion are the stuff of the politics of accusation, and these are the last things that should be called upon in the name of mental health.

Throughout *Compassion and Self-Hate,* conscience is portrayed as, in King's words, a hate-filled policeman. Under the color of medical authority (the author being an M.D.), the book inveighs against American culture as a "reign of terror." Characteristic of its argumentation is the following paragraph:

> *People's consciences are almost always much too strong.* We need freedom and the renewed ability to be spontaneous. The basic good of people and of human substance is a much better guarantee of satisfying behavior both in terms of self and society than the unrequited yearnings and frustrations produced by self-hate. Freedom "to be" invariably produces more constructive behavior than any kind of tyranny, either internal or external in origin.

What seems an authoritative statement grounded in clinical experience reveals itself, upon rereading, as a piece of rhetoric whose principal figure is exaggeration. "Almost always." "Much too strong." "Much better." "Invariably." "Any kind of tyranny." The author simply protests too much. Indeed, in the next lines he likens a strong conscience to an SS guard.

One is reminded of the rhetoric of exaggeration in *The Aquarian Conspiracy*: "Just as hostages sometimes become fond of their abductors, we become attached to the factors that imprison us: our habits, customs, the expectations of others, rules, schedules, the state." "Just as"? Similarly distorted for polemical purposes is Anne Wilson Schaef's sketch of the unliberated woman who "gets her identity *completely* from outside herself; she has *no* self-esteem or self-worth. . . . She is controlling because she has *no* self and is so dependent upon others." From King's compelling portrayal of one fighting a sense of nobodiness, we pass to one who has become nobody in full. Perhaps the cause of all this overstatement is that the authors (and they are not alone) attempt to make a political argument under the name of a therapeutic one, and such arguments, as I have said, favor caricature and excess. The claim that ours is an addictive society certainly has the resounding hollowness of a political slogan.

Where Marxism once argued that the abolition of slavery left wage slavery untouched (an allegation that Charles Reich extended still further, claiming that "machine slavery, extending upward to the white collar and professional ranks, became the key reality of twentieth-century existence"), pop psychology argues that the rights revolution will be complete only with every person's emancipation from psychological slavery, or the tyranny of should. Run your eye down a page of Dyer's *Pulling Your Own Strings*: "domination," "slaves," "being owned," "slavery"—an entire rhetoric of hyperbole. Dyer rejects tradition as a thing external to the self even as he plays on the traditional associations of language. But it is the psychologist of the moment, Phil McGraw, who most effectively appropriates and universalizes King's rhetoric of oppression. We have simply all suffered too much, we are all bruised by injustice and cruelty, we have all been denied our birthright, we have all reached the crisis point and are now ready for liberation. In the rhetoric of McGraw as of King, the time for patience is past. "If now is not the time to reconnect with your authentic self, when will there be a better time? . . . The time is ripe for reopening these beliefs for confrontation and change. . . . *Start now.*"

Writes McGraw in a typical passage in *Self Matters*:

To redefine your life and your self-concept, you must do two things. First, you must acquire some very specific tools. Second, you must commit to being totally and courageously honest in evaluating and using all of the information you have amassed thus far. Some of that which you have identified has been ugly and unpleasant to acknowledge and now is the time to do something about it. Insight without action is worse than being totally asleep at the switch. At least when asleep, you can cling to the old "ignorance is bliss" argument. To do the hard work necessary to figure out your life . . . and then just stagnate and go right back to the same old grind is not okay. . . . You must be accountable and action-oriented to effectively deal with the unvarnished truth and make important changes. To do any less is a waste of your time. What I'm saying is that if you want to maximize the quality of your life and escape from the traps that have contained you thus far, you're going to have to find the courage to continue to be real. . . . It is time to sort the fictional crap from the authentic truth, so that you can reject it and finally uncover and live consistently with who you truly are. . . . Remember that not everyone will be excited about you rejecting some of the roles that you have passively been accepting, in favor of those you truly and actively choose.

* "Totally and courageously honest": like Martin Luther King stating his case in the Letter.
* "Now is the time": so says King.
* "Ignorance is bliss": the purpose of civil disobedience, according to King, is to make it impossible for the public to continue to ignore oppression.
* Hard work and stagnation: "without hard work," says King, "time itself becomes an ally of the forces of social stagnation."
* "Action-oriented": the fourth and final step of civil disobedience is direct action.
* "A waste of your time": "We must use time creatively," says King.

* "The courage to be real": Paul Tillich, cited in King's Letter, and the subject of part of his doctoral dissertation, wrote *Courage to Be.*

* "The roles that you have passively been accepting": in King's phrase, "the paralyzing chains of conformity."

Underlying these correspondences is McGraw's intuition that each and every reader has endured an oppression somehow equivalent to racial injustice, and that the moment has come for them to confront and overcome their oppression and reclaim their God-given rights, just as in the rhetoric of civil rights. King explicitly states that we have not merely a right but a duty to disobey unjust laws; McGraw says, "You don't just have a right to find your way to the authentic and true you; you have a responsibility to do it." King's "We Shall Overcome" becomes McGraw's "you must prevail." King, however, gives voice to his people's impatience while McGraw seeks to stir up grievance, to rouse readers from their state of passivity and discouragement:

> There are a lot of people who are ready, willing, and able to take from you that which is rightfully yours. It might be your property; it might be your space; it might be your very right to think, feel and believe in a certain way. Why would you want to make it easier for them? . . . Once you have strength and resolve enough to believe that you deserve what it is that you want, then and only then will you be bold enough to say, "It is my time, it is my turn; this is for me, and I claim it, here and now."

Once you believe (the therapeutic version of salvation by faith), you will know that the time has come to reclaim your right to happiness, as King's people learned that the time had come for them to reclaim *their* rights.

Much is lost in the conversion of King's plea for equal rights into pop counsel. Consider this passage from *The Language of Letting Go*:

> Being patient does not mean we go through the sometimes grueling process of life and recovery without having feelings! Feel the frustration. Feel the impatience. Get as angry as you need to about not having your needs met. Feel your fear. . . . We find patience by surrendering to our feelings.

It is as if King's Letter legitimizing the impatience of his people had been shorn of its audience, its argumentation, its biblical allusions and resonance, its thought.

☞ The constant theme of pop psychology is that your uniqueness is threatened by rules and roles you never created, that you must not subject yourself to these things, that all pre-existing models menace the self. On that much positive thinkers, astral theorists, recovery counselors all agree. In view of the therapeutic emphasis on "wiping the slate clean"—that is, canceling all that society has imprinted on you—is it not ironic that works in this genre should themselves be so derivative? Would Phil McGraw's crusading rhetoric of rights have been so well received if he had actually invented it, rather than reproducing language long familiar? How could his oratory resonate if there was nothing for it to resonate with? Might not the very aim of wiping the slate clean have seemed an outlandish fantasy if the disavowal of "the very idea of the past" had not been the talk of the sixties and a commonplace of pop psychology ever since? Had the genre of pop psychology that McGraw considers so much rubbish not been in existence—that is, had readers not been accustomed to its idiom—might not a typical McGraw declaration such as "It is time to sort the fictional crap from the authentic truth, so that you can reject it and finally uncover and live consistently with who you truly are" sound like ranting? For all of his contempt for convention and for the world, McGraw employs the established conventions of the self-help genre, such as writing a book about its own reader, and borrows heavily from a rhetoric that predates his own writings. First Ferguson's argument, itself standard "brainwashing" rhetoric, that "just as hostages sometimes become fond of their abductors," so we bond with all that oppresses us; then McGraw's claim that the reader is "just like a prisoner of war or a cult member."

A genre so heavily indebted to pre-existing sources insists on the present moment—"now"—as the only reality. Now is the time for me to end my unhappiness and liberate myself from the tyranny of the past, says the therapist. But while drawing on the rhetoric of rights as it appears, for example, in the writing of King, pop psychology often radiates a resentment that is far from King's spirit of reconciliation.

> "I go through revenge periods. I imagine walking into my parents' house with a shotgun aimed right at my father's balls. 'Okay, Dad. Don't move an inch. Not one step, you sucker. I'm gonna take 'em off one at a time. And I'm gonna take my sweet time about it, too!'"

(This victim's narrative in fact bears an epigraph attributed to Martin Luther King, Sr. [sic]: "No matter what you do to me, I will not give you the power to make me hate.") Phil McGraw suggests that a woman address these words to her victimizers:

> "You need to know the pain you caused me. You need to know the crippling effect what you did had on me. You need to know

what it's done to my life and my marriage and my relationship
with children, you no-good, rat-bastard son of a bitch."

Here then is the note of "*ressentiment*"—of a desire for revenge
that has soured the mind and taken possession of the imagination. Late in the *Odyssey*, when the loyal servant Eurycleia dis-
covers that all the suitors have been killed at last, she breaks
into a cry of triumph; but so ugly is her passion that she is si-
lenced at once by Odysseus. The voices just cited are Eurycleia-
like voices—ugly, intoxicated outcries by sufferers who for too
long have been dreaming of revenge.

The critic Walter Benjamin theorized that for the oppressed
at the moment of revolution, time suddenly electrifies; no
longer a succession of empty moments, it fills with meaning and
becomes "Now-time." ("Now is the time for their dinner to be
served," says Odysseus of the suitors, just as he is about to
slaughter them at the table.) With its rhetoric of oppression, its
affection for phrases like "now is the time," its idealization of
"the moment" as if it were the consummation of time itself, and
indeed its dreams of revenge, pop psychology plays on this conception of revolutionary time. Where a Marxist would once
have urged the oppressed to rise to their destiny as the makers
of history, Phil McGraw urges readers to rise up and create
their own life.

> It's time for you to stop being passively shaped by the internal
> and external forces in your life. It's time to start consciously
> and actively challenging and directing those very same forces.
> . . . Now is the time.

Here as elsewhere, McGraw does all he can to induce a sense
of "Now-time." As I have argued, the pop psychology whose

conventions McGraw follows faithfully owes much to the utopianism of the 1960s, with its revolutionary mood of "Now." That era's foremost theorist of revolution, Herbert Marcuse, has been cited with Walter Benjamin as among "the most important ideologists of revolutionary messianism" in the twentieth century.

Conceptually it is not that far from the revolutionary rhetoric of the 1960s to that of a work like Gloria Steinem's *Revolution from Within: A Book of Self-Esteem*. But in the self-help movement, "Now is the time" conveys not only the hope or promise of a life transformation, and not only impatience and even contempt toward the past, but resentment of the past's interference with my invention of myself. The past is the shadow hanging over the present—a curse to be lifted, an oppressor in its own right. "Live in the moment." But as pop psychology's own derivation from pre-existing sources suggests, the past makes the present possible in the first place. Martin Luther King may have cited Socrates, Luther, and Jefferson among others in the "Letter from Birmingham Jail" not to endear himself to white readers by honoring their heroes, but because he knew that the past is the soil and source of the present and that he did not create himself. He also knew the virtue of patience. The author of *Why We Can't Wait*, the maker of the argument that the time for patience has expired, nevertheless undertook to answer his critics in the "Letter from Birmingham Jail" in what he called "patient and reasonable terms."

☞ As a gauge of the generic nature of the language of pop psychology, consider a student essay, used as an example by the Educational Testing Service, that faithfully reproduces the clichés of the genre. Asked to discuss the choice between doing what you want and doing what you ought to do, the student wrote in part,

> My friend Bob was a very intelligent man. He went to college and excelled in everything he did. All of his life his parents gloated in the spotlight of their son "the genius." They all had high hopes of him becoming the doctor of the family. He had one more month until graduation, yet something was plaguing him. Bob had an obsession for jet skiing. And he had a chance to buy a little shop on Marina Blvd. and start his own business. In order to do this, he would have to drop everything and start on his new business right then. I'm sure Bob thought he should finish college and become a doctor, but he really wanted to open that jet ski shop. He went with what he truly wanted. I believe in this case what he wanted to do was a better choice than what he should do. Bob is extremely happy now. And I wonder if he would be happy if he chose to become a doctor? Probably not, because that isn't what he wanted.

Here then is the story line of pop psychology: If you forget ought and should, and follow the promptings of your authentic self, all will be well. So conventional is the story of Bob, right up to its statutory happy ending, that one can't be sure Bob wasn't invented for the purpose of the essay. The conflict between parental expectation and heart's desire, the little shop—it all seems scripted. But perhaps the most scripted touch in the story is the coincidence of a dreamed-of opportunity presenting itself just as Bob is about to graduate. Not only must Bob "drop everything and start on his new business"—or, in the language of the genre, wipe the slate clean—but he must to do this "right then." It is the rhetoric of urgency that certifies this story as a portrait not of Bob but of pop psychology itself, with its message that "Now is the time." "*Start now.*"

Choice

A century after the end of the Victorian era, in the press and in intellectual circles alike, the word "Victorian" is still an epithet of opprobrium. Victorianism thus understood is so much sexual hypocrisy, bad taste, and strenuous moralism, all of it offensive in the eyes of the modern. That Victorianism, quite unlike modernism or for that matter romanticism or classicism, is named for a person suggests something of the special animus directed toward it. (I once saw a production of Oscar Wilde's *An Ideal Husband* with a giant medallion of the ugly queen presiding over the stage.)

If today we periodize history to our own advantage, claiming in effect to have emerged from the ignorance and darkness of the past, just as the Renaissance once emerged from the Middle Ages, the Victorians themselves not only periodized but acclaimed, or else decried, the emergence of their own society from the ways of the past. Even while making the Victorians the special objects of odium and caricature to celebrate the progress we have made since then, critics today still invoke the great

Victorian ideal of progress itself. Self-help writers, depreciating as they do everything received and not created by oneself, voice an especially strong bias against tradition; yet the very title of their genre is a Victorianism. Writing of Samuel Smiles's immensely popular book *Self-Help*, Asa Briggs notes that

> On both sides of the Atlantic in the middle years of the nineteenth century there was a great wave of "success" literature, designed to provide its readers not only with a message but with a practical guide to the problems of city life and the right tactics for "getting on."

For all its rhetoric of erasing the past, the how-to literature of today clearly descends from these success stories; indeed, it is filled with success stories of its own. The person who can design his own being (the hero of pop psychology) is the self-made man of yesterday made absolute. Many who would be embarrassed by the poverty of the Samuel Smiles stories do not seem to find psychological success stories equally impoverished.

Maybe the real reason the Victorians are such an embarrassment is that they embarrass the modern, and postmodern, fantasy of self-creation. As if keeping a family secret, Phil McGraw nowhere in *Self Matters* or *Life Strategies* mentions the name of the Victorian whose powerful argument he reduces, rewrites, and retails: John Stuart Mill. Mill's classic essay *On Liberty* was published in the same year as Samuel Smiles's *Self-Help*, 1859.

☞ Such is our debt to the past that even the prejudice against it is inherited. As hostile to tradition in his own way as were the revolutionaries of France who declared a Year One in 1792,

Mill's godfather, Jeremy Bentham, "begins all his inquiries by supposing nothing to be known on the subject; and reconstructs all philosophy ab initio [from the beginning], without reference to the opinions of his predecessors." In the spirit of those in the 1960s who sought "to disavow the very idea of the past" and declared their own Year One, Phil McGraw would have me erase my own history and reconstruct it from the beginning, rewriting even my birth. ("If you hadn't inherited the status quo; if you weren't born into a certain family and station in life and weren't buried so deep that you seemed to have no choices, what would you choose?") When the same author impresses on the reader the urgent necessity "to maximize your quality of life," he uses a verb invented by Bentham, just as the mixing of quality and quantity recalls a charge brought against Benthamism, that it can tabulate but not evaluate, count but not judge. For its part, the Weight-and-Balance Happiness Scale, which made its appearance in the best-seller *Looking Out For #1* (1977), is an unintended parody of Bentham and of itself.

Why is pop psychology so derivative? One reason has already been noted: being unable—contrary to its own rhetoric—to invent its own foundations, it must rely on what already exists. But in addition, *being* rhetoric, addressing the reader directly ⬤n the manner of promise, exhortation, and warning, it must necessarily deal in commonplaces. From Aristotle on, the commonplace has been understood as practically the unit of rhetoric. In order to strike a chord with its audience, rhetoric must play on sentiments and ideas already in the audience's possession; and pop psychology does so continually. (Two primary features of self-help writing—its repetition and exaggeration— are not only common and virtually inescapable features of rhetoric, but in this case serve in lieu of traditional rhetorical adornments such as figures of speech.) It is ironic that one of the sources exploited by pop psychology in its search for received ideas is the work of a great critic of the commonplace, John Stuart Mill.

Mill's essay *On Liberty* celebrates the few who choose rather than merely inherit or follow a way of life. When M. Scott Peck asks, "What distinguishes the few from the many?"—meaning, what separates the few who courageously venture into and complete therapy from the many who fear, shun, and desert it?—he appropriates Mill's concept of the enlightened minority even as he defines enlightenment psychiatrically and redefines it to include "peership with God." In many ways, Mill's terms and rhetoric have indeed passed into the hands of psychotherapists. "Progress depends on individuals who are innovators, who reject convention," writes Wayne Dyer in *Your Erroneous Zones* (1976), paraphrasing *On Liberty*, which he elsewhere cites by name. Or as Dyer writes in *Pulling Your Own Strings*,

> To live your life the way you choose, you have to be a bit rebellious. . . . The central insight must be that individuals have the *right* to decide how they will live their lives, and that as long as their exercise of this right does not infringe on the equal rights of others, any person or institution that interferes ought to be viewed as a victimizer.

So states Mill, except that he declines to bring rights into the discussion (perhaps knowing what rights rhetoric does to the argument), doesn't use emotive labels like "victimizer," to which we are intended to react like puppets, and doesn't tell readers to their face that they have to do this or see that.

The principle that society's precepts threaten the self has remained constant through all the variations of pop psychology. Where Mill, writing in 1859, maintained that the prevailing

standard of character was "to be without any marked character; to maim by compression, like a Chinese lady's foot, every
part of human nature which stands out prominently," a psychologist now maintains that "anorexia signifies that a young
woman is so delicate that, like the women of China with their
tiny broken feet, she needs a man to shelter and protect her."
And just as Mill's rhetoric of nonconformity has been appropriated in self-help literature, so too is the concern with the
despotic power of fathers voiced in *On Liberty*. "As a society,
we have traditionally considered the discipline of children a
private matter, to be handled within the family, usually at the
father's discretion," writes one therapist, paraphrasing Mill:

> The State, while it respects the liberty of each in what specially
> regards himself, is bound to maintain a vigilant control over his
> exercise of any power which it allows him to possess over oth-
> ers. This obligation is almost entirely disregarded in the case of
> the family relations, a case, in its direct influence on human
> happiness, more important than all others taken together. The
> almost despotic power of husbands over wives need not be en-
> larged upon here. . . . It is in the case of children that misap-
> plied notions of liberty are a real obstacle to the fulfillment by
> the State of its duties.

But it is not just on this or that point that pop psychology
owes a debt to Mill. The very terms that preside over pop psychology in all its forms—terms like "growth" and "discovery"
and "progress" and "individuality"—descend from the liberal
tradition classically instanced in Mill's essay. Attached as they
are to the image of themselves as emancipators, however, pop
psychologists rarely acknowledge debts to tradition. After all,
in the stories they tell, people who choose to be happy make a

decision to walk away from the past. And to say that the rhetoric of pop psychology plays on Mill doesn't mean it is faithful to Mill's intent. While Mill certainly affirms the act of choice, he does not speak of people who make a choice to be happy— indeed, his autobiography reports that he made it the "basis of [his] philosophy of life" that one cannot pursue happiness directly at all—still less portray the choice to be happy as the critical act of human life.

"He who does anything because it is the custom makes no choice," writes Mill—a statement that pop psychologists find congenial. (Mill's next words, however, find little reception among the therapists: "He gains no practice either in discerning or in desiring what is best. The mental and moral, like the muscular powers, are improved only by being used.") Mill continues, "He who lets the world, or his own portion of it, choose his plan of life for him, has no need of any other faculty than . . . imitation." Those who do not choose their plan of life for themselves follow like sheep, or automatically reproduce patterns laid down by others, but in any case they surrender the possibility of self-determination to an external regime. They are conformists. By now this message, suitably retouched, has been reproduced so widely and invariantly as to constitute a regime in its own right. Phil McGraw: "You may well have been conditioned to give your power away and make your own individual wants and needs secondary in determining the choices you would make, because you sensed or convinced yourself that conforming was essential to your very survival." Theodore Rubin in *Compassion and Self-Hate*: "People who are particularly individualistic . . . must be prepared to fight for the compassionate *I am I* principle, against the popular and tenacious forces of conformity." McGraw: "So what is this authentic self I keep talking about? . . . It is all of your strengths and values that are uniquely yours and need expression, versus what you have been programmed to believe that you are 'supposed' to be and do." Joseph Campbell: "What is the nature of the wasteland? It is a land where everybody is living an inauthentic life, doing as other people do, doing as you're told, with no courage for your own life." Dissent has become orthodoxy.

Human nature, writes John Stuart Mill, is not a machine "but a tree, which requires to grow and develop itself on all sides, according to the tendency of the inward forces which make it a living thing." The self-help movement has claimed this, the classical language of liberalism, so that now it is the patient who achieves growth under the guidance of a therapist. That our nature is "always in its essence developing" is the stated premise of Gail Sheehy's argument in *Passages*. We are not done developing after our emergence from childhood, as if the language of Mill had somehow authorized a conception of adult life as a prolonged adolescence. Commenting on *Passages*, Christopher Lasch wrote in 1979 that while generous in spirit, "it rests on medical definitions of reality that remain highly suspect, not least because they make it so difficult to get through life without the constant attention of doctors, psychiatrists, and faith healers." Between medical doctors and faith healers extends a vast amorphous region now claimed by psychotherapists, social workers, counselors, and personal coaches, many of whom associate themselves somehow with the authority and good name of medicine. (Confusing the matter further are the medical doctors who themselves write pop psychology.) At the moment the most influential of the public therapists may be Dr. Phil McGraw, who is probably thought by many of his devotees to be a medical doctor (but is in fact a psychologist), and whose voice indeed rings with the accent of the revivalist—the faith healer.

According to McGraw, we must liberate ourselves from patterns "automatically adopted." "Stop being the silent and obedient sheep." The self-determining individual risks unpopularity. Growing up, "you had to conform to the values, patterns, and demands" of the community. "Individual expression" breaks the power of "conformity." This is the story McGraw tells ad infinitum. A hostile world, a world demanding the suppression of your individuality and obedience to its own mechanisms, has robbed you of well-being and never will you recover this well-being, which is your birthright, unless and until you cease to conform to those demands and instead heed McGraw's prescriptions. (Other healers urge the same thing. "Stop being so damned nice. . . . Assert yourself. Stand up for yourself. You are here and you are real. Let the world know it.") Naturally we are to believe that when people stop being obedient sheep, their revolt against the world's unjust laws will be innocent. When they repudiate what the world calls moral, then and only then will they become truly moral. Except perhaps for this last point, the key terms in McGraw's myth—individuality, unpopularity, conformity, mechanism—reproduce the letter if not the spirit of Mill's language. Mill says, "Human beings are not like sheep; and even sheep are not undistinguishably alike."

And so Mill's

> Not only in what concerns others, but in what concerns only themselves, the individual or the family do not ask themselves—what do I prefer? . . . It does not occur to them to have any inclination, except for what is customary. . . .

becomes McGraw's

> You need to ask yourself: "Is what I'm doing today really what I *want* to do, or am I doing it, not because I want to, but because it is what I was doing yesterday?"

This example typifies the exploitation of the tradition of liberalism in pop psychology, which continually inveighs against "tradition" and "the Western model." How can McGraw borrow so freely from tradition while instructing the reader to "adopt the attitude of questioning and challenging everything in your life that you can identify as having been . . . adopted out of tradition or history"? If his rhetoric did not tap into sources long in existence and themes well established, it would not have the resonance and reception it does. Indeed, McGraw tirelessly repeats others in the self-help genre, who themselves appropriate the long-familiar language of nonconformism. It is as if the genre as a whole took the view that human beings are extremely simple creatures who must be told the same things over and over again in order to learn. Even the figure of a flock as an image of a conformist society is unoriginal. Wrote Wayne Dyer in 1976,

> You do not have to be always as your culture expects you to be. If you are, and feel an inability to be otherwise, you are indeed a follower, one of a flock who allows others to determine his course. . . . [A healthy person will let others] go through their sheep motions.

When self-help authors echo John Stuart Mill, or quote an aphorism from Emerson, these are almost invariably not conscious borrowings; they are unconscious debts to tradition. Pop psychology does not and cannot live up to its own rejection of tradition, though by the same token it adulterates what it borrows.

☞ In his nonconformism and his poor opinion of existing morals, manners, and sexual institutions, John Stuart Mill is in the tradition of Mary Wollstonecraft, and for her, women bear responsibility for their own conduct despite being the products of bad education. Hence the unexpectedly strong note of reproach of women themselves in Mary Wollstonecraft's *Vindication of the Rights of Woman* (1792). Women bear responsibility because without it they would sink beneath the level of rational beings. In a sense, the readership of the *Vindication* is expected to perform the same sort of transformation as the readers of a self-help manual, in this case turning themselves into responsible agents in spite of being reared in a thoroughly corrupt system.

But I believe it is not so much utopianism as moral ardor that inspires in Mary Wollstonecraft the belief that women must and can break the vicious circle that seems to entrap them—the circle by which corrupt institutions fashion corrupt women who then perpetuate the institutions themselves. At the point where the mother begins to train her girl-child in affectation, grooming her for the marriage market—at that point Mary Wollstonecraft holds the woman responsible, regardless of her own upbringing, for she has failed her duty and chosen to become the agent of depraved institutions. When a trenchant critic of pop psychology, replying to its exaggeration of human helplessness, argues that "Somewhere along the line we still become accountable for ourselves; the factors that shaped us are moot," she takes a position close to that of Mary Wollstonecraft. And unlike a self-help author, Mary Wollstonecraft never thinks of choice without thinking also of responsibility. So too Mill.

For Mary Wollstonecraft as for Mill and others both before and after who invested great importance in the act of choice, that act was not content-free and all-transforming, like the waving of a wand, as now portrayed in the literature of self-help. "Reason is but choosing," says Milton in "Areopagitica," a direct precursor of *On Liberty* (and a work that ridicules political measures suitable only for "Atlantic and Utopian polities"). Endowed with the gift of reason, Adam and Eve in *Paradise Lost* must each choose whether to eat the apple or refrain; neither can claim that the choice to eat is valid simply *as* a choice, nor can Adam point to Eve's choice as a precedent or extenuation of his own. Milton is the epic poet of choice. Of the great theorist of prose literature M. M. Bakhtin, it is said that he "above all . . wanted to give body and weight to an understanding of the world in which selves create, exercise choice, take responsibility, and develop unpredictably," with the implication that the act of choice is a morally answerable one. Choice does not absolve from responsibility; it *incurs* responsibility. So great is pop psychology's aversion to moral responsibility that at times it sacrifices the very principle of choice: "We cannot choose or be held responsible for choice if we do not have the necessary qualifications for making that choice." According to *The Portable Therapist*, people without a conscience lack such qualifications and are therefore not responsible for their actions. The Grand Inquisitor might have agreed.

☞ According to the romantic picture of choice in the self-help literature, to lead an authentic life is to break free of the patterns and precepts imposed on you, and then choose patterns and precepts for yourself. This story of the passage from bondage to freedom echoes endlessly through the pages of pop psychology, where "the supreme act is the act of choice," as Charles Reich put it in his manifesto of advanced consciousness. "The past may feel like a prison, but you do have the key and you can walk away whenever you choose to let go," advises *The Portable Therapist*. "We have choices, more choices than

we let ourselves see," declares *The Language of Letting Go.*
"The sense of being trapped is an illusion." Phil McGraw, using identical rhetoric, maintains that the only thing keeping us
in prison is our own failure to choose freedom. In a single paragraph of *Self Matters,* I count ten variants of "choose" and
"choice." In a single paragraph of Rubin's *Self-Hate and Compassion,* I count fourteen.

In the choice-obsessed world of pop psychology, people
choose to feel the pain of the dentist's drill ("You could make
the whole experience work for rather than against you by
choosing to make it a pleasant, exciting procedure"), and cancer patients choose their own tumors ("There is a burgeoning
amount of evidence to support the notion that people even
choose things like tumors"). You choose your sensations, your
perceptions, your thoughts. If anything not chosen represents
something imposed, in order to be free you have to choose
everything. (Do pop psychologists use a kind of alternative language in order to free themselves of their mother tongue?)
Choosing is thus exaggerated just as the injustice of the existing
order, which represses your power of choice, is exaggerated.
When Oprah Winfrey was sued by the beef industry, "she had
a choice": fight or not fight. She fought and won. "Just like
Oprah, you face problems and challenges each and every day.
. . . Just like Oprah, you have to help you." Choice will make
you free.

In so idealizing the act of choice, pop psychology appeals to
a powerful strain in our culture. From the shopper to the existentialist theorizer, the act of choice has been celebrated across
the expanse of modern life. In Charlotte Perkins Gilman's feminist utopia of *Herland,* heroic women choose to allow child-
longing to grow within them, or else they choose not to and
"put the whole thing out of [their] mind"; and so they keep

their population to the level the land can sustain. Their very commonwealth is a hymn to choice. A popular classic of the advice genre revealingly inverts the Gospel's "few are chosen" into an affirmation of the power of choice. "Christ's assertion 'Many are called, but few are chosen' I would translate to mean 'All of us are called by and to grace, but few of us choose to listen to the call.'" Under the influence of the exaltation of choice, guilt itself, once portrayed as a terrible force impossible to evade, becomes an optional experience. Those who profess guilt over, say, the extinct institution of slavery do not suffer guilt so much as they choose it. They choose to listen to the call of enlightened opinion. Where the psychologically informed reader "never has to feel guilty again," the choice to feel guilt over slavery is politically honorable precisely because one *doesn't* have to feel it.

Who doesn't want choice? If it goes against the grain to speak on behalf of blame, what could possibly be said against choice? Isn't to speak against choice to speak for bondage?

Only if anything not explicitly chosen represents bondage; only if we "really have to choose between an image of total freedom and an image of total determinism." Like one who proposes desperate measures in an emergency ("Remember," says one author, "*your life is at stake*"), the therapists argue that we really are hopelessly determined unless and until we break free—a state of emergency indeed. "After childhood the self-hating process has an autonomy of its own and unless active and, yes, heroic, intervention takes place, it goes on unabated in the same automatic, choiceless way as the heart beats." The therapist therefore resembles the deprogrammer who liberates a youth from the cult that has made an automaton of him, except that in the eyes of pop psychology our entire culture is that cult. It renders us choiceless, though once we decide to throw off our chains, its dominion over us is at an end. I would say of the romanticization of choice in pop psychology what Iris Murdoch says of the exaltation of choice in modern philosophy: "The existentialist [that is, exaggerated] picture of choice, whether it be surrealist or rational, seems unrealistic, over-optimistic, romantic, because it ignores what appears at least to be a sort of continuous background with a life of its own." In other words, ordinary life is not just a black field punctuated by occasional bursts of brilliance in the form of acts of choice. It is far richer than that. "Here neither the inspiring ideas of freedom, sincerity and fiats of will, nor the plain wholesome concept of a rational [or Kantian] discernment of duty, seem complex enough to do justice to what we really are."

Still less adequate are the prescriptions of pop psychology, often framed in the language of the primer. How just can a philosophy be that speaks of our having been born as an insult to our power of choice? "You didn't choose to be born, but the reality is that you're here," observes Robert Ringer. Phil McGraw agrees. It is because we never chose to be born, and anything not chosen violates the self, that McGraw exhorts readers to unwrite and rewrite the story of their life from day one. "Without question, a defining moment of overwhelming significance for you was the moment of your birth. You didn't get a vote; it just happened. . . . All of the choosing was done for you." The task of self-help is therefore the recovery of the freedom you lost when you came into the world. The Grand Inquisitor takes over the freedom "with which the ill-fated creature [that is, man] is born," and for Phil McGraw too, the human misfortune seems to begin with birth.

But we cannot unwrite and rewrite ourselves. We cannot possibly face a choice between total freedom and total determinism because we don't possess unlimited freedom to begin with. Perhaps it is this all-or-nothing attitude toward freedom that accounts for the receptivity of the self-help movement to the demeaning plea of addiction, as though we had become slaves not only to tobacco and alcohol but sex, food, gambling, whatnot. For if we are not unconditionally free in our choice-making, says pop psychology, are we not then determined? If we are not the master, are we not the slave? However that may be, and in spite of the myth of choice-making as a transformation of the chooser, it is clear that my power to make choices extends only so far. I can choose a pen, a car, a course of action, but despite the aggressively promoted notion that I can new-model myself by an act of will, I do not and cannot choose the person doing the choosing.

☞ Limits on the human power of choice do exist.

In the campaign against Catholicism waged in the days of Shakespeare, many an Englishman and Englishwoman must have been compelled to repudiate the old faith and choose the new way of Protestantism. One of the satires of John Donne, himself raised a Catholic, has been described as "an excited, disturbed reflection on his own need to choose" a religion. Compounding the ordeal of choosing a religion under the pressure of historical circumstances, such as those that bore upon Donne, is the fact that religion doesn't really lend itself to choice at all. Even Milton, who not only took the new way but vilified Catholicism as a conspiracy against human liberty, would have recognized some limits on the power of choice. His "Areopagitica" depicts England as a new Israel, a nation favored by God and, like its original, given to disloyalty and impiety. ("God is decreeing to begin some new and great period in his church, even to the reforming of the Reformation itself: what does he then but reveal himself to his servants, and as his manner is, first to his Englishmen? I say, as his manner is, first to us, though we mark not the method of his counsels, and are unworthy.") But the Israelites were a chosen, not a choosing, nation. Some consider those new Israelites, the Puritans, to be the originators of improvement literature as we know it; certainly Benjamin Franklin was not far removed from the Puritans.

Suppose that Charles is thinking of dedicating himself to a religious faith but wavering in his choice. The improvement literature of his own time instructs him that "you have to decide deliberately, instead of drifting unthinkingly into action or inaction—you have to know what options are available, and you have to check them out," and this principle he takes to heart. Eventually he narrows the possibilities to two: the Southern Baptist faith and Buddhism. He investigates what each asks of him and has to offer, considering his options in the spirit of one who believes we make ourselves what we are by our choices. He appreciates the magnitude of the decision. What is absurd here? Clearly, that one doesn't choose to join a religion in the way one chooses, say, to take out a mortgage. Someone calculating whether or not to join a religion has already proven definitively that he or she does not and cannot belong to that religion, if only because a religion does not return benefits on investments.

Now suppose that Charles is endeavoring to decide whether or not to marry Lydia. As in the case of his religious deliberations, he carefully considers the magnitude of the choice and weighs the benefits and liabilities of the married state. Among the benefits of being married to Lydia are that it will satisfy Lydia, it will help if and when they decide to have a child (but that is another choice), and it will lay to rest the nagging question of whether or not to marry. Among the liabilities of marriage are that it will complicate the dissolution of the relationship if and when it does dissolve. Is it not clear that Charles had better not marry Lydia—that getting married is not an act to be contemplated in the spirit of choice-making recommended in the help manuals?

The reason most advice manuals cannot accommodate either of these cases is that they cannot really envision human beings joined by strong bonds, or cannot conceive of bonds except as bondage. The explicit message of Phil McGraw is that you have no true bond with anyone whomsoever except your counselor and deliverer Phil McGraw, amazingly the only other person on this earth with your interests at heart. "Your parents, teachers, friends, spouse, employers" make their demands "without consideration of what you truly want." Only Phil McGraw respects what you truly want. In contemplating his choices, Charles asks himself what he truly wants; but how could one with such an impoverished sense of human connection possibly enter into a deep and lasting bond?

On some matters we may find we have no choice, but this isn't to say that we experience the impossibility of choice as subjection. Sissela Bok's fine study of lying, curiously entitled *Lying: Moral Choice in Public and Private Life* (as though even morality were defined by choice-making), ends with a consideration of lies by doctors to patients. The traditional rationale for medical lies, namely, that the informed physician believes they are in the patient's best interest, is examined and found far too permissive. Sissela Bok argues—persuasively, to my mind—that the traditional presumption in favor of the physician in these matters must be reversed, and that lies by physicians to patients must be prohibited unless the case meets a narrow and demanding set of conditions. Indeed, the tradition that accords doctors the *choice* to lie—that places the issue in their discretion—is exactly what the author argues against.

By now, the author contends (writing in 1978), "the doctor's choice to lie increasingly involves co-workers in acting a part they find neither humane nor wise." But isn't this to say that the conscientious doctor really has no choice? "For the great majority of patients . . . the goal must be disclosure, and the atmosphere one of openness." Good medical practice, keeping the patient's perspective in mind, "requires a stringent adherence to honesty." "Must be," "requires"—contrary to the title of the work, responsible physicians know that in questions of truth and falsehood they rarely have a choice. Conversely, the physician who thinks he has been presented with choices, who starts asking himself if he ought to tell the truth or conceal it, or perhaps reveal it in part, simply does not feel the force of Bok's argument. Told that he had the obligation to be truthful, such a physician might chafe and complain of a loss of rights; but someone who felt the obligation and appreciated its force would not complain.

☞ Like a wand waved over an object to make it disappear, choice in pop psychology cancels all else, from the world's expectations to one's own history. By the act of choice we become free. The critical therapeutic act, after all, is to make a choice to change your life. Once the choice is made, the change has already begun. Has literature ever celebrated an antinomian force as pop psychology celebrates choice?

In Shakespeare, love is indeed an antinomian force, heedless of parental prohibitions, common sense, the law, social differences of all kinds (as with Othello and Desdemona), even language (as with Mortimer and his Welsh wife in *Henry IV, Part I*). Precisely because of its independence of all laws and considerations, however, Shakespeare portrays love not just as a comical ecstasy but as a potentially tragic force. The doubleness of love as portrayed in the sister plays *A Midsummer Night's Dream* and *Romeo and Juliet*, both dated to 1595–1596, may help explain why the former contains so much strange tragic potential, as in the inserted story of Pyramus and Thisbe. (The Knight's Tale, evidently one of the sources of Shakespeare's Theseus, *is* tragic except for its ending.) But being an overpowering force, Shakespearean love is not chosen. We fall in love, after all, and falling is the definitive experience of helplessness. The lovers in *A Midsummer Night's Dream* accordingly appear as the comical thralls of their own passion—at least the young men do, once under the spell of the love liquor. If we could escape the dominion of common sense and the world's laws simply by choosing to, the experience would be too shallow and the exemption too easily had: so Shakespeare suggests.

Pop psychology portrays the world itself as a kind of unjust law. In the opening scene of *A Midsummer Night's Dream*, we learn of a law dictating that a daughter marry the man of her father's choice or else face harsh penalties—a law so absurd and tyrannical that for Hermia there is simply no possibility of obeying it. Pop psychology tells us that whatever we want is in our power. Prospero in *The Tempest* remarks that both Miranda and Ferdinand are in *love's* power. In Shakespeare, only in love—a power that claims us and not the other way around, just as Cupid's arrow finds us instead of us finding it—do we transcend law, common sense, the world. And we do so at considerable risk.

Fixated as it is on choice (because anything not chosen represents subjection), pop psychology depicts even love as choice.

"If we choose to love ourselves and to behave lovingly toward ourselves, if we choose to have Self-Esteem, than [sic] we have control over ourselves." The same manual actually proposes exercises to make the reader *fall in love* with him- or herself. Love of others is similarly depicted as a choice in advice literature. "The highest forms of love are inevitably totally free choices and not acts of conformity," as though even love must conform to the terms of Mill's *On Liberty*. Again, "Love is as love does. Love is an act of will—namely, both an intention and an action. Will also implies choice. We do not have to love. We choose to love." Love in Shakespeare is beyond choice. As hyperbolic as the Shakespearean portrayal of love may be, I think it is closer to love as we know it than the portrayal of love as an act of will.

 8

Morality

The German expatriate who served as perhaps the foremost intellectual patron of the student revolt of the 1960s, Herbert Marcuse, wrote in 1970 that "the new theory of man . . . implies the genesis of a new morality as the heir and the negation of the Judeo-Christian morality which up to now has characterized the history of Western civilization." Assured by his knowledge of human needs and his insight into the logic of history, Marcuse was prepared to affirm that the destruction of existing morality would only bring about something better. Today few remember Marcuse's utopian polemics, and his reconciliation of Marx and Freud—two men who might well have detested each other—stirs little interest even within the academic world. His attack on Judeo-Christian morality, however, has gone mainstream. For it is a stated tenet of the pop psychology movement that Judeo-Christian—sometimes called puritanical—morality is repressive, self-defeating, and obsolete (quite as Marcuse said). The all-but-stated implication is that doing away with such a burden on human life can result in nothing but good.

Also in 1970, Charles Reich argued that morality belongs to Consciousness I while the present belongs to Consciousness III. Citing Marcuse, Reich distinguished between "those needs which are a product of a person's authentic self, and those which are imposed from the outside by society," and as crude as it is, this distinction is axiomatic for pop psychology.

☞ With its direct address of the reader, pop psychology fails to cut through convention and artificiality; on the contrary, it defines itself as rhetoric. Rhetoric, after all, is speechmaking. Part of the art of rhetoric, according to Aristotle, is the expression of the speaker's character—ēthos, from which we derive "ethics." Confessing that he once "betrayed who I was and instead accepted a fictional substitute that was defined from the outside in," Phil McGraw not only assures readers of his fidelity to the tenets of pop psychology by using its language; he also establishes the character of one who knows what he's talking about when he orates on the betrayal of the true self, one whose concern for the reader is authentic because he learned the hard way what authenticity is.

But the speechmakers of the self-help world don't just claim to be worthy of trust and belief: they claim to be uniquely worthy, because uniquely concerned with the reader's innermost being and truest interests. In a world that threatens the self, only the therapist is free of bad motives. Only the therapist understands the weapons and tactics used against the self—chief among them moralistic language, a cover story for a campaign of repression. In pop psychology, the ēthos of the therapist is exalted and the institution of morality deplored in the same degree.

All that the self-help movement finds destructive and retrograde is summed up in the word "morality," or as it is sometimes rendered, "judgment." Dostoevsky may have worried about what would happen if everything were permitted, but pop psychology is sure that with the abolition of morality, people will be happy and innocent, and indeed moral, as the great obstacle in the way of the good will have been swept away. Morality is immoral because blame is blameworthy, because traditional norms of obligation obscure the supreme obligation to self, because patience accustoms us to suffering. In the therapeutic version of "We Shall Overcome," it is morality that will be overcome. If all the worst problems stem from a lack of self-esteem (as pop psychologists are prepared to argue, to the point of deriving Hitler's maniacal evil from cruelty inflicted on him as a child), and if morality's harsh judgments damage self-esteem, getting rid of this source of misery, self-contempt, and cruelty will instantly improve the human condition.

Pop psychology takes for granted the virtue of morality's elimination. Reich's *Greening of America* in fact made the case that the end of morality means the birth of a beautiful age, but this is a work so cartoonish that it cannot be named, much less cited as authoritative, in a genre that speaks in the voice of professional knowledge. Similarly, the polemics of R. D. Laing, the Marcuse of psychiatry, are too mad to be cited anymore by authors who still claim that we are brainwashed and our authenticity sacrificed. When Laing says that "a child of two is already a moral mover and moral talker and moral experiencer," the word "moral" is filled with sarcasm and even hatred.

The same spirit of inversion that makes morality immoral in the eyes of pop psychology also generates, in one notable work, the reversal of the Golden Rule. According to Theodore Rubin, because injustice to others pales before injustice to self—because we are "much more compassionate . . . to other people than we are to ourselves"—the Golden Rule is misguided. "More often than not," writes Rubin, as though offering a sound empirical conclusion based on the widest observation, "the problem does not involve, 'Do unto others as you would have others do unto you,' but rather: *Treat yourself at least as well as you treat other people!*" The author's reverse alchemy yields a rule that means: Treat others any which way, provided only that you don't blame yourself.

Rubin offers no discussion and apparently gives no thought to the implications of this original maxim. Yet the Golden Rule is no incidental principle but a foundational one, "basic to . . . many religious and moral traditions," as Sissela Bok notes in her study of *Lying*, citing Confucian, Jewish, and Islamic versions. The thesis of *Lying* itself rests on the Golden Rule, just as it is the habit of making allowances in our own favor, not others' favor, that the argument of *Lying* takes account of and guards against. (Pop psychologists incessantly make allowances in their own favor, urging the reader not to heed any prescriptions whatever—except theirs. They allege that family, friends, society, the world—all except them—have an interest in the suppression of your true self. In a work whose title, *Compassion and Self-Hate*, poses a stark antithesis, Rubin criticizes the practice of "polarizing issues into absolutely good and absolutely bad categories" as a serious pathology.)

To overwrite the Golden Rule with *Treat yourself at least as well as you treat other people* is to say that everything is permitted, except that this Dostoevskian watchword of rebellion has been recast as a counsel of health. Nor is Rubin alone. According to M. Scott Peck, those who have advanced far enough in psychotherapy "will one day suddenly realize that they have it in their power to do whatever they want." This too seems like a way of saying, Everything is permitted. According to Wayne Dyer, "You can do anything you want just because you want to, and for no other reason." According to the authors of *Self-Esteem*, it is therapeutic to say to oneself, "I can do anything I want, but what I want is determined by my awareness." Pop psychologists bend the principle that we each have a right to our feelings—a principle they hold sacred—into the argument that we have a right to *do* anything and everything. Outside the pop psychology movement, not everyone agrees that we have a right to our feelings in the first place. "One is almost never right to feel envy," argues Joseph Epstein; "to be envious is to be, *ipso facto*, wrong."

In Charlotte Perkins Gilman's Herland, "the best and wisest were ready to give help," that is, counsel, at all times. In our world that role is performed by therapists who not only claim to provide the help that the world doesn't, but shield the client or patient or reader from the world's cruelty. From one manual to another, pop psychology offers readers reassurance of their own worth, as though a vulnerable self were being protected from an overwhelming menace. In the eyes of pop psychology, that menace is morality.

After hearing the story of one Danielle, the reader of a self-help manual is asked, "Who in your extended family was . . . like Danielle's father? Who tried to tell you the right and wrong way to think and feel? Who tried to tell you what you should be thinking and feeling?"—with the implication that such judgments are atrocities. (Self-help works tell readers exactly what they should be feeling. Recall Wayne Dyer: anyone who interferes with you "ought to be viewed as a victimizer.") It is as if the therapist interposed himself as a human shield between the reader-patient and an inhuman force. In the eyes of pop psychology, judging others—except those condemned by pop psychology itself—is almost always an imprisoning fallacy. "By giving up judging others, we set ourselves free. We waste a tremendous amount of our power judging others." Thus we do not cease to judge others for their sake but for our own, so as to conserve or liberate our power. And if our judgments of others are ruinous, still more so, of course, are judgments of ourselves— hence pop psychology's emphatic repudiation of guilt. Not only are words like "guilt," "judgment," and "morality" virtually printed in red in self-help literature, but so too is any term denoting an obligation to something other than oneself.

> Fixed beliefs express themselves through concepts like "should" and "must." They are, in truth, demands: demands for your compliance with a particular vision of what life is, demands for you not to make waves or disrupt the roles that others play. . . . A fixed belief keeps you within your assigned place in this world. It establishes the boundaries of what you are willing to accept from life.

The belief that obligations, or shoulds, violate the self is itself solidly fixed in the genre.

Well before Phil McGraw came forward as the sole truth-teller in a world of liars, Wayne Dyer, for one, argued that we need to recognize and liberate ourselves from "the folly of shoulds, musts, and oughts." Presumably it is because Dyer does not recognize shoulds that he disregards the caution in the Declaration of Independence that governments long established should not be changed for casual reasons. If we are slaves to morality, Dyer is an abolitionist. "Man invents terms that say this behavior is right, and that is wrong, this event is right, that wrong. But reality has no use for such judgments."

> Many people have been sent off to die in stupid wars because it was "the right thing to do," even though both sides end up shaking hands when the whole thing is over. . . . People vic-

timize each other by saying that loyalty to family members is *always* right, or that one must always tell the truth because it is the right thing to do. . . . You must decide for yourself not whether your behavior is right or wrong, but whether it is effective or ineffective in the pursuit of legitimate goals.

Clearly this man regards morality as mere name-calling and thinks humanity would be better off without it. As fantastic as his conviction is that with the elimination of morality one great pretext for victimization will be removed from the world, it is widely shared in the self-help genre. "Forget concepts of right and wrong," state the authors of *Self-Esteem*.

The proposition that with the disappearance of morality, cruelty will crumble and humanity will come into its own, is never really elaborated in pop psychology. But the vision and promise of such a transformation are always present in and between the lines of pop psychology, like a half-heard air on Prospero's island. "We invariably relate better to other people when we relate better to ourselves," meaning that when we stop judging ourselves morally, we begin to treat others morally. All depends on the abolition of guilt. Thus a social worker teaches that "if you can learn to receive each moment . . . without criticism, blame, guilt, or judgment, you will be well on your way to a deeply confident sense of self." Once the curse of morality is well lifted, you will experience profound peace. At ease with yourself, suffused with the feeling of being all there, lost in the contemplation of "how wondrous and interesting you can be," you will show the world that there is nothing to fear from the shattering of moral prohibitions. Ivan Karamazov agonizes over what it really means to do away with such prohibitions; not so the readers projected by the help manuals. They must never concern themselves with the possible costs of eliminating morality, never wonder how bonds can hold and trust can be maintained in the absence of that sense of responsibility which pop psychology deems a deadly artifice.

At one point in *The Brothers Karamazov*, Ivan is taunted with his own belief that with the old morality gone, "everything will begin anew. . . . Man will be lifted up with the spirit of divine Titanic pride, and the man-god will appear. . . . His pride will teach him that it's useless for him to repine at life's being a moment, and he will love his brother without need of reward." In William Morris's *News from Nowhere*, published some ten years after *The Brothers Karamazov*, we are conducted to an England of the future where the old morality based on private property has been abolished and happiness has taken its place.

> "Well, private property being abolished, all the laws and all the legal 'crimes' which it had manufactured of course came to an end. Thou shalt not steal, had to be translated into, Thou shalt work in order to live happily."

In pop psychology, "Thou shalt not" gives way to "Thou shalt live happily." It is simply assumed that the extinction of morality will be all to the good, just as *News from Nowhere* asks us to assume that a great "Clearing of Misery" took place in England some time in the twentieth century. Pop psychology tells stories, one after the other, of the clearing of misery. Its vision of the clouds of morality lifting to let in the rays of happiness is a utopian one in its own right.

☞ Whether or not rebelling against morality makes a person moral, those who stop conforming like sheep to the prescriptions of society, and start conforming to those of pop psychology, appear to act in ways that can only be described as sheepish. How else to characterize the mother who dare not tell Jill not to eat all the cherries lest she scar Jill for life? So loaded is the portrayal of parental cruelty in self-help literature that any parent who takes it seriously will be in a state of continual paralyzing dread. In the irony of retrospect, Dr. Spock, author of *Baby and Child Care*, once wrote, "In the twentieth century parents have been persuaded that the only people who know for sure how children should be managed are the child psychiatrists, psychologists, teachers, social workers and pediatricians—like myself." A potent tool of persuasion is the story of the child injected with lifelong guilt.

In the world of pop psychology, where morality is at once the cloak worn by, and the wound left by, human cruelty, the worst abusers of children cover their crimes by leaving guilt, once again, in the mind of the victim. In the definitive example of therapy as the protection of a vulnerable self from hostile judgments, self-blaming survivors of sexual abuse are folded in a protective embrace by the healing literature. The guiding presumption here is that anyone who believes she or he was abused as a child, and a great many others with the appropriate symptoms, were indeed abused. To question charges or diagnoses of abuse is to violate the victim all over again.

Behind such thinking stands the premise that if skeptical questioning were abolished along with the rest of the machinery of hostile judgments—if all claims of abuse were simply accepted—no fabricated atrocities, no unfounded accusations, no miscarriages of justice would result. The therapeutic doctrine that "there is no reality; only perception," as Phil McGraw puts it, will not open the gates to false charges, because patients guided by therapeutic benevolence do not make false charges. And such benevolence demands the transformation of morality. In an influential guide for women survivors of child sexual abuse, moral terms like "honor" are accordingly transformed completely, as if they had been made over from the oppressor to the victim. You, the victim, must learn to honor your pain where before, perhaps, you were enjoined to honor your father and mother. As one proclaimed victim says, "I had to learn to honor all my feelings, especially the anger and the outrage. . . . I trust the validity of my outrage. The outrage is because I honor and value and love life." With honor now conferred by the victim onto herself, the healing of a wounded self has begun.

Overcoming morality is the way to well-being. Having neutralized conscience, I will not act like a person without a conscience: I will become happy and harmless.

> Lingering guilt robs you of your natural state of innocence and keeps you from feeling a healthy sense of worthiness and entitlement. Instead of knowing and acting from what you want, you act too much for others, you accommodate too much, and you do not feel comfortable asking for or asserting your wants and needs. You are a good and nice person, but have a hard time saying no to others.

Letting go of morality thus allows me to be the moral person I actually am. There are "moments when we are able to let go without having to watch over and judge ourselves. At times like these we feel inspired by a secure sense that if we just take ourselves as we come, that will be quite good enough." From the abolition of morality follows not transgression but contentment, not license but peace. With prohibitions gone, well-being succeeds.

In accordance with the practice of clipping inspirational phrases from works of literature, the author of GUILT Is the Teacher; LOVE Is the Lesson quotes William Blake's "If the doors of perception were cleansed, every thing would appear to man as it is, infinite." The source of this dictum (not provided) is *The Marriage of Heaven and Hell*, a sort of high satiric manifesto of antinomianism etched by Blake in the early years of the French Revolution. Taunting more conventional Christians in the manner of a provocateur, Blake argues through the person of a devil that Jesus broke every one of the Ten Commandments.

> Did he not mock at the sabbath, and so mock the sabbath's God? murder those who were murdered because of him? turn away the law from the woman taken in adultery? steal the labor of others to support him? bear false witness when he omitted making a defence before Pilate? covet when he pray'd for his disciples, and when he bid them shake off the dust of their feet against such as refused to lodge them? I tell you, no virtue can exist without breaking these ten commandments.

The showmanship, the circus leaps and stretches of this polemic signal that it is not to be taken too literally. When Phil McGraw proclaims, "You must challenge . . . limiting beliefs, rather than living in obedience to them, as though they were commandments etched in stone," he means "must." It is left to us to puzzle out just how far to pursue our rebellion against the original commandments etched in stone. When pop psychology argues for the overthrow of morality, we are simply to assume that morality will survive its own abolition. The entire genre makes that assumption, just as Marcuse assumed that the overthrow of existing morality would mean the advent of a superior morality. Only because pop psychology is insulated against independent thought by a doctrinal myth of natural innocence is it able to assume that the disappearance of morality will be the lifting of a curse. Pop psychology has no need to argue this notion out, and never does so, because it is already built into its most cherished beliefs.

So too, pop psychology hesitates to confront the immediate implications of its rejection of laws, rules, standards, prohibitions—anything binding. As if issuing a disclaimer, Wayne Dyer in *Your Erroneous Zones* declares, "Nowhere is it being implied or in any way suggested that you become contemptuous of the law, or break rules simply because you see fit to do so"—but this is exactly what he urges a few lines later in the same paragraph. "Often rules are foolish, and traditions no longer make any sense," he observes. "When this is the case, and you are unable to function effectively because you must follow senseless rules, that is the time to reconsider the rules and your behavior." Break the rules as you see fit. You can do anything you want just because you want to. Perhaps Dyer is not troubled by the tendency of his own doctrine because, like his counterparts, he tacitly assumes the survival of the same institutions of morality he deplores.

How can a reader be sure that the antinomianism of the self-help genre—its expressed contempt of rules and prohibitions—will prove as innocent as the authors believe? It is said that in order to preserve the progressive associations of the color red, the Red Guards during the Chinese Cultural Revolution changed red stoplights to mean Go—a classic instance of deprogramming and reprogramming. Phil McGraw also changes Stop to Go: "You have to be willing to challenge, test, and try virtually everything that up until now you may have treated with habitual and automatic resistance." "You shall not" is transmuted into "You must." If McGraw's words are to be taken seriously—and he repeats them practically verbatim elsewhere—how could they not terminate in some other mad cultural revolution? If we have to be willing to try virtually everything we are averse to, do we then have a duty to cheat and steal? parachute jump? spy for a hostile power? experiment with incest? (Lest the reader think this flippant, R. D. Laing actually argued that "if all through school the young were provoked to question the Ten Commandments . . . the laws of incest, and so on, there would be such creativity that society would not know where to turn.") Or does the author really mean that we should try virtually everything, taking care all the while to stay within the bounds of the law, common sense, and human decency? Like Dyer disclaiming his own argument, McGraw, immediately after lamenting the human tendency to judge, denies that he is calling on the reader "to suspend good judgment." McGraw *indicts* good judgment. The root of his favorite word, "authentic," bears remembering. "*Authentes*: not only a master and a doer, but also a perpetrator, a murderer, even a self-murderer, a suicide." Only the rigging of language allows McGraw and many others to predefine authenticity as a synonym for health and harmlessness.

Here the image of Phil McGraw rises before the eyes of the reader as if to say, "Trust me." If you recollect the happy moments when you were living fully *in* the moment and cared nothing for the judgments of others, you will recall the sense that "it was you that mattered, not in a selfish way, but in a confident way." Converting red to green and emancipating ourselves from morality will therefore result not in license or lawbreaking but serenity.

Yet one of McGraw's heroes *was* a lawbreaker—not Martin Luther King but a bootlegger. In *Self Matters* we are introduced to Gene Knight, a pilot who flew cases of Jim Beam into the dry counties of Oklahoma in the 1950s, a folk hero who

> could have passed for Errol Flynn. He had coal-black hair, wore a leather flying jacket, and stood about six foot four. He hopped down from the plane, grinning ear to ear. As he shook

hands, slapped backs, and exchanged stories with all of the men, there was an air about him, an air of absolutely infectious joy. As the men dashed about to offload the cases of whiskey, Gene was just grinning away, as if to say, "Isn't this the greatest? Could it get any better than this?"

What if the portrait had been of a cocaine runner, also with the looks of Errol Flynn, also a born pilot, who loved the dangerous game of flying his cargo up from South America— a daredevil who lived in the moment and cared nothing for the judgments of others? "Believe me," Phil McGraw seems to answer. "It can't happen. No criminal could emanate such a natural sense of joy." Pop psychology places too much faith in its own stories and too much stock in a fantasy of natural innocence that undermines the validity of any law, custom, or standard whatever. Certainly subscribers to the doctrine that prohibitions violate the self are in no position to prohibit their children from using cocaine; the best they can do is ask if the children are sure they authentically want to use the drug, or if they just want to use it because their friends do.

In the eyes of some therapists, nothing, not even murder, should be allowed to sour our all-important relationship with ourselves. If I understand it, that is what is meant by the following paragraph in *Compassion and Self-Hate*:

> Hating oneself, one's actual self or any aspect or part of oneself, is always part of an ongoing active process. If we hate our looks, the way we move, particular inabilities, culturally unacceptable characteristics such as jealousy, envy, possessiveness, fragility, vulnerability, duplicity, lying, stealing and even murdering, perversions, sexual and otherwise, we are engaging in the process. We engage in self-hate when we hate

any aspect of ourselves and whenever we have feelings of self-contempt generally.

Only the peculiar conventions of the therapeutic make it possible to reduce murder to a culturally unacceptable characteristic on a par with fragility. Although this author has a theory that "all murderers are latent, chronically depressed people," he is less interested in murder per se than in "the little murders we inflict on ourselves on a daily basis" in the form of self-hatred.

What of the principle proclaimed by Phil McGraw, but also throughout the genre from decade to decade, that "there is a whole other level of existence, distinct from what you do, that is the real, true, genuine sum and substance of who you are"? The ability to disengage from one's own deeds as if they were not one's own at all is a well-known technique of moral dissociation; it has enabled many to commit crimes while pretending that their actions did not belong to them, and another self remained within, distinct from what they did, untainted.

But the acts authorized by the antinomian teachings of pop psychology are not confined to the spectacular or the illegal. The genre gives a license to abject self-pity; to poisonous accusations of friends, parents, society, the world; to thoughtless credulity.

Imagine someone whose vocabulary runs from "self-nurturing" to "self-affirmation" to "self-actualization" to "self-alienation" and so on through the innumerable coined compounds (except "self-obsessed") that run through the self-help literature. Someone too who feels that he and his therapist stand against the world—that only with the help of the therapist can he recover his true self and find relief from the lies that engulf him. Suppose, again, that this person has been persuaded that his true self resides apart from his deeds, that no matter what he does his goodness is unimpaired—a principle that has held constant over the decades through all the trends and variations of pop psychology. What sort of trust can be placed in this person? What sort of relations can he enter into? What would it mean to be the co-worker, friend, spouse, or child of one who believes that any obligation to anyone or anything beyond himself spells treason to himself, and that no deed however disloyal or dishonest can possibly compromise him?

It is said that Rousseau convinced himself that he was the victim of a "massive plot" and confronted "enemy forces" that were committed to his destruction. As the imaginary victim of such great injustice, Rousseau acquired "absolute justification. He offers his neck to the sacrificial knife in order to acquire the purity of the victim." We know that conspiracy theories foster delusions accompanied by a conviction of superior insight and a bizarre sense of justification that depends, as in Rousseau's case, on the wickedness of an imagined adversary. Conspiracy theories make for wild judgments and false accusations, reinforced against reason and reflecting great imaginary credit on the mind bold enough to conceive them. The prevailing ideology of the self-help movement verges on conspiracy theory. Sometimes it explicitly becomes such theory. "Other people conspire to manipulate or control your behavior," writes Wayne Dyer on the first page of *Pulling Your Own Strings*, to be followed years later by Phil McGraw, among others. The problem, says McGraw to the reader, is that

> You have gone right along with the expectancies imposed by other people. You have actively participated in your own seduction by selling out for what you don't want. You've gotten used to living an assigned role, rather than living true to who you really are. You have participated in a devastating conspiracy, with you as the unwitting fall guy.

In this passage, painfully typical of the genre, the reader is envisioned as living practically behind enemy lines, with his or her true identity concealed from an implacably hostile world. But what sort of behavior can be expected from those who imagine the world to be a conspiracy against them? Perhaps the kind of righteous accusations and demands that the reader of self-help is said to be surrounded by.

In *Little Dorrit* we meet one of Dickens's most striking creations, Miss Wade, consumed with resentment of a world whose plot against her she believes she can see right through. Tyrannized by her own imagination like many another in Dickens, Miss Wade really does suppose herself living behind enemy lines. "From a very early age I have detected what those about me thought they hid from me." Eventually she undertakes to "release . . . from bondage" a girl she identifies as a victim of the same cruel hypocrisy encircling her. Miss Wade is something like the therapist who takes the patient under his charge, liberating him or her from the falsehood of everyone else. But she is also the reader addressed in many a manual of recovery, seething with resentment and accusation, victim of an imaginary world conspiracy.

☞ How refreshing it is to turn from the loaded portrayal of morality in self-help literature to the writings of a philosopher who never proposes to deprogram and reprogram, and who understands morality not as a system of repression but as the field and element in which human life takes place, and which calls forth the human capacity for evaluation. The very title of Iris Murdoch's *Metaphysics as a Guide to Morals* establishes that she is no prosecutor of morals. Language, she writes, must be truthful, and the work to make it so falls to "everyone, every moral being, that is every human being."

According to Iris Murdoch, our very consciousness is morally animated. Our speech too is "moral speech, a constant use of the innumerable subtle *normative* words whereby (for better or worse) we texture the detail of our moral surround and steer our life of action." If this is so—if our very speech and thought are morally quickened—then to seek to eliminate moral judgment from speech and thought, as pop psychology does, is to expurgate and impoverish our own nature. Iris Murdoch was of course also a remarkable novelist, and it may be that it takes a novelist "to display how deeply, subtly, and in detail, values, the various qualities and grades between good and bad, 'seep' through our moment-to-moment experiences."

In her philosophical capacity, Murdoch contends that

> Philosophical doctrines which profess neutrality, whether they are professedly analytic (against preaching) or scientific (against value) cannot help, by what they obliterate or what they emphasize, making moral judgments. . . . Moral philosophers should be frankly and realistically high-minded in the sense of recognising the unique and profound presence and importance of a moral sense.

Without a moral sense, the human mind, according to Murdoch, is largely consumed with fantasy.

> Neurotic or vengeful fantasies, erotic fantasies, delusions of grandeur, dreams of power, can imprison the mind, impeding new understanding, new interests and affections, possibilities of fruitful and virtuous action.

Pop psychology, with its almost demagogic appeals to resentment ("You've suffered long enough and now it's time to take back your life"), its way of fanning the flames of delusion ("Your parents, your friends, the world are all against you"), its flattery of dreams of power (or "empowerment")—pop psychology represents exactly what, in Iris Murdoch's view, the human mind must struggle against.

And if as human beings we evaluate or act morally, it only follows that as pop psychology inveighs against morality, it propagates its own evaluations (shielded against criticism by the rhetoric of benevolence). Even pop psychology cannot help making moral judgments. Theodore Rubin's *Compassion and Self-Hate* is so filled with condemnations of our culture as a reign of terror—the sort of sentiment scrawled on walls in the 1960s, now conveyed with an air of medical authority—that after a few pages the very phrase "our culture" primes the reader for what comes next. As an example of the sort of judgment that can be delivered in the name of health, consider a comment in a footnote in another popular classic, *The Road Less Traveled*, first published in 1978.

> My work with couples has led me to the stark conclusion that open marriage is the only kind of mature marriage that is healthy and not seriously destructive to the spiritual health and growth of the individual partners.

(*Open Marriage*, by Nena and George O'Neill, appeared a few years before.) One is struck immediately by the use of the mantra words of therapy—"healthy," "mature," "growth," "individual"—to lend an air of authority to a disputable statement about the way human beings should live. Just as morality will flourish when everything traditionally known as morality has vanished, so, it seems, marriage will come into its own when marriage as the world has known it withers away.

Self-transformation

In a fine critique of the philosophical fantasy of removing ourselves from the institutions that house us, the better to evaluate them from without, Frederick Will likens thinkers to sailors at sea engaged in the rebuilding of their own ship. Simply belonging to a philosophical institution (or tradition) doesn't preclude us from engaging in the reconstruction of that institution; it is not as if the investigation, building, and rebuilding of knowledge could be reliably conducted only from some vantage point outside the world as it is. We human beings in general could also be likened to mariners rebuilding a vessel on the open sea, though by the same token there are limits to our powers of reconstruction. While at sea, we can't remove our own keel.

Among the theories marketed by pop psychology is the elementary delusion that it is possible to transform oneself completely, keel and all. Self-help literature abounds with tales of transformation where people go from misery and failure to happiness, deprogramming and reprogramming themselves in a few strokes. The self undergoes a revolution. Some books pretend to change the reader from one chapter to another, as when Phil McGraw observes at the start of Chapter 11 of *Self Matters* that "it would be fair to say that you are a different person now from the one who started this book." (This from the same author who ridicules self-help programs that promise results "fast, fast, fast.") Psychological Cinderella stories certify the doctrine that a truer self dwells within us, waiting only to come forth, as well as the corollary doctrine that our highest obligation is to this inner tenant. Ordinary experience, however, affords few examples of people who change their character either swiftly or radically. Most seem to remain much as they are. Recently I wrote that "In spite of the unlikeliness of the notion of shedding one's character, and the oddity of being at once the manager of this change and the entity being changed, few seem willing to question the project of remaking ourselves from the inside out by some sort of therapeutic program."

As a way of driving a punitive sense of shame out of their minds, readers of one self-help manual are told to write out "new statements" such as "I am lovable" and "I am strong," and post them on their refrigerator—an exercise that typifies the genre's ideal of reprogramming the self. In holding out the prospect of a complete reconstruction of the self, pop psychology promises more than it can possibly deliver; the rewards it does deliver may well be illusory. Intended to make a reader feel better, and using every rhetorical means at their command to recommend themselves, works of pop psychology after all practically target the placebo effect. In the island utopia of pop psychology, however, no questioning of the official fables is permitted, and placebo effects are never mentioned.

☞ In the desire to transform themselves, men have donned the robes of the Romans, as Machiavelli did upon entering his library and other imaginary sons of the ancients did less literally. A man named Dzhugashvili became Stalin. One Jack Rosenberg, a used-car salesman, refashioned himself as Werner Erhard and began offering seminars. Since the Renaissance, Westerners have indeed explored "radical new spheres of elected existence," but does this mean there are no limits on our power to invent ourselves? Can we actually elect our existence? In Gatsby, for all his urban dealings and suburban festivities, there remains the rusticity of the boy Jay Gatz. The Jews who refashioned American comedy in the twentieth century may have anglicized their names or acted like assimilated citizens, but beneath all that ran something deeper than name or manner, intractable, and beyond choice. At some level the prevailing myth of choice and will was satirized by these comic artists who seemed to be saying, "You may think you can, think you can, but that's your problem—I know I can't." And in truth we cannot choose ourselves. Certainly we can choose a new name, an imaginary ancestor, or indeed a self-improvement program, but that we can reinvent our own character—choose the way we make choices—defies the possible. You can't outrun your shadow. It may have been something like that shadow that Hannah Arendt had in mind when she wrote that the disclosure of one's uniqueness in speech and act

> can almost never be achieved as a wilful purpose, as though one possessed and could dispose of this "who" in the same manner he has and can dispose of his qualities. On the contrary, it is more likely that the "who," which appears so clearly and unmistakably to others, remains hidden from the person himself, like the *daimon* in Greek religion which accompanies

each man throughout his life, always looking over his shoulder from behind and thus visible only to those he encounters.

What could be farther from the doctrines of pop psychology, which tells us that we can determine our own being and change who we are by an act of will?

Perhaps the most radical reconstitution of the self occurs in the experience of conversion, as in the transformation of Abram and Sarai to Abraham and Sarah, and of Saul to Paul. Conversion is an experience that befalls the converted person. ("It was as though a sharp dagger had pierced me right through," says Father Zossima in *The Brothers Karamazov* of the moment of his conversion.) In *The Greening of America*, Charles Reich maintained that a generation was arriving at Consciousness III by conversion. Pop psychology would have me design and manage my own conversion. But even if observation didn't suggest the improbability of people reconstructing themselves in this fashion, there would seem to be some logical objections to the notion. I can design a new house, but does it make sense to say that I can "design a new life," as the author of *Take Time for Your Life*, for one, says? The mariner cannot will, pretend, or design a new keel into being. Besides, if I am in such disarray that I need to be rebuilt completely, how can I be the one to conduct this process? For I am in disarray. If I am badly confused, possibly even my decision to commit myself to the seven-step program of *Take Time for Your Life* will be misguided. In any case, I just can't change my skin, or play the puppet and the puppet-master at once, as in *Pulling Your Own Strings*. Advice-givers themselves seem to recognize that there is something wrong with self-help—in the words of Phil McGraw, "Has anybody noticed over the last fifty years that this crap doesn't work?"—though they point to the triviality of others' advice or the reader's inadequate commitment, rather than to the impossibility of designing one's being.

Like much else, the power of realization is exaggerated in pop psychology, as though an instantaneous revolution had taken place. According to M. Scott Peck, the knowledge that they can do anything comes to advanced minds in just this way. "If people progress far enough in psychotherapy they will . . . one day suddenly realize that they have it in their power to do whatever they want." On the first page of the same work we are told that "Once we truly know that life is difficult—once we truly understand and accept it—then life is no longer difficult. Because once it is accepted, the fact that life is difficult no longer matters." A verbal trick (something like "freedom is the recognition of necessity") is presented as a first principle. In the world as it is, difficulty—say, the difficulty of cancer—does not vanish with the realization of difficulty; nor does the model of sudden transformation have much application in moral life. When Hamlet urges his mother to begin a regimen of self-purification, instructing her to

> Refrain tonight,
> And that shall lend a kind of easiness
> To the next abstinence; the next more easy;
> For use can almost change the stamp of nature,
> And either master the devil or throw him out
> With wondrous potency,

he seeks to put to good use the power of habit that elsewhere in the play accustoms people over time to the inconceivable. M. Scott Peck went on to attend exorcisms where the devil was thrown out on the spot.

Surely change of self is evolutionary, not revolutionary. At times in great novels of the nineteenth century, a character—

say, Dickens's Pip or Dmitri Karamazov—will dream of some complete transformation of his existence, only to be instructed by experience that no such leap, no such release from the prosaic conditions of life, is possible. Reflecting the exaggeration and exaltation of will in modern culture, the idea that I can will a new self into being, and quickly, is in fact utopian. As Iris Murdoch writes, "Moral change for the better happens, if at all, slowly, as new modes of outlook and new desires come into being." Such change is less likely to flow from the antinomian rejection of roles and duties, as burdens on the self, than from their acceptance. Responsibilities may call forth a capacity for responsibility: a good nurse learns dedication from the practice of nursing, a parent patience and love by being a parent. In both cases, only because of continuing difficulty is the role a source of enrichment.

☞ In the first utopian work of literature, the *Odyssey*, the Phaeacians live in a sort of island paradise, feasting and playing games, attended by servants of gold (an idyll shattered when their ship is turned to stone after conveying Odysseus to Ithaca). But so too is the conclusion of the *Odyssey* utopian, telling as it does of the overthrow of the suitors and the hero's reclamation of his palace and patrimony. In More's Utopia there are no taverns or brothels and none of the parasitism that flourishes in Europe, where consumers live off of the producers of things. The suitors who infest Odysseus's palace in his absence convert it into their own tavern and brothel, and their death is portrayed as the elimination of insolent parasites who have fed on stocks not their own. Here too there are to be no taverns, brothels, or parasites. The utopian ending of the *Odyssey* was picked up, in effect, by Marxism, which portrayed all of history as tending toward this kind of cleansing and which, in the Soviet Union at least, "officially acknowledged the entire tradition of utopian thinking as its predecessor." Vilifying class enemies as parasites, Marxism told of the oppressed of the earth rising up to take possession of their legacy in accordance with the laws of history: a utopian version of the archetype of repatriation and revenge laid down in the *Odyssey*, where long privation indeed changes into its opposite in a single dramatic moment.

Even in the face of this great reversal of fortune, however, the character of Odysseus remains the same. Hence, perhaps, the strong emphasis over the latter books of the *Odyssey* on the tokens or proofs of the hero's unique identity: his pin, scar, bow, and bed.

In a deservedly famous essay devoted in part to the *Odyssey*, Erich Auerbach discusses the leisurely digression on the hero's scar in Book 19, just as the action of the poem reaches high tension—the tension of a drawn bow. Observing that the purpose of the digression seems to be to relax this tension, Auerbach points out the poem's remarkable absence of suspense. It seems to me, though, that the story of the boy Odysseus venturing into the den of a boar and so acquiring the scar that later identifies him does more than entertain us and dispel tension. The boy who strode across the threshold of a boar's den, and did so first, was already showing traits that would mark him later in life, in particular the boldness to cross into enemy territory. That boy would become the spy who slipped behind Trojan lines and the tactician who smuggled a band of warriors, including himself, through the gates of Troy; he would become the man who in sheer daring, perhaps an excess of daring, ventured into the cave of Polyphemus, the Cyclops; and he would become the hero bathed by Eurycleia in Book 19, who smuggled himself into the very den of his mortal enemies at great risk before destroying them. The boar scar is Odysseus's character. Perhaps it was Odysseus's strong attraction to highly charged threshold locations like the door of a cave, the gates of a city, the entry to the underworld, and the porch of his own palace that inspired later authors—authors now hostile to the figure of Odysseus—to place him at other thresholds: among the Greek tragedians the scenes just before and just after the Trojan War (each a moral no-man's-land where, it seems, everything is permitted), and in Dante the pillars of Hercules marking the boundary of the known world and the limits of the permissible.

What is striking about the character of the hero in the *Odyssey* isn't any transformation of his nature but the opposite: his amazing consistency over time and in the face of the most varied and trying circumstances. Here, we might say, is the point of origin of the romance tradition in which heroes and heroines go through their adventures unscathed, as though able to pass through fire, like Shakespeare's Marina maintaining her purity in a brothel. Dramatized in Odysseus is the ideal of one who remains himself in both action and suffering because he masters himself, who undergoes the most severe trials without breaking, as Odysseus endures years of delay on his journey home only to endure the insults of the suitors upon his arrival in Ithaca. So fundamental in Western moral thinking is the power to bear adversity that it takes forms Hellenic and Hebraic, stoic and Christian, fictitious and philosophical, ancient and modern. (In pop psychology, whose note is "you have suffered long enough," endurance not only has little value, it is the problem you are to be cured of. Stoicism of any sort suggests an unhealthy condition of repressed emotion.)

But if Homer meant us to follow a trait of Odysseus's character from boyhood forward, why didn't he tell Odysseus's story from boyhood forward, that is, chronologically? Had Homer been a modern, he might have done so. But not even the homecoming of Odysseus is recounted in a chronological manner, nor of course does Homer narrate the Trojan War from start to finish. The sort of retrospective narration introduced into the *Odyssey* with the hero's recital of his own adventures would become a feature of epic composition, incorporated into the *Aeneid* with the hero's recital of *his* travails (modeled in part on the *Odyssey*), and into *Paradise Lost* with the belated narration of the war in heaven. Perhaps the naturalness of chronology and the merits of narrative streamlining are over-rated. Shakespeare created Richard III before Richard II, and of the two it was the latter, his consciousness doubled back on itself as a result of his loss of the crown, who pointed the direction of Shakespeare's art. Not any soliloquy of Richard III, as memorable as they are, but that of Richard II, near the end of his play, has been accounted "the first of Shakespeare's great soliloquies," as if the poet discovered how to turn consciousness inward when he turned history itself back and portrayed the event (the overthrow of Richard II) that sets in motion the action of no less than seven of the history plays. Reminiscent of the *Odyssey* in its depiction of exile and reunion, among other things, Shakespeare's last romance, *The Tempest*, contains a lengthy narration of events that happened twelve years before. As for the narrator of the retrospective sections of the *Odyssey* itself, he is the only one of Homer's heroes endowed with reflection, with inwardness, a quality that makes him and not, say, Achilles or Hector, the archetypal literary character.

As with the continuing reverberations of the overthrow of Richard II, or indeed the retelling of adventures in the *Odyssey* or the echoes of the *Odyssey* through the world of fiction, literature reminds us of the continuing presence of the past. Never was Homer going to tell the story of Odysseus chronologically, from cradle to grave, anyway; but perhaps one reason he didn't tell the story of Odysseus's boyhood scar early on is to avoid giving the impression that once told, such a story is done with. Instead he delivered the story of boy and boar in a way that implies that just as the hero carries it at all times in the form of a scar—the visible mark of his unchanging character—so the body of the poem carries it in the form of memory.

☞ "Live in the moment," says pop psychology. "Don't dwell on the past." Practically by its nature, narrative *does* dwell on the past. In an essay on "The Novel and the Sense of the Past," the biblical and literary scholar Robert Alter examines a passage from *Anna Karenina*, concluding that its "psychological portraiture . . . depends essentially on Tolstoy's ability to show [Karenin] shuttling back and forth between different moments in his past, and it is no accident that the passage should abound with terms like recollection, memory, recalling, reviewing the past, down to the final assertion . . . that Karenin 'would forget what he did not wish to remember.'" As in the *Odyssey*, the present is rich with recollection.

At the end of Melville's *Benito Cereno*, the title character, a sea captain who had been taken hostage and terrorized in a slave revolt, engages in a colloquy with the American captain through whose dim eyes we receive most of the tale. "The past is passed," says the American, sounding a note that has become familiar. "Why moralize upon it? Forget it. See, yon bright sun has forgotten it, and the blue sea, and the blue sky; these have turned over new leaves." "Because they have no memory," answers Don Benito. "Because they are not human." Literature is with Don Benito in this argument. As the *Odyssey* is the song of the Muse (the Muses themselves being the daughters of Zeus and Mnemosynē, or Memory), so is literature itself in some sense a song of remembrance.

To the degree that narrative is dedicated to remembrance, to the degree that time in narrative reflects the presence of the past, narrative itself contradicts the therapeutic fantasy of wiping the slate of time clean in order to live in the moment. One reason for the poverty of the life-stories serving as illustrations of doctrine in the self-help genre is that they violate the nature of narrative itself. Another is that they *do* illustrate doctrine.

10

Literature Rewritten

Subjected to the changing moods and modes of literary criticism, the objects of literary study seem to shift like images in
water. So it was that a critic in the 1960s, interpreting *Great
Expectations* in the light of Freud's *Civilization and its Discontents*, could portray Pip, the hero narrator, as a study in discontent with civilization. According to the critic, Pip is

> a hopeful young man with a strong animal body and powerful
> desires who is called on at every turn to display, in the com-
> monest actions of his everyday life, the ideals of the civilization
> into which he was born: continual self-restraint, self-control,
> forgiveness of enemies, fortitude in withstanding . . . boredom
> and frustration and insult. He is the perfect model of moral de-
> portment because he is "morally timid and very sensitive"—
> because he is so utterly persuaded of the validity of these ideals
> that he never finds any adequate opportunity for expressing, or
> even recognizing, his own interests and his own self.

Whatever its merits as a description of Pip, this is a superlative portrait of the sort of person projected by pop psychology from decade to decade: a victim of repression who internalizes perfectionism, sacrifices his own interests and his own self to something called morality, and has learned patience ("fortitude in withstanding") only too well. The rhetorical style of the critic— "at every turn," "continual," "perfect," "utterly," "never"— becomes the pop psychologist's rhetoric of exaggeration. Literary criticism becomes psychological counsel, just as psychological dogma and speculation feed literary criticism.

☞ A few years ago, with the publication of *Reviving Ophelia: Saving the Selves of Adolescent Girls*, essays on Ophelia as an adolescent girl began to appear in my Shakespeare courses. Surprisingly, though, except for the following passage, *Reviving Ophelia* barely mentions Ophelia:

> The story of Ophelia, from Shakespeare's *Hamlet*, shows the destructive forces that affect young women. As a girl, Ophelia is happy and free, but with adolescence she loses herself. When she falls in love with Hamlet, she lives only for his approval. She has no inner direction; rather she struggles to meet the demands of Hamlet and her father. Her value is determined utterly by their approval. Ophelia is torn apart by her efforts to please. When Hamlet spurns her because she is an obedient daughter, she goes mad with grief. Dressed in elegant clothes that weigh her down, she drowns in a stream filled with flowers.

In what version of *Hamlet* does Ophelia drown in a stream filled with flowers? But for that matter, what version says that

Ophelia was happy and free as a girl only to lose her happiness and freedom in adolescence? Clearly, the author of *Reviving Ophelia* has read into *Hamlet* the master myth of pop psychology, that we sacrifice to the tyrannical demands of others the authentic self that is rightfully ours. At the hands of pop psychology, any and all literature yields this message, or some variant of it, because pop psychology reads it into literature in the first place. Wayne Dyer quotes with approval a therapist's view of Don Quixote as a rebel against a stifling conformity: "It greatly upset the other members of Don Quixote's family and his community to learn that he had chosen to believe in himself." In Cervantes, however, Don Quixote is half mad.

Although the Freudian myth brought forth a school of literary criticism in its time, few scholars and fewer students employ Freudian categories and machinery anymore. Those drawn to the exposure of unavowed motives are likelier, nowadays, to investigate the political motives presumed buried in literary and subliterary texts. Neither have I seen the once-familiar name of Abraham Maslow in student work for years, perhaps because the notion of self-actualization now has such general currency that it no longer attaches to Maslow. Even as Freud and Maslow recede from view, however, psychological trends continue to color the thinking of readers of literature. A few years ago, shortly after "social anxiety disorder" passed into common parlance and (not coincidentally) a pharmaceutical remedy hit the market, a student in one of my courses claimed in an essay that the Yeoman in the General Prologue of the *Canterbury Tales* suffers from this disorder, as shown by all the unnecessary weaponry he carries on his way toward Canterbury in the company of the other pilgrims. Let this instance, then, stand for a multitude in which the tools of pop psychology are brought to bear on works of literature.

The Yeoman is portrayed, in part, as follows:

A sheef of pecok arwes [arrows], bright and kene,
Under his belt he bar [bore] ful thriftily [skillfully],
(Wel koude he dresse [prepare] his takel [tackle] yemanly:
His arwes drouped noght with fetheres lowe)
And in his hand he baar a myghty bowe.
A not heed [cropped hair] hadde he, with a broune visage.
Of wodecraft wel koude [knew] he al the usage.
Upon his arm he baar a gay bracer [arm-guard],
And by his syde a swerd and a bokeler,
And on that oother syde a gay daggere
Harneised [mounted] wel and sharp as point of spere;
A Cristopher on his brest of silver sheene.
An horn he baar, the bawdryk [sling] was of grene;
A forster was he, soothly [truly], as I gesse.

Certainly the Yeoman's weaponry—bow and arrows, sword and dagger—stands out in this description. What then is wrong with the argument that he suffers from social anxiety disorder?

For one thing, even if the condition existed six hundred years ago while escaping notice and comment, no reason exists for the Yeoman of all people to suffer from it, considering that he is attached to the highest-ranking pilgrim of all, the Knight. (The first words of the Yeoman's portrait, omitted above, read "A YEMAN hadde he," where "he" refers to the Knight; the line implies a definite connection between the two men.) Far from lacking a secure place in the world, the Yeoman has a place in the entourage of a powerful man, the only other member of this elite company being the Knight's own son, the Squire. As the Knight's forester or woodsman, the Yeoman presumably enjoys a strong personal bond with his lord, a bond not subject to the uncertainties of contract relations, just as he must be presumed free of anxiety over the possibility of losing his post. The Yeoman's is a position others might well envy. Then too, in context there is nothing so unusual about the Yeoman's show of weaponry. Other pilgrims display weapons like ornaments—for example, the Guildsmen who proclaim their social importance with their silver-adorned knives, and who cannot possibly be suffering from social anxiety as they are described en masse, as a single unit of five. Most of the Canterbury pilgrims are portrayed, for better or worse, as masters of their trade. The Yeoman's weapons are simply the tools of *his* trade as woodsman, the equivalent of the Clerk's books, and they appear, it seems to me, in a fully affirmative light and not a suspect, ominous, or pathological light. Both his dagger and arm-guard are said to be "gay," and the same description might be applied to all his other trappings and armaments, declaring as they do his joy in what he does and who he is. His arrows are triumphs of craft, and he sports them, like his mighty bow and his gay dagger, with pride—not the sinful pride that preachers like the Parson warned of, but an innocent delight in the place one fills in the greater order of things. The horn, which is no weapon at all, is another instrument and sign of his craft. It is the hunting horn whose music sounds through the great hunting scenes of the contemporary romance *Sir Gawain and the Green Knight*. When Theseus enters Act Four of *A Midsummer Night's Dream* to the sound of a horn, at the head of a hunting party, and proceeds to call for the forester, he confirms the linkage between knights, hunting, horns, and foresters richly implied in the portrait of the Yeoman. (The tale told by Chaucer's Knight, also featuring Theseus, seems to be in the textual background of *A Midsummer Night's Dream*.)

And so the thesis that the Yeoman suffers from anxiety induced by the presence of other people appears to be wrong in every way: the Yeoman is secure and not anxious; he travels as a member of a small retinue, not as a lonely or alienated figure; he wears his weapons as emblems of his way of life and not as threats to others or defenses against others; his portrait is affirmative in tone, not satirical; and it is meant to be read with an eye to its context, especially its immediate context in the General Prologue, not to the latest edition of a manual of certified disorders.

What if jurors construed evidence, physicians interpreted histories, or citizens in their everyday lives made inferences as loosely as my student? But on reflection, what seemed to me most erroneous about his argument was not its inattention to evidence (as the synopsis of Ophelia's story cited above omits the killing of her father) but its driving assumption that only now, six hundred years after the composition of the *Canterbury Tales*, with the identification of a suddenly fashionable disorder, has it become possible to understand the Yeoman. What was denied all others has been granted us. Before now, people peered through a glass darkly; with the coming of pop psychology all is revealed. Those before us, trapped in ignorance, prisoners of history, could not see; now we see. This is utopian literary criticism, inspired by the belief that the sun of psychology burns off illusion and that we can now therefore survey all things, including the past and its errors, from a position of privileged understanding. The theory flatters us, the enlightened, as abjectly as self-help manuals do their readers.

To be sure, psychology often speaks of literature as a trove of symbols and archetypes whose meaning was profoundly if obscurely understood before being decoded by psychology. Freud said the poets read the secrets of the unconscious before he did; and self-help authors embellish their pages with literary quotations as though enlightened rationality had finally understood what the intuition of the poets knew all long. Under such shows of deference, however, runs the belief that psychology in fact holds the master key to literature, now reduced to an illustration of therapeutic doctrines. Only as an illustration of its own thesis (and scarcely even then) does *Reviving Ophelia* take an interest in Ophelia. Read in context, the story of Ophelia is not a parable of "the destructive forces that affect young women" in general. It is a tragedy of double grief in keeping with other doublings in the play, a commentary on a tyrannical and foolish father—one of many in Shakespeare—and a dramatization of the heightened possibilities and dangers of youth precisely because it falls in between more settled and defined phases of human life. It was also as an illustration of a preconceived thesis, and not as a text in context, that my student approached the Yeoman, who in his own way enjoys a well-defined position.

Underlying my student's thesis was the belief that under the guidance of psychology we have passed from the realm of myth to that of clinical understanding. Self-help literature transposes the same story to the level of the person, telling of patients reborn as they pass, with expert help, from error and confusion to insight.

11

Constructing Stories

Holding out the promise that the abolition of morality will mean the advent of goodness, pop psychology reflects the utopian movements from which it springs. To my mind, the illustrative stories everywhere in its literature are by and large as lacking in reality as accounts of utopia, such as this typical passage in Charlotte Perkins Gilman's *Herland*:

> We talked and talked. We took long walks together. She showed me things, explained them, interpreted much that I had not understood. Through her sympathetic intelligence I became more and more comprehending of the spirit of the people of Herland, more and more appreciative of its marvelous inner growth as well as outer perfection.

The reader of pop psychology also walks through a revealed world accompanied by a sympathetic and knowing guide, and at the end of it all is supposed to say of the author, "She showed me things, explained them, interpreted much that I had not understood." (Of all that the narrator sees in Herland, nothing leaves him "so really awed" as the natives' working knowledge of psychology.) Before Gilman wrote *Herland* she wrote *Women and Economics*, whose arguments *Herland* dresses in a thin garment of fiction. Before William Morris wrote *News from Nowhere* he wrote the *Manifesto of the Socialist League*, which the former illustrates. In a similar way, the lesson of a story in the self-help genre is always given before the story comes into being. The first words of Stephen Covey's *Living the 7 Habits: The Courage to Change* state as much:

> *Living the 7 Habits* is a book of stories—stories about people from all walks of life dealing with profound challenges in their businesses, communities, schools, and families, as well as within themselves—showing how they applied the principles of *The 7 Habits of Highly Effective People* to these challenges, and the remarkable things that resulted.

☞ In pop psychology, theory precedes evidence. Only because of the priority of theory can Phil McGraw tell me about myself without having met me, that is, in the absence of any evidence whatever. "I do think I know a lot about what may be going on in your life." "I'm going to show you exactly, precisely why and how [independence, passion, and so on] have been robbed from you." The psychologist knows I have been robbed because his theory calls for this to be so. Others assert with evangelical certainty that child abuse had to take place in a given instance, whether or not evidence independent of their theory exists.

A psychologist maintains that "ninety percent of all incest victims never tell anyone what has happened, or what is happening, to them"—an absence of evidence that does not deter the psychologist because her theory makes evidence unnecessary. Incest became general when the general attributes of people in the life-stories of self-help books, such as guilt, a poor opinion of themselves, and dependence on others, were defined as presumptive symptoms of incest. A psychiatrist can declare positively that "horrendous human acts are . . . always the outgrowths of self-hating, overwhelming, castigating consciences" not because he knows all there is to know about the horrors committed in all times and all places, which would mean omniscience, but simply because his theory purports to be the key to everything. A renowned psychologist, one who served as president of the American Psychological Association, can state positively that "the truth is that the average American citizen does not have a real friend in the world" for the simple reason that he possesses a theory giving him the imaginary power to say what the truth is. Because advice authors deem child-rearing a skill to be learned at the hands of experts like themselves, they can simply presume children were raised poorly (as expansive as this assumption is) until their expertise came onto the scene. That people liberated from morality will behave more morally than ever is not an observation or even a hope but a doctrine dictated by the theory of human life that governs every page of pop psychology. The educational theory that achievement follows from self-esteem, and not the reverse, seems to retain its credit regardless of evidence, as if theory had made evidence simply unnecessary. The principle that difficulty will vanish once realized is presented not on the last page of *The Road Less Traveled* but on the first, for it precedes argument and does not follow from it. Similarly, only because pop psychology dictates that inhumanity flows from wounded self-esteem is the argument made that Adolf Eichmann did what he did because his father wounded his self-esteem.

And just as theory precedes evidence in self-help literature, so do sweeping assumptions govern the stories.

Assume that parents are "toxic"; assume that society promotes "addiction"; that "the Western model" is soul damaging; that at birth we are "filled with . . . creativity, wisdom, love, joy, enthusiasm, and contentment," which we proceed to lose—assume any of these things and the story is all but written already. In each case the individual can either manage to overcome the odds and achieve well-being (and given the generally uplifting tone of self-help, this will be the usual outcome), or not. A story dominated by such vast assumptions really has no chance. So too, the persons told of in self-help stories, identified by first name if at all, often seem to be invented for the sole purpose of illustrating the author's message. Just as such persons have no existence beyond their modest function, so too the meaning of these fables is exhausted in the doctrines they exemplify.

The first story recounted in *Letting Go of Shame* tells of a two-year-old who

finds a special place in the garden where she digs happily in the soft soil. She feels proud of her accomplishments. "Look at me," she wants to tell the world. "Look at what I can do. I am good."

"Just look at you!" shouts her mother. "Look at this mess. You are dirty. Your clothes are ruined. I'm very disappointed with you. You ought to be ashamed of yourself."

The child feels very small. She drops her head and stares at the ground. She sees her dirty hands and clothes and begins to feel dirty inside. She thinks there must be something very bad about her, something so bad she will never really be clean. She hears her mother's disdain. She feels defective.

How can the authors read the thoughts of a two-year-old? How do they know she thinks she is so bad she will never really be clean? Because they invented this precociously farseeing youngster for the purpose of illustrating their own theory of shame. Perhaps because this theory agrees with the master theory of pop psychology—that the authenticity we bring with us into the world is cruelly undermined by the world—it is assumed true and placed beyond question.

The story of Happiness Lost, or Authenticity Lost, runs through the pages of the self-help genre. A less accusatory version appears on the first page of GUILT Is *the Teacher;* LOVE Is *the Lesson*:

> I remember how special it was to pick up my children from their cribs in the morning, when they were so full of vitality about the day to come. Living in the present moment, they approached life with wonder, anticipation, and honesty. If they were hungry or wet, they cried or screamed. If they were content, they laughed and smiled. They were authentically human and free to express themselves in a way that adults often cannot. As we grow older, our duties, responsibilities, and roles too often assume control of us.

Consider now this passage from the last pages of *The Death of Ivan Ilych*, whose author, Tolstoy, was a disciple of Rousseau:

> The further [Ivan Ilych] departed from childhood and the nearer he came to the present the more worthless and doubtful were the joys. . . . Pictures of his past rose before him one after another. They always began with what was nearest in time and then went back to what was most remote—to his

childhood—and stopped there. If he thought of the stewed prunes that had been offered to him that day, his mind went back to the raw shrivelled French plums of his childhood, their peculiar flavor and the flow of saliva when he sucked their pits; along with the memory of that taste came a whole series of memories of those days: his nanny, his brother, and their toys. "No, I mustn't think of that. . . . It's too painful," Ivan Ilych said to himself, and brought himself back to the present—to the button on the back of the sofa and the creases in its morocco. "Morocco is expensive, but it doesn't wear well: there had been a quarrel about it. It was a different kind of quarrel and a different morocco that time when we tore father's portfolio and were punished, and mamma brought us some tarts. . . ." Once again his thoughts dwelt on his childhood; again it was painful and he tried to banish them and fix his mind on something else.

Then together with that chain of memories another series passed through his mind—of how his illness had progressed and grown worse. There too the further back he looked, the more life there was. There had been more of what was good in life and more of life itself.

While the passage from GUILT *Is the Teacher* as well as this excerpt both concern a grave loss of authenticity over time, as though it bled out of us as we mature, the first is written in vapid clichés, the second with strong detail. It is as if Tolstoy's fidelity to the particular would not allow his ideological program, as forceful as it is, to overrule his sense of reality or obligation to the truth. In the same essay in which she identifies every human being as a moral being, Iris Murdoch contends that "utopian political theories . . . flourish when we lose the ordinary fundamental sense of contingency and accident which belongs with the concept of the individual." Ivan Ilych, a definite individual, lies on his deathbed haunted with recollections of his childhood because of an accident on a stepladder—an event so ordinary, and presented with such a complete absence of portent, that at the time it scarcely registers as an event. Contingency and contingency alone accounts for the flow of consciousness, narrative, and recollection from the leather of the couch to the leather of the portfolio to the gift of tarts. The passage from GUILT *Is the Teacher* is bathed in utopianism; that from *The Death of Ivan Ilych*, for all of the author's dedication to Rousseau, in a rich and rigorous sense of the real. Nor does Tolstoy anywhere imply that all would be well with us adults if only we let ourselves cry and scream. And in contrast to one who forgives another in order to release himself from resentment, as in the counsels of pop psychology, Ivan Ilych in the end asks his family to forgive *him* and dies to release both them and himself from suffering.

The attachment to the real that I refer to manifests itself in (among other forms) the details strewn through the text of *The Death of Ivan Ilych*: a caught shawl, a cigarette case, a medallion, a striped leather ball. So strong was Tolstoy's sense of the contingent detail, and of the obligation of art to the depiction of contingency, that he repudiated all conventional forms of plot construction on the ground that they misrepresented the nature of the real. It is his rejection of literary plotting that accounts for the feeling of plotlessness, of narrative wandering, in *War and Peace*. As Gary Saul Morson has written:

> Tolstoy objected to the traditional plots of novels and histories, which he believed falsified the nature of reality, and, therefore, of the events they sought to describe. To summarize his objections: Incidents in these narratives derive meaning from their

place within a generically given structure and in relation to an ending, but for Tolstoy such meanings are necessarily false. Foreshadowing, a source of narrative irony and aesthetic power, smuggles additional false meanings into events because, in Tolstoy's view, not just one but many possible futures spring from any given moment. [Hence the absence of foreshadowing in *The Death of Ivan Ilych*.] Each event figures in many possible sequences even though only one sequence is realized.

If we investigate the construction of psychological success stories with these strictures in mind, we find them to be invariably "generically given structures"—standard products—whose highly edited content is dictated by the program, and in most cases the happy ending, stamped upon them. The second of Stephen Covey's "seven habits of highly effective people" is "Begin with the end in mind," and the rigidly stylized stories in his follow-up volume, *Living the 7 Habits,* like innumerable other products of pop psychology, are constructed accordingly. As if life itself were a story whose end is given in advance, Eric Berne, psychoanalyst and author of *Games People Play*, once said that we each write the story of our life, right down to the bed we will die in, in early childhood. Tolstoy objected to conventional plots precisely on the ground that they were constructed with the end in mind. A hundred years ago the convention of the closed ending had become not only intolerable to many novelists, now inventing ways around it, but (in England at least) tiresome to the reading public. "There was a change, a recognition," Frank Kermode notes, that conventional narrative closure "may falsify the truth." This recognition has not reached the authors of self-help stories, however.

Neatly packaged and processed, the life-stories of the self-help genre go down easily, like coated pills. A self-help book for cancer patients introduces us to Ellen B., a second-grade teacher, of whom we learn:

> Ellen's life was full. She was an excellent teacher. Her lesson plans and projects were well organized and her students liked her. . . . Ellen was a wonderful mom. She was a Girl Scout leader while her daughters were enrolled. She helped them with their studies, drove carpools, and even practiced soccer with them.

How diminished, how uninformative such language is! Not even a bare outline of an actual person emerges from this generic structure. Does it take no more than being organized and being liked to be an excellent teacher? But perhaps the most serious defect of this kind of story is that it allows no way to assess its judgments because the little information it conveys comes prejudged. No sooner do we learn Ellen is a teacher than we are told she is an excellent teacher. No sooner do we learn she is a mom than we find she is a wonderful mom. Neither judgment is supported in a remotely convincing manner. Nor do we possess any independent information about Ellen that we might draw on to evaluate the conclusions we are fed. It is as if the story of Ellen B. had been written in a utopia where the thought of doubting did not and could not exist. How would it have been constructed by Tolstoy, whose Ivan Ilych is just as conventional but who bursts into being over the course of his ordeal with cancer? That question must remain open, but it is certain that Tolstoy's version would not have terminated in clichés like "she found herself living in the present," or in Ellen's words, "Today is my first priority," for in Tolstoy's view a story governed by its ending, and all the more such a conventional ending, must be false.

In *Compassion and Self-Hate* we encounter "a forty-four-year-old man who, as it turned out, was terrified of growing old." At the very moment we are introduced to this man we are told what his trouble turned out to be. The specimen comes labeled. Turning the tables on the author, a psychiatrist, one suspects that his way of putting the conclusion at the beginning is symptomatic of a larger problem: a habit of reasoning in a circle, allowing a theory to dictate the evidence that supports the theory. Such circularity is typical, I believe, of self-help stories. Also typical is the story's resolution. Within two paragraphs, under the guidance of the psychiatrist the man has lost his terror of aging.

Both the original utopian work of literature and the stories of pop psychology tend toward closure. Unlike the *Iliad*, which ends with Troy still standing, the *Odyssey* ends with resolution. The stories of pop psychology race toward resolution, as in the case of a tale in *The Road Less Traveled* of a woman who goes from neurosis to success in half a page. Once brought to understand "that her loneliness, while her problem, was not necessarily due to a fault or defect of her own," the woman was "ultimately . . . divorced, put herself through college while raising her children, became a magazine editor, and married a successful publisher." That is, once having undergone therapy, she lived happily ever after. How many potential stories lie concealed in the end to this story! Any of the authors who, a hundred years ago, resisted the conventions of narrative closure, any of the readers who came to suspect that such conventions falsify—any of them would have recognized that the word "ultimately" as used here is particularly false, that it closes what is not closed, editing and expurgating in the interest of narrative neatness, converting a woman into an illustration of the healing power of therapy. Such an illustrative fable has little more truth in it than the black-bordered death notice for Ivan Ilych published by his wife, which is also conventional, highly expurgated, and neatly packaged.

Inasmuch as we know nothing about the people in self-help fables except the very little we are told, it is hard to say what has been left out for the sake of the message, but in the case of a story anthologized and possibly edited by Stephen Covey in *Living the 7 Habits*, one can guess. The narrative, which runs to three pages, tells of a minister who one day decides to clean his shotgun. "As I was cleaning the gun, it discharged and shot my wife. The doctors were unable to save her or our unborn child." Over the remainder of the story the word "remorse" appears once and "guilt" not at all. Along with the locution "the gun shot my wife" in place of "I shot my wife," the whitewashed wording of this story (which ends with the minister "happily remarried") suggests a determination to exclude the topic of guilt. In the eyes of pop psychology, guilt, after all, is an error that takes root in our minds and consumes us from within.

As we know, Covey insists that the principles illustrated by his stories are indisputable. "You can't really argue against them," he says, any more than you can dispute the law of gravity. The demand that the reader accept a highly edited and possibly fictitious account as factually true, and accept it without question or argument, becomes especially coercive in purported accounts of sexual abuse, where doubting the story is said to mock the victim's suffering. So ingrained in the therapeutic imagination is the figure of the abused child that fictitious cases of abuse call forth the same language of outrage as real ones. Addressing the reader directly, in the manner of pop psychology, *The Portable Therapist* proclaims,

It is not your fault that you were abused. You did not deserve
it. You could not control it. You are completely blameless. . . .
Let go of all guilt—it is not yours.

But of course the reader of these words may not have been
abused at all. Consider too the story of a woman known only
by the pseudonym of "Gizelle," as it appears in the influential
guide for women survivors of child sexual abuse, *The Courage
to Heal*. Four brief paragraphs into her story, "Gizelle" reports,

The rape [no rape has been mentioned to this point] happened
the month of my third birthday, right after Daddy returned. I
was sound asleep in my bedroom. I woke up with my father's
penis in my mouth. The impact of it thrust my head back and
literally cut off my wind and I thought I was dying. I didn't
know what was in my mouth. I didn't know what a penis was.
I just woke up with this whatever-it-was shoved down my
throat, suffocating, gagging.

This sets the tone for the narrative. The reader is simply not permitted to do anything but experience the pain and outrage of
the writer. Who is the reader to question Gizelle's account? Not
even knowing who Gizelle is, how *could* a reader question it?

Years later, after a serious crisis, Gizelle writes, "I hooked
up with Frank Lanou, who has been my counselor and guide
through this whole thing." At the same time she begins to have
flashbacks, connecting them with a drug called MDMA that she
is now taking under the counselor's guidance. At this point a
footnote informs us that "although Gizelle had a powerful healing experience, MDMA is not always helpful in recovering memories. . . . When Gizelle used MDMA it was legal and she had the

support of a skilled therapist. At present, use of the drug is illegal." During the first MDMA session, "within twenty minutes it all started coming up. . . . I said, 'Frank, this sounds crazy, but I feel like I'm being raped. That's the feeling in my body.' And then I said, 'Who would do this to me?' And then the next moment, I said, 'Oh my God, it's my father.'" During the second MDMA session Gizelle achieves total recall. "We have in our bodies exact 100 percent recall of what's happened to us. All we have to do is connect with it." As it happens, one of the street names of MDMA is Ecstasy. And so it is on the strength of an Ecstasy-induced recovery of a latent somatic memory that the reader of this account is commanded, as it were, to believe every word of it.

Less sensationally and with less at stake, other self-help stories also prejudge all information received by the reader and thus dictate, or attempt to dictate, the reader's response; indeed, almost all such stories do. The assumed reader of these fables, like an inhabitant of some island kingdom cut off from all outside sources of information, knows nothing of the persons mentioned except what he or she is told, and in theory can respond only in the manner prescribed. Amid Stephen Covey's anecdotes of people who live by his seven principles, we meet a man who at the age of thirty-four reads the Alcoholics Anonymous book. "It was the first book I'd ever read cover to cover. *The 7 Habits* was the second." In a sense this man already is cut off from information; he has nothing to read Stephen Covey's "universal, timeless, and self-evident principles" against. The ideal reader of self-help stories never reads them against anything. The ideal reader of a work of literature reads with an interest in the sources it draws on, the traditions it takes part in, the debates it enters, the works it parodies, the accents and discordances of its own voices.

☞ Trimming the meager information they convey so that it supports a single predetermined conclusion and nothing else, self-help stories deny readers the ability and even the right to draw their own conclusions. In spite of pop psychology's unctuous regard for every reader's inner wisdom, the stories show the reader scant respect. In a work of fiction any such attempt to prescribe conclusions would be intolerable. Among his last notes, the literary theorist M. M. Bakhtin reflected that not only modern (that is, postmedieval) literature but the modern languages themselves have broken away from "high, proclamatory genres—of priests, prophets, preachers, judges, leaders, patriarchal fathers, and so forth." The proclamation "retards and freezes thought." It demands "reverent repetition," not a thinking response. It is monologue. I would argue that all of this is true of the generic language of our own high priests, the therapists: it is proclamatory ("The world has attacked your authenticity"), injunctive ("Stop taking care of others. Seek help"), repetitive, one-toned, at odds in every way with the literature of the imagination. It is worth noting that the last and greatest work by Bakhtin's favorite author, Dostoevsky, contains the most powerful indictment of child abuse in world literature—and that the author makes us question not only the justice of the world but the very prosecutor of these crimes, Ivan Karamazov.

To illumine the nature of self-help stories in particular, we might consider some principles of literary construction. First, and most generally, a work of fiction cannot illustrate a set of doctrines and beliefs (in the way that, say, *Herland* illustrates those of *Women and Economics*) except at the cost of its independence as art. One reason *The Color Purple* caught the imagination of the 1980s—it was said to be the work of literature most widely taught in universities at the time—may be that it *does* illustrate the doctrines of pop psychology. It illustrates them with fidelity and flair. Telling of Celie, a young woman sexually abused, trampled, and deprived of a sense of worth, who overcomes oppression and achieves empowerment, *The Color Purple* confirms fictionally the allegations of incest made by the recovery movement and dramatizes the doctrine of self-esteem as the determinant of emotional life that pervades and defines pop psychology. Passages in *The Color Purple* mirror the doctrines of pop psychology so closely that they could serve as illustrative fables in a manual:

> I can't even remember the last time I felt mad, I say. I used to git mad at my mammy cause she put a lot of work on me. Then I see how sick she is. Couldn't stay mad at her. Couldn't be mad at my daddy cause he my daddy. Bible say, Honor father and mother no matter what. Then after while every time I got mad, or start to feel mad, I got sick. Felt like throwing up. Terrible feeling. Then I start to feel nothing at all.

This passage could be correlated point for point with therapeutic doctrine, but as the two are one the exercise is moot. Even the heroine's venture as a pants maker agrees with self-help doctrine. "Turn Your Hobby into a Business," advised Wayne Dyer a few years before the publication of *The Color Purple*, offering this example among others:

> Marilyn was interested in macrame. She did it as a hobby until she saw the business opportunities available. Her friends wanted specialized items made, and they were willing to pay her. After one year, she had turned a hobby into a full-time fun job, and was making a very nice income.

And so it is, more or less, with Celie.

If *The Brothers Karamazov* provokes us to question Ivan even though (or possibly because) he catalogs crimes against children, the reader of *The Color Purple* is allowed to do nothing but react when, on the novel's first page, the heroine is raped by her stepfather. Readers of a work of fiction ought to be permitted to think for themselves. Certainly we should be presented with enough information about the characters to be able to form our own judgments, and for that matter evaluate the judgments made about them by the narrator or other characters. In part this is simply a matter of quantity. The informational famine that rules the world of the self-help story has no place in literature. Even if the author writes with a strong moral purpose, as Tolstoy does in *The Death of Ivan Ilych*, the reader may reach conclusions other than those prescribed, provided the work is honestly constructed and enough information finds its way to the reader—conditions met in *Ivan Ilych*. Here, for example, Tolstoy tells us exactly what to think of the hero's wife: she is to be condemned in strict Rousseauvian terms as a figure of dissimulation, identified with the poisonous falsehood of the theater, the press, the social world, and the regime of public opinion. Nevertheless, as I have argued elsewhere, the powerful sense of contingency that fills the tale also fills it with uncertainty, making it impossible for the reader to share the absoluteness of the author's judgment of this woman. In other ways, too, it seems to me, this great novella transcends the narrow program stamped upon it so forcibly and legibly. That a work of fiction could outgrow or escape the intention of the author is a possibility Tolstoy himself cited in his discussion of Chekhov's story "The Darling."

Much as a novel needs to allow its characters to breathe, literature must allow its readers freedom. Why is it that irony is missing from pop psychology? Possibly because irony would interfere with its heart-to-heart style, or because irony hints at resignation, at acceptance of the inconceivable (as in Jane Austen), and such acceptance runs contrary to the genre's can-do spirit. But irony also leaves us with a perplexing freedom, as the reader of the *Canterbury Tales* confronts many uncertainties because of the poet's studied use of equivocation and disguise. Inasmuch as irony is not what we would expect, it causes us to think (as though philosophy were originating anew in wonder), and sometimes we are not even certain of what is ironic and what isn't. Moreover, because readers of literature are expected to think for themselves, the literary text allows for, even ironically provokes, the possibility of misreading. Like uncertainty and surprise, which are also summoned into play in literature, error is not merely the accompaniment but the very condition of human freedom. In his investigation of the moral implications of reading literature, Wayne Booth attaches great importance to the "practice of subtle, sensitive moral inference, the kind that most choices in daily life require of us," and a skill the reader of Henry James or Jane Austen is called on to exercise. But to venture into the fictional world of James or Austen is to enter a field of uncertainty where our customary assurance fails us and we must learn moral inference all over again. It is this loss and gain, in good part, that makes the experience of their fictional worlds at once a chastening, a revelation, and a delight. Perhaps it stands to reason that a psychology that vilifies morality does not allow for the textual trials and errors that educate morally.

To keep us from uncertainty, everything in illustrative self-help stories comes explained, identified, interpreted. A prominent self-help book names "recognition" as the first step toward emancipation from the power of self-hatred, and such stories make sure the reader recognizes what's what at every point. Recognition is a powerful literary device going back to the *Odyssey*, its latter books punctuated by the revelation and proof of the hero's identity to his son, herdsman, nurse, wife, enemies, and father in what can only be called recognition scenes. So important is recognition to literature that authors and styles characterize themselves by their handling of the convention's potential. According to Aristotle, recognition lends power to tragedy. So it does in Shakespeare; but think too of the recognition scenes at the conclusion of Shakespeare's romances; of conventional discoveries of ancestry in the novel; of the ironic comedy of recognition in Jane Austen; of Pip's shattering recognition of his patron's identity in *Great Expectations*; of the nonrecognition of Smerdyakov as a brother in *The Brothers Karamazov*; of a juror's recognition of the prostitute-defendant as the servant girl he once seduced, in Tolstoy's *Resurrection*; of the reader's recognition (or not) of Homer under the text of *Ulysses*. Alone among literary forms, the novel often deliberately places the reader in the same position of not understanding and not recognizing as the characters under these limitations. It does so, I believe, to engage the reader more fully, to cultivate humility, and to preclude the sort of pretense that claims to know all motives, see through all disguises, and possess the master key of interpretation.

Literature conveys vastly more, but in one or two respects perhaps less information than self-help stories. As though they could not abide the unknown, self-help stories not only label all things but reveal all their characters' secrets. Authors of fiction are unlikely to do this, at least in the flat manner of advice literature:

Roseanne resented her ex-husband for leaving her. She had given him the best years of her life, and he left her to marry a younger woman. She felt deprived of love and support throughout the marriage, but when she thought about his being happy in his new marriage, she felt resentful.

It is said that there is intimate knowledge about their characters that both Tolstoy and James, among other authors, withhold out of respect for those characters. Some authors may believe that baring the soul of a character in the summary manner of the psychologist not only violates but actually misrepresents that person. Others may veil a character's motives or history in order to deepen the enigma of the person's being, an extreme case being Bartleby the Scrivener, who never discloses exactly why he prefers not to work, speak, or in the end live. It should also be noted that any author who delivered a story as one-sidedly and uncritically (not to say as briefly) as the story of Roseanne would fail to meet the standards of the art.

Just as an author is unlikely to reveal a major character's innermost nature, as though tagging a specimen with a label, so too an author may wait, and ask us to wait, for a character's nature to come forth. The correlate of reticence is patience. Only deep in the middle of *Crime and Punishment* do we learn that Raskolnikov was imitating Napoleon when he committed murder:

> I wanted to become a Napoleon: that's why I killed the old woman. . . . You see, what happened was that one day I asked myself this question: what if Napoleon, for instance, had been in my place and if he had not had an Egypt or the crossing of Mont Blanc to start his career with, but instead of all those splendid and monumental things there had simply been some ridiculous old woman . . . who had to be murdered to get the money from her box (for his career, of course). Well, would he have made up his mind to do it if there were no other way?

Would he have felt disgusted to do it because it was far from monumental and—wicked, too? Well, let me tell you, I spent a long time worrying over that question, so that in the end I felt terribly ashamed when it occurred to me (quite suddenly, somehow), that he [Napoleon] wouldn't have felt disgusted at all and that indeed it would never have occurred to him that it was not monumental. In fact he would not have understood what there was to be squeamish about. And if he had had no alternative, he would have strangled her without the slightest hesitation, and done it thoroughly, too. Well, so, I too hesitated no longer and—and murdered her, following the example of my authority [that is, Napoleon].

Instead of revealing this to us at the time of the event, it is as if the author waited for Raskolnikov himself to make the revelation in his own time (just as Raskolnikov originally spent a long time contemplating the Napoleon question). Some would say that such a statement made *about* Raskolnikov, rather than *by* Raskolnikov, would be an act of violation.

Some characters in literature are indeed meant to be seen through. Incapable of keeping their nature to themselves, they wear their secrets on their sleeve, living exemplifications of this or that form of folly. In this category belong the types that populate the world of satire. Like Erasmus's self-identified Folly, though, the best types somehow overfulfill their role, coming to life in spite of their own identifying label or the satiric program that supposedly governs them. Chaucer's Wife of Bath does not exemplify the talkative, appetitive, ungovernable woman; she so overfulfills that definition (her speech a Niagara, her appetites many and conflicting, her will to govern matched only by a desire to submit) that she leaps into life and dominates the better part of the *Canterbury Tales*. As though she had achieved independence of her own author's intention, we simply cannot tell whether the poet viewed her with approval or disapproval, revulsion or delight, or all of these at once. The reader of a psychological vignette is told exactly how to interpret it; indeed, the vignette and its interpretation are the same thing. Readers of Chaucer are on their own. Pop psychology instructs us that men are from Mars, women from Venus. The Wife of Bath is from both.

> For certes [certainly] I am al [all] Venerien
> In feelynge, and myn herte is Marcien.
> Venus me yaf [gave] my lust, my likerousnesse [lecherousness],
> And Mars yaf me my sturdy hardynesse.

In part because readers are on their own, literature encourages a searching mind. Readers of self-help are spoon-fed conclusions, as in this passage in *Toxic Parents*, which readers are intended to accept word for word:

> Children who are not encouraged to do, to try, to explore, to master, and to risk failure, often feel helpless and inadequate. Overcontrolled by anxious, fearful parents, these children often become anxious and fearful themselves. This makes it difficult for them to mature. When they develop through adolescence and adulthood, many of them never outgrow the need for ongoing parental guidance and control. As a result, their parents continue to invade, manipulate, and frequently dominate their lives.

Readers alive to the possibilities of irony may wonder about parents consumed with fear of their own toxic influence; parents so dependent on the guidance of professed experts that they remain, morally speaking, children themselves.

☞ In addition to stories that flow from a single pen, there are those we might call common stories—for example, the story a generation might tell itself about its own place in history. In the world of American poetry, the story goes that in the mid-twentieth century the rule of impersonality was triumphantly broken, the model of the breakthrough being furnished by Robert Lowell, who

> after writing several books of highly praised [impersonal verse] . . . understood that poetry could be fragmentary, subjective, personal, and the result was *Life Studies*, a watershed in twentieth-century poetry. *Life Studies* itself tells this story; the volume begins with formal poems that recall the high-church values of Lowell's earlier work, moving on to the free verse anxieties of poems about his family and his mental collapse. Lowell sometimes spoke of this movement as a "breakthrough back into life," as if free verse were not one kind of form among many but a movement beyond the merely literary. Psychic and political health, it seems, could be achieved by breaking the pentameter.

I quote here from James Longenbach, who contends that this thumbnail story of liberation, which has acquired the status of a master myth, is erroneous and misleading even with respect to Lowell.

If the story of Lowell's breakthrough was false, how could it have caught on and become the story of a generation of poets? Perhaps because it resonated with the larger narrative of our emergence from repression into the open air of freedom and experimental understanding. And just as the Lowell story tells of the mind's collapse and reconstitution, so the liberation myth associates liberation itself with therapy. Longenbach designates the oft-told story of the evolution of American poetry after modernism as a "breakthrough narrative," and breakthrough is exactly what is celebrated to this day in pop psychology in all its forms. Breakthrough is what transforms us from unfulfilled, habit-bound persons to happy, free persons. Breakthrough is what M. Scott Peck's patient Marcia experienced when, after a moment of truth, she was "immediately" and permanently cured of her promiscuity. Phil McGraw's Claire broke through. "Once this woman reclaimed her authentic self, it was as if floodgates had opened." (The flooding is conventional. Wrote William Schutz of an encounter group in 1967, "The dramatic reliving of . . . situations exploded the cork and the repressed feelings flooded out." One of his encounter games was called "Breaking Out.")

Therapy itself made a breakthrough not long after the publication of *Life Studies* in 1958, going from the recourse of a few to a possibility for millions—as it were, from a rarity to a commodity. It was as if floodgates had opened. In 1962 the film *David and Lisa*, based on a clinical history by Theodore Rubin (the author later of *Compassion and Self-Hate*, among other works), made its appearance. Read about the film and you will see that David has a breakthrough, that Keir Dullea, who plays David, made his breakthrough as an actor, that the film marks a first in its depiction of emotionally disturbed teenagers, and that the actor Howard Da Silva had a breakthrough of his own in the film—appearing on screen for the first time since he was blacklisted. Breakthroughs everywhere. The breakthrough, the critical moment in therapy, had itself broken through. "Break through" is now a Cadillac slogan.

Under the influence of this myth, even guilt, pop psychology's nemesis, has had a breakthrough. A special form of guilt has been synthesized that is not toxic but beneficial, that is not to be hidden in shame but displayed with honor, even promoted. This too calls for investigation.

12

Liberal Guilt

In one of the stories nested within *Frankenstein* we read of a woman whose conscience is troubled after her three beloved children die, leaving alive only a despised daughter, Justine. "She began to think that the deaths of her favourites was [sic] a judgment from heaven to chastise her partiality." But if in her contrition "she sometimes begged Justine to forgive her unkindness . . . much oftener [she] accused her of having caused the deaths of her brothers and sister," in turn giving more cause for contrition. Trapped in what certainly looks like a vicious cycle, Madame Moritz goes into a decline from which she never recovers.

As brief as it is, the story of Madame Moritz plants the idea that guilt is but the other side of the worst forces in our nature, and that it leads not to redemption but only to more guilt. Spiraling guilt is also, after all, the image left in our minds by the great tragedy of guilt, *Macbeth*. Seized with guilt over the murder of Duncan, Macbeth proceeds to compound the offense by arranging the murder of Banquo and then, in a refinement of evil with strong parallels in *Frankenstein,* the family of Macduff. From guilt comes more guilt. But is guilt then cursed? In the tragic history of Victor Frankenstein, it appears so.

Here too a vicious cycle sets in, as intense guilt over his creature's crimes hardens him against the creature, driving the latter to more and more crime. The story of Frankenstein becomes a story of all-consuming guilt.

> Remorse extinguished every hope. I had been the author of unalterable evils, and I lived in daily fear lest the monster whom I had created should perpetrate some new wickedness. . . .

> I, not in deed, but in effect, was the true murderer. . . . I was encompassed by a cloud which no beneficial influence could penetrate. . . .

> I shuddered to think that future ages might curse me as their pest, whose selfishness had not hesitated to buy its own peace at the price, perhaps, of the existence of the whole human race. . . .

> William, Justine, and Henry—they all died by my hands. . . .

> In my Elizabeth I possessed a treasure, alas, balanced by those horrors of remorse and guilt which would pursue me until death.

Ironically, however, the more bitter Frankenstein's remorse, the more remorse it engenders, until in the end Elizabeth is murdered for the sake of the torture it will cause him. Since it is bound indissolubly with moral abhorrence of his creature, and the pain of being abhorred drives the creature to crime, guilt in the moral economy of *Frankenstein* only produces more of the same. (As *The Portable Therapist* says, guilt "can be thought of as an evil circle: a snake with its tail in its mouth.") As the creature takes out the pain of rejection by his maker on Clerval and finally on Elizabeth, the agony of Frankenstein's guilt is redoubled. Where the torments of guilt in *Macbeth* point unclearly to the workings of divine justice, those in *Frankenstein* seem pointless, in the sense of being contrary to the self-interest of the sufferer. Only if Frankenstein had been less moralistic, less condemning of his creature as the cause of his guilt, could he as well as the creature have achieved something of the happiness whose force as an ideal is everywhere felt in *Frankenstein* even as the ideal goes unrealized. Guilt in *Frankenstein* is the mind's curse, the nemesis of human wishes, the enemy of happiness.

Guilt is counterproductive; it is also, the novel suggests, useless, in that its place could be taken by other, more benign affections. John Stuart Mill once observed that Bentham seems to have had no concept of conscience "as a thing distinct from philanthropy, from affection for God or man, and from self-interest in this world or in the next." As shown by the tale of his benevolence toward the De Laceys, Frankenstein's creature is animated with the sincere love of man. Hatred of his creator is the measure of his capacity for love. In the name of his own rightful self-interest, he entreats Frankenstein to provide him a mate. The creature possesses, in other words, just those endowments that do the work of conscience without the traditional moral and metaphysical machinery, and, from a certain progressive point of view, do it better, with greater efficiency and humanity. Once he falls into the kind of agonized reflection that distinguishes guilt, the creature is lost. Indeed, he seems caught in a cycle very like his maker's; at least his tortures over the taking of life ("Think you that the groans of Clerval were music to my ears?") do not stand in the way of doing so again and again. This is not the world of Dostoevsky, where remorse is capable of producing moral transformation. Written from a political position seemingly antithetical to Dostoevsky's, *Frankenstein* finds guilt sterile, or if productive, only in the empty and mocking sense of producing ever more of itself.

The story of *Frankenstein* has entered popular lore, albeit in a distorted cinematic form, and with the name of Frankenstein made over to the creature denied, in the original, any name at all. In another respect *Frankenstein* has penetrated more deeply into our culture. "I am malicious because I am miserable," says Frankenstein's stalker. The horrors of prejudice, the hurt of wounded self-esteem, the imperatives of sex, the very principle of simple causation—the lessons of *Frankenstein* are the ABCs of pop psychology. When the creature calculates his murders for psychological effect, culminating in the strangling of Frankenstein's bride on the night of their wedding, he dramatizes in his own way the bias of the work that has made it a virtual index to pop psychology today—one of the doctrines of the latter being that guilt is toxic. Speaking with a sort of pastoral concern, the already-cited 1977 Department of Health, Education, and Welfare pamphlet observes that "nobody knows how much suffering, and even tragedy, has been triggered by needless feelings of guilt, one of the commonest— yet most powerful—emotions that rule our lives." Such a direct assault on guilt could not have been launched without a great deal of preliminary shelling, as by the sort of philosophy conveyed some two centuries ago in *Frankenstein*.

One distinctive form of guilt, however, is portrayed in *Frankenstein* as sweet and noble. That he was the innocent cause of his family's downfall "preyed on the heart" of Felix De Lacey. Elizabeth blames herself for the murder of young William—of which she is entirely innocent—because she gave him the locket taken by his killer. "She weeps continually and accuses herself unjustly as the cause of his death." So far from being a potent toxin as in the case of Victor Frankenstein, this kind of guilt is seen as perfectly harmless, the outpouring of a generous nature. Here, then, is innocent guilt—what we know today as liberal guilt.

☞ If anyone in the world is unfree, then no one is free—so it is said. But what if, despite the unfreedom of someone somewhere, I feel free anyway? Recently Denis Donoghue wrote:

> Granted that the Parthenon and the Egyptian pyramids were built by slaves who, most of them, did not survive to admire the fruits of their labor. I feel uneasy, perhaps even dispirited, by that reflection, but I can't feel guilty. I didn't whip those slaves into their compulsions.

By the same reasoning I don't feel guilt over distant abuses and sufferings today. At this point, though, a still small uneasy voice of humanity somewhere in my head speaks up as if to say, "You should."

But if liberal guilt has so much to do with the imagining of others, it may be best to begin an inquiry into its nature with an example from the world of the imagination.

Having broken up with her husband, a woman feels "riven with guilt" over their child's plight, though she can't decide whether the collapse of the marriage was her husband's fault or hers.

A successful writer imagines himself feeling miserably guilty if he buys a certain fancy car, but still can't forgo it. "Can you believe it? While war raged in Yugoslavia, thousands died daily of AIDS, bombs exploded in Northern Ireland and the unemployment figures rose inexorably in Britain, I could think of nothing except whether or not to buy this car."

The writer later asks his philandering agent "if he didn't sometimes feel a qualm of guilt" over his affairs.

These cases come from David Lodge's satiric novel *Therapy* (1995), its hero, Tubby Passmore, a Narcissus of anxiety peering into the pool of his own discontent. As a caricaturist in the tradition of Dickens, Lodge heightens the features of his types, among them the sort of person oppressed by the strangely weightless guilt we know as liberal guilt. One of the defining moods of our age, liberal guilt is an uneasiness of conscience, but an uneasiness cultivated rather than just suffered. Accordingly, in each of the cases just cited, guilt is more of an entertained possibility than a preying force. Like a kind of play experience, it is somehow juggled, pretended into and out of existence. Said to be torn with guilt, the now-single mother is not so sure she is really to blame. The moment her guilt is mentioned, it is thrown in doubt. As for the writer, the hero or anti-hero of *Therapy*, he goes ahead and buys the car regardless of any moral pains lying in wait for him. For the war in Yugoslavia and the other horrors of the world he of course feels no responsibility. When, later, he asks his agent if he feels any guilt over his amours, the guilt referred to is nothing but a conversation point, a thin if interesting possibility. Tubby Passmore writes for a sitcom, and the kind of guilt he immerses himself in resembles a script in its own right, a story the mind tells itself. If pop psychology teaches that we can script our very selves, liberal guilt is constructed accordingly.

Why should such a dubious sentiment of misgiving be called liberal guilt? If liberalism cultivates a heightened sympathy with suffering, Tubby Passmore thinks of the world's miserable even as he contemplates a new car. (Tubby reports that he votes Labour but confesses to feeling "secretly relieved" when they lose.) If liberalism calls into question traditional superstitions, a guilt like that practiced by the hero of *Therapy* reduces guilt to an archaism. Guilt one makes no secret of, guilt one advertises like a fashion or badge of honor, is not what used to be called guilt. Liberal guilt is guilt not endured but entertained, theorized, fashioned, as if it were up to us to make the most of its possibilities. Karl Mannheim once observed that liberalism, at its origin, "lives on the potential and possible." Made over in the image of its source, liberal guilt is no longer an implacable force but a mode of free play—an option, an exercise in as-if, a mental experiment. When I claim to feel guilty over America's racial record, it is not as though I incurred great costs and consequences as a result. (So too, the Germans who claimed that all Germans were guilty of the Holocaust didn't mean they all should be tried as war criminals.) Liberal guilt is guilt denatured—its reality questionable, its shame cleared, its horror muted.

The first chapter of *Anna Karenina* has Stiva saying to himself, "It's all my fault—all my fault, though I'm not to blame"; two chapters later he is identified as a liberal. Liberal guilt as we know it also says, "It's my fault, though I'm not to blame." Identifying himself as a liberal, Leslie Fiedler once wrote that for decades "the implicit dogma of American liberalism" was that a person of liberal views was incapable of being wrong. In the ethos of liberal guilt, this conviction of blamelessness leads a strange afterlife, the troubled conscience itself becoming a kind of proof of being in the right. Liberal guilt not only survives the loss of innocence that followed the exposure of the Soviet Union as a totalitarian state; it survives the loss of guilt. It is guilt that continues in good repute after "Most of us have been brought up to believe that all guilt is harmful, unnecessary and should be eradicated," in the words of the pamphlet on guilt cited above. Liberal guilt, then, reflects a bad social conscience that is somehow exempt from all the criticisms of conscience as an oppressive force in self-help literature and beyond. Maybe the very concept of guilt was rooted too deeply in Judeo-Christian sources to survive transplant into the realm of the secular in any but the thin and tenuous form known as liberal guilt. Maybe the Enlightenment attack on priests and kings was bound to spill over eventually into a critique of conscience as an internal priest-king, the last redoubt of superstition. And if it is true that the liberal ideas of the Enlightenment appealed to a feeling of open possibility, guilt embarrasses the vision of the possible because it cannot be escaped or denied. How strong the attachment to the voluntary principle to make even guilt an elective experience, and how different the guilt you entertain in imagination from the guilt that pursues you relentlessly and claims you as its own. "An evil conscience," says St. Augustine, "cannot flee from itself; it has no place to which it may go; it pursues itself."

As guilt is liberalized, it is brought under control—tamed, played on, now raised, now reduced. The sort of enlightened policy toward guilt that appeals to our social conscience in the name of the oppressed, even as it casts guilt as a blight on happiness—such a policy realizes with stark clarity the managerial attitude toward our own selves that is everywhere apparent in the self-help literature. To this day, nothing is more distinctive of the liberal style than to discount guilt as an irrational survival of an authoritarian age (a senseless blame game) even while siding with the hapless and the victimized as a matter of social conscience and professing guilt over any enjoyed privilege. In a self-help manual you read that guilt poisons happiness and causes self-hatred. But a news report describes Africa as a scar on the conscience of the world, and spokesmen for the social conscience tell you to feel guilty over burning too much gasoline and buying things made in a sweatshop. That guilt should be juggled in this way, diminished one moment and heightened the next, suggests we really are dealing with the management of the self. Hence too the experimental attitude sometimes taken toward guilt, as if one were uncertain whether to feel more or less of it, or any at all. "I don't know if I should feel guilty about this," someone says, the pains of guilt having become purely optional. ("I don't know" is a comic refrain in Lodge's *Therapy*.) Even when taking the form of a kind of moral headache, liberal guilt isn't experienced like the guilt that pursues and punishes. The great dramas of the power of guilt— *Oedipus Rex*, *Hamlet*, *Macbeth*—after all feature riddles, witches, ghosts, things that offend the enlightened mind as evidences of superstition. Some readers recoil at John Ruskin's famous purple description of Turner's painting of a "guilty" slave ship after a storm, a passage that ends with an allusion to Macbeth's bloody hands.

While remorse works on us from within, only in the condition of liberal guilt does guilt really become, as we say, subjective, terminating in the figure of the neurotic afflicted by "guilt feelings" for reasons unknown. As though the play character of liberal guilt had come back to haunt him, his guilt has become objectless, a game played for its own sake. Liberal guilt, being of the mind's own making, is by the same token weak in comparison to guilt less volitional, less made to order. A classical tragedy where the guilt of the hero is all in the mind is unthinkable, but under the modern order guilt may well be just this. The reader of Locke's seminal *Essay* learns how many of the mind's ideas are its own coinages, without an original in Nature. But if guilt is a product of the mind, by the same token it is theoretically under the mind's control. So it is that readers of the HEW pamphlet already cited (it is entitled "Plain Talk about Feelings of Guilt") are counseled to ask themselves if they really ought to feel guilty and are spoon-fed examples of people suffering guilt needlessly. Guilt, readers are advised,

> is a civilizing force that, when unbridled, can cause much hurt. But with wisdom, fortified by knowledge, this pervasive emotion can be tamed and used to your advantage as you go on with the business of life.

Just as economic pursuits were once thought to promote civility by taming passion and channeling it into the business of life, so, it seems, guilt properly modulated makes the world a better place. Liberal guilt is guilt in its most civilizing aspect. About it, however, there hangs the suggestion of something fictive or fashioned, something, as Locke might say, of the mind's own workmanship.

As Charles Taylor has written, "when we decide that we oughtn't to feel guilty for something we do or feel and treat the spasms like some irrational holdover from our childhood training"—and the pamphlet just cited takes this view of guilt precisely—we typify the style of the Lockean self. Here then is a simplified example of the managed reduction—the other side of the cultivation—of guilt. Characteristic of the Lockean self at the foundation of "the modern identity" is the instrumental position it takes toward its own properties and habits "so that they can be *worked on.*" In the spirit of filling out a general type, let me propose that the Lockean self also manages the balance of pleasure and pain (as in the sweet pains and sorrowful pleasures of sentimental experience); works up feelings as well as working on them; entertains suffering that is not its own and disengages from burdens that perhaps are; and both modulates its own sense of guilt and attunes it to that of others. In liberal guilt, the racking experience of guilt yields to the agreeable pain of an induced or professed sorrow, and the first-person nature of guilt is displaced by a cultivation of the vicarious.

Between Locke and the present come what I think of as three phases of humanitarianism: the idealization of compassion in the eighteenth-century culture of sentiment; the troubling of consciousness with the emergence of the social question in the nineteenth century; and the critique of guilt itself, as an inhibitor of happiness and poison of well-being, in our own age. The figure of Tubby Passmore, advertiser of his own unhappiness, belongs to our time; a few nineteenth-century figures will be cited presently. As an example of the literature of sentiment, consider the famous episode of the caged starling in Laurence Sterne's *Sentimental Journey*, a work of the strangest mannerism but much loved in its time and well after. (The young Tolstoy thought of translating it into Russian.)

Worried that he is soon to be thrown into the Bastille and struggling to argue down his fears, Yorick suddenly hears a small voice complaining, "I can't get out—I can't get out." It is a starling in a cage. "I vow, I never had my affections more tenderly awakened." All his fear of the Bastille comes back to him, along with a wave of sympathy for the world's enslaved.

> Disguise thyself as thou wilt, still slavery! said I—still thou art a bitter draught; and though thousands in all ages have been made to drink of thee, thou art no less bitter on that account— 'tis thou, thrice sweet and gracious goddess, addressing myself to LIBERTY, whom all in public or in private worship.

With the image of the caged bird in his mind, Yorick retires to his room to give his imagination full liberty to depict the horrors of slavery. Finding that he cannot figure to himself "the millions of my fellow creatures born to no inheritance but slavery," he dwells instead on the image of a solitary captive wasting away in prison. It is as if the entire episode had been specially constructed to bring Yorick's sentiments into play. In a sense the true protagonist is Yorick, the man of sensibility, not the starling, the captive, or the slave. (Seeing that the bird was brought up in captivity, it would do it no good to be set free anyway. Yorick doesn't release it when it comes into his possession.) The narrative revolves around Yorick, his attempts at reasoning with himself, his affections, his power and deficiency of imagination. Note too that, unlike one who discerns a connection between the slave system and the sugar in his tea, Yorick's sympathy with slaves is unmixed with any sense of responsibility for their condition. If he did feel in some way responsible, perhaps he would be less free to sympathize.

If Tubby Passmore is a type, Yorick is an original, in some ways the original of Tubby himself. Yorick is a man of the Enlightenment, Tubby seeks light in the office of his cognitive behavior therapist. Yorick commiserates with the captive and the oppressed, Tubby pretends to remember the world's casualties. Yorick goes wherever his heart takes him (a freedom reflected in Sterne's disregard of the laws of sequence, making his narrative wanderings strangely indeterminate and open-ended); Tubby does from moment to moment whatever he wants to do, finally making his own pilgrimage of the heart by tracking down an old girlfriend on the way to Santiago de Compostela. Inasmuch as liberal guilt is not just suffered but chosen and worked at (and therefore honorable), Yorick's most notable and attractive feature, his plain freedom, bears special emphasis in this inquiry into liberal guilt.

Dostoevsky may have been right to say that in his time "the 'higher liberal,' that is, a liberal without goals, [is] possible only in Russia," but something of this character is already present in Yorick, his only program being the lack of one. If, as Karl

Mannheim suggests, liberalism prefers the possible to the actual, this figure of impracticality is the purest of liberals in the sense that his principles have not been committed to anything like a program of action. Once the age of revolution arrived, such indifference would be harder to maintain. It arrived but a few years after the publication of A *Sentimental Journey*.

☞ The Declaration of Independence was crafted by one who deemed the work of Sterne "the best course of morality that was ever written," and whose private correspondence while in Europe on his own journey of the heart rings with echoes of A *Sentimental Journey*. About that work Jefferson wrote,

> We neither know nor care whether Lawrence Sterne really went to France, whether he was there accosted by the poor Franciscan, at first rebuked him unkindly, and then gave him a peace offering: or whether the whole be a fiction. In either case we are equally sorrowful at the rebuke, and secretly resolve *we* will never do so: we are pleased with the subsequent atonement, and view with emulation a soul candidly acknowledging its fault and making a just reparation.

Generosity of spirit like Yorick's would seem to be the very thing Jefferson looked for in the "candid world" to which the Declaration of Independence is addressed.

Dominated by the catalogue of abuses committed by the British Parliament and the Crown—acts of "Cruelty & perfidy scarcely paralleled in the most barbarous ages"—the Declaration offers an account of suffering comparable in sentimental effect to a Sternean tale of sorrow, though in a political register. (Infamously oppressed by the mother country, the colonies take their place in the tradition of the abused child.) Implied

in the Declaration, moreover, is one of the themes of sentimentalism: that sensitivity to distress, our own and others',
proves us moral agents.

> What can be more nobly human than to have a tender senti-
> mental feeling of our own and other's misfortunes? This degree
> of sensibility every man ought to wish to have for his own sake,
> as it disposes him to, and renders him more capable of practis-
> ing all the virtues that promote his own welfare and happiness.

Such sensibility has become one of the insignia of the liberal
ethos, though liberal *guilt* is a more voluntary and constructed
response than the instinctive compassion that was of such interest to the Enlightenment. If the theme of pop psychology is
that we either choose or blindly receive our values (which I have
argued is a false and coercive dichotomy), liberal guilt represents a chosen pain, a pain conceived in the name of the great
ideal of the Enlightenment, freedom.

In the tradition of the Declaration of Independence making
its case to the world, speaking to everyone of feeling, is a bill of
indictment already cited in these pages because of its high importance in the civil rights revolution—a document that quotes
the Declaration and in fact enumerates a long train of abuses:
Martin Luther King's "Letter from Birmingham Jail." Instead
of censuring Jefferson as a slaveholder, as we might have expected, King cites him as an inspiration, and where Jefferson
appeals over the heads of the British Parliament and the Crown
to the tribunal of all candid minds, King appeals over the heads
of the Birmingham authorities to the court of public opinion.
By forcing the nation to face up to its own racial record, the
"Letter from Birmingham Jail" raises guilt, but probably not in
those most immediately to blame—the lynch mobs, the canine
squads, the false promisers, and all the others arraigned by King

for the crimes of oppression. Whatever its reception by the handful of clergymen addressed in the first instance, the real effect of the "Letter," I imagine, was felt by thousands far from the scene and in no way responsible for the atrocities cited by King. Much as Yorick seems to sympathize all the more readily with those he meets on the road because he is soon to proceed down that road; so in the case of the readers I envision, the fact of being well removed from direct guilt makes it easier to extend compassion and even entertain a kind of vicarious or secondary guilt. With this in mind, we might reinterpret the eighteenth-century belief (cited in Chapter 2) that commerce makes us more gentle, civilizes us. The branching networks and remote connections introduced by modern commerce—links so indirect that it takes an Adam Smith to work them out—make sympathy easier by removing the terrors of direct responsibility. (Sympathy is the key term of Smith's *Theory of Moral Sentiments*.) It is a perfect stranger—one passing down the road like Yorick—who binds the wounds of the man who fell among thieves. It was nonslaveholders who worked to outlaw the slave trade and at last slavery.

☞ For the sake of contrast with liberal guilt, consider a poem of guilt, Coleridge's "Ancient Mariner." Here, as in the starling episode of *A Sentimental Journey*, a bird is one of the persons of the drama, its killing an unprovoked and unexplained act so "pure" in a negative sense that it has something of the primal quality of the Fall.

> "God save thee, ancient Mariner!
> From the fiends, that plague thee thus!—
> Why look'st thou so?"—With my crossbow
> I shot the ALBATROSS.

208 / Fool's Paradise

(Can the Mariner be imagined saying, "I don't know if I should feel guilty about this"?) To those who think the idea of responsibility belongs to a premodern world where causation is assigned to persons rather than to systems or abstractions, the real if unintended message of this poem might be that guilt exists only in a mind so fixated on persons that the very sun becomes a person. "The Sun now rose upon the right; / Out of the sea came he." Traditional guilt is certainly personal.

Since the "Ancient Mariner" evokes a certain presence of Middle English, it is worth recalling what guilt refers to in Chaucer's tongue. According to the Parson of the *Canterbury Tales*, "Seint Ambrose seith that Penitence is the pleynynge [sorrowing] of man for the gilt that he hath doon, and namoore [no more] to do any thyng for which hym oghte to pleyne. . . . Penitence . . . is verray [true] repentance of a man that halt [holds] hymself in sorwe and oother peyne for his giltes." Guilt in the progressive sense of a diffuse regret or the feeling for another's suffering has no existence within this definition. For the Mariner there is nothing indirect, pretended, or pleasant about guilt. For the reader, though, the Mariner's experience is transfigured in something like the way meter tempers and sweetens passion, according to the Preface to the *Lyrical Ballads* in which the poem originally appeared. The air of the mythic and the remote enveloping the poem, the affectation of Middle English, the re-creation of some pre-Newtonian cosmos—all contribute to this effect. Here is a poem sentimental in the special sense of being belatedly and affectedly naive, its archaism a reminder, perhaps, that under the modern order guilt is liable to take on the character of a holdover from the past (as indeed it is portrayed throughout the self-help genre). In keeping or not with the author's intent, the poem, by removing the Mariner's experience to a mythic past, seems to say that guilt belongs to a pre-enlightened age. Like the witches in *Macbeth*, the sphinx in *Oedipus*, the Ghost in *Hamlet*, guilt is rooted in superstition.

Even if guilt weren't associated with the archaic, its power alone would frustrate the pursuit of happiness, and still more the right to happiness. Maybe it is because guilt binds us indissolubly to the past where its origin lies, while the ideal of progress has a tropism toward the future, that our culture has such a problem with guilt. Putting the past behind you is the one thing guilt will not permit. The Ancient Mariner relives his crime. From a progressive point of view, there must be something wrong with a force that keeps you so painfully stuck in the past. Guilt seems particularly out of step with the utilitarianism that supplies modernity's prevailing philosophy. If a utilitarian like Bentham seeks to institute an economy, a sort of rational minimum, of punishment, there is something distinctly irrational in that mode of punishment called guilt that goes on and on after the offense has become a memory—again as in the case of the Ancient Mariner—and perhaps after punishment has lost its point. Once guilt comes to be seen as regret for imagined offenses, as the dictionary puts it, it loses all sense whatever. But even if the offense took place, the fact that it lies in the past makes dwelling on it seem pointless. In the 1950s there were many in West Germany who felt the task before the nation was not to confront the crimes of the Nazi era but to get on with economic reconstruction. Under the Covey system, one who causes the death of his friend by driving drunk does not dwell on this horror (which would be "reactive") but sees to his drinking problem and works toward a goal ("proactive").

What can be more futile than fretting over the past? As self-help literature reminds us, the past is over and done with. It would be surprising if skepticism toward punishment (such a conspicuous feature of the liberal ethos, rooted as it is in a dislike and distrust of brute methods that goes back for centuries) didn't carry over to a distrust of the self-punishment of guilt, all the more because of the wasted energy that goes into playing the roles of both judge and offender. Liberal guilt, then, marks the actual erosion of guilt at the hands of an ethos whose sense of the rational is offended by this effect that outlasts its cause, and whose partiality for words like "growth" (one of the thematic words of pop psychology) causes it to regard guilt as a drag on the human capacity for change. Certainly the liberal project couldn't be complete without the transformation of a force that acts on the self as powerfully and intimately as guilt.

So little actual remorse is shown in the mode of feeling called liberal guilt that it is fair to ask why it should be thought of as guilt at all. After all, as a form of sentimentalism it traces back to the Enlightenment culture of sympathy symbolized by the man of feeling whose heart goes out to a perfect stranger—someone whose suffering he has not caused. The guiltless guilt of today's humanitarian, the aroused conscience accompanied by no real conviction of blame, recalls an Enlightenment ideal of innocent commiseration. With the coming of the social question in the nineteenth century, something more like guilt enters into humanitarian feeling. Says the title character in Anthony Trollope's *The Prime Minister*,

> How can you look at the bowed back and bent legs and abject face of that poor ploughman, who winter and summer has to drag his rheumatic limbs to his work, while you go a-hunting or sit in pride of place among the foremost few of your country, and say that it all is as it ought to be? You are a Liberal because you know that it is not all as it ought to be.

And yet in context the prime minister's qualms of conscience are not really credible, coming as they do from nowhere. Liberal guilt in general has a similarly equivocal character, being guiltlike and yet short of guilt per se. Hence the lawyer's offer of a few dollars—guilt money—to Bartleby the scrivener (and the former too tells us, virtually in these words, "I vow, I never had my affections more tenderly awakened"). Hence the vague sense of Arthur Clennam, in Dickens's *Little Dorrit*, "that there was some one with an unsatisfied claim upon his justice." Hence all those preoccupied (in the words of Richard Rorty) with "doubt about their own sensitivity to the pain and humiliation of others, doubt that present institutional arrangements are adequate to deal with this pain and humiliation, curiosity about possible alternatives." Doubt and curiosity: we are in the land of the indeterminate, where guilt loses its definiteness and becomes, as I have said, a kind of weightless oppression. Only one thing is Tubby Passmore sure of—that all is not as it ought to be; and that is why he seeks therapy.

Perhaps the best representative of liberal guilt in our literature is Clennam, the troubled hero of *Little Dorrit*, of whom Dickens writes, "The shadow of a supposed act of injustice, which had hung over him since his father's death, was so vague and formless that it might be the result of a reality widely remote from his idea of it." How indeterminate is this guilt. No crime of his own but a supposition of one committed by his father—a fact twice displaced, as it were—hangs over Clennam. For most of the novel, Clennam lives in the mode of as-if, a topic of running comment in this most ambitious of Dickens's satiric works, and the same scenes that show him tenderly concerned also expose him, in the manner of satire (a tradition also at work in *Therapy*), as blind and self-deceived. By the end of *Little Dorrit*, Clennam experiences guilt in his own person. No longer is it a thought experiment and he himself a third party to human experience.

When guilt becomes hypothetical and virtually imaginary, its terror—our helplessness either to escape or deny it—is reduced. In the most fantastic episode of *The Brothers Karamazov*, Dostoevsky turns liberal guilt inside out by making its vague and formless character a torture and not an anodyne. In view of the suppositious or as-if nature of liberal guilt, it is remarkable that the apparition of the devil that haunts Ivan Karamazov in his crisis of guilt deals in hypotheticals and pretending, specializes in the noncommittal, dreams of taking on a more definite identity. According to Mannheim, liberalism tends to think abstractly, "lives on the potential" as opposed to the actual. Ivan's devil identifies himself as an "x in an indeterminate equation. I am a sort of phantom in life who has lost all beginning and end, and who has even forgotten his own name." Asked whether God exists, the devil replies in the words so favored by Tubby Passmore, "I don't know. There! I've said it now!" A caricature of a liberal, this garrulous phantom is also a mocking double of Ivan, situated in no-man's land, willing to finance Dmitri's escape with guilt money and yet unconvinced of the validity of guilt itself. Dostoevsky's supreme caricature of a liberal soul, though, may be Stepan Trofimovich Verkhovensky of *Devils*, given to delusions all at once noble, pathetic, and mad. At one point likened to a "sentimental court jester," Stepan is another Yorick.

Figures of liberal sensibility are not necessarily figures of the ridiculous, as Dostoevsky's ideological rival Turgenev illustrates. The fathers in *Fathers and Sons*, though subjected to a certain light irony, are men of genuine feeling whose simplicity is all the more welcome to the reader next to the ultra-cynicism of Bazarov. Set on the eve of the emancipation of the serfs,

Fathers and Sons depicts both fathers as liberals, with the elder Kirsanov "doing everything to keep up with the times" and worrying over his own "serf-owning mentality" and the elder Bazarov giving up land to the peasants in return for rent. But about their views on the land question and their political ideals, *Fathers and Sons* has little to say. What makes these men so admirable in the eyes of the reader is not their sympathy with humanity but their deep love of their own sons. And whatever they might say, they love their sons not because the young represent progress but simply because Arkady and Yevgeny are their own flesh and blood.

☞ From a certain perspective there can be little more unprofitable than punishing yourself over and over again for a deed already done. Some might say, however, that guilt is worse than profitless: it is dangerous. Undeniably, guilt introduces an element of risk into human affairs. "Will all great Neptune's ocean wash this blood / Clean from my hand?" Haunted by guilt, Macbeth steeps himself in crime. Claudius, after attempting to cleanse his conscience in prayer, has Hamlet sent to England to be executed. Victor Frankenstein's guilt over bringing his creature into existence drives the creature to compound one murder with another. The mysterious Mihail in *The Brothers Karamazov*, carrying within him a hell of guilt, comes close to killing his confessor. Of the aged Tolstoy a biographer writes,

> He had felt guilty his whole life long: to his wife, because he could not live according to his ideal and give her the life she desired; to the peasants, because they were poor while he had everything he could ask for; to his readers, because he preached virtue while living in vice; to his disciples, because they were sent into exile while he stayed on at Yasnaya Polyana [his estate].

Eventually, when these contradictions could no longer be borne, Tolstoy abandoned his estate, fled, fell ill, and died.

Thinkers in the early modern era were struck with the failure of homilies and threats, including the threat of hell, to restrain passions and stabilize human affairs. In view of the risks of guilt, some today may choose a peaceable existence where citizens harmless to themselves and others enjoy their lives in tranquility, their conscience managed and if need be medicated.

As the therapists say, guilt can cause much hurt. But I do not think anyone set out to invent liberal guilt with the aim of defusing a dangerous force. Liberal guilt represents an unintended consequence of the program of reducing human suffering. The sort of guilt captured satirically by David Lodge has been stripped of everything that associates guilt with "abhorrence and detestation" and makes guilt an implacable force and an agent of suffering. It is the shell that remains after the psychologist, speaking with the authority of enlightenment, assures me that guilt is nothing but a spell cast over the self by social edicts and parental prohibitions. Liberalism does not seek to abolish conscience so much as to place it under the enlightened management of therapists and educators. To be educated in this sense is to have certain feelings raised and others lowered; it is to be told what to feel good about and what to feel bad about, to heed the counsels of psychologists, the appeals of advocates, the urgings of experts; to be liberated from the priest only to enter the therapist's confessional, and from the magistrate only to deliver yourself to the demands of enlightened opinion. Some think liberal guilt, properly administered, is actually good for you. From a poison comes a medicine.

13

Epilogue:
Distinctions and Boundaries

As hearts melt in compassion, so in pop psychology differences of all kinds simply dissolve. Pages in which Samuel Johnson is quoted along with Kahlil Gibran, where "the wisdom of the East" becomes a prescription for success, give the impression of highly wrought artifacts of gold being melted down for some other use. If liberal guilt, as opposed to actual remorse, is vague, formless, and indeterminate, pop psychology has a shapelessness all it own.

In *The Road Less Traveled*, the most widely read work of its kind, we meet Gibran and Seneca, Ann Bradstreet and Buckminster Fuller, Benjamin Franklin and Carl Jung. Space and time melt, differences dissolve, as if things had returned to some primordial state. In the 1960s, Martin Luther King spoke for an oppressed race afflicted with fear and self-doubt. In pop psychology ever since, everyone is portrayed as so afflicted. "We are not second-class citizens," declares Melody Beattie in the name of her readers. King proclaims that the time has come for freedom, Phil McGraw that the time has come for well-being. King confronts the legacy of slavery, pop psychology the influence of self-hate, under which, in the words of Theodore Rubin, "we are reduced to a slavelike status and must obey the commands of an implacable slave master." Consciousness III, wrote Charles Reich, "proposes to abolish . . . involuntary servitude." After suddenly becoming aware that "the world of conventional activities and socially accepted interpretations of reality was shallow and unrewarding," a sociologist cited in *The Aquarian Conspiracy* "attained freedom just as fully and really as a runaway slave might have in the pre–Civil War period."

As slavery loses its definition at the hands of pop psychology, so does much else. In *Compassion and Self-Hate*, the very term "compassion" liquefies, becoming completely shapeless. "Compassion is any and all thoughts, feelings, moods, insights and actions that serve the interest of actual self." Post-traumatic stress disorder, which originally pertained to veterans of war, was soon extended to cover presumed victims of child abuse. Co-dependency, which originally referred to the plight of women married to alcoholics, was quickly broadened to encompass a multitude of ills. Indeed, in some sense PTSD and co-dependency have become the same thing, like two streams forming one.

Addiction, originally linked to alcohol, now extends to gambling, shopping, sex, "anything we feel we have to lie about." Leo Buscaglia looked into himself one day and discovered seventy-three addictions. Some trace co-dependency itself to addiction. By the estimate of one professional, 96 percent of the American population are co-dependents. (Maybe this is the same 96 percent who, according to the divinations of Thomas Harris, have had "I'm not OK" experiences in early childhood.)

In the judgment of another professional, the very attempt to define co-dependency constitutes "a manifestation of the disease process." Number melts, boundaries blur, things run together. M. Scott Peck, who designates addiction "the sacred disease," speculates that science and religion are on the way to becoming the same thing. For many, religion and psychology come to the same thing. In the general convergence, societies become addicted persons (hence *When Society Becomes an Addict*) and families become police states. The claim that the abused suffer their own "private holocaust" exemplifies pop psychology's inflationary rhetoric as well as its denial of differences, as if they represented what the age of Sterne and Jefferson called artificial distinctions.

Why is it that words like "illness" or "neurosis" are rarely found in advice literature? Perhaps because most of the authors, not being medical doctors, are reluctant to use terms associated with medicine or psychiatry. Probably too, the authors wish to avoid giving the impression that the ill constitute a category distinct from everyone else. (Extending the same principle, one theorist-practitioner alleges that most mental-health professionals are themselves untreated co-dependents.) But by the same token, this policy of delicacy opens the possibility that everyone can be considered ill in some way, just as everyone can lay claim to the woe of oppression. By not distinguishing the ill from the well, the authors refrain from stigmatizing the ill even as they open a field for the expansionary tendency of their own rhetoric—the same tendency that extends human rights into a right to be happy. Reading a self-help passage like

> Jean is a human being. As a human being she must be free to engage in encounters in which she may either be accepted or rejected without recriminations of any kind,

one has the sense that liberation rhetoric, which once meant something, has been reduced to vacuity. In the world of pop psychology, one possesses all kinds of rights without content. "You have a right to become the person you were destined to become." "If I'm not yet certain who I am, I will affirm that I have a right to that exciting discovery." "We have a right to be here. We have a right to be ourselves." "We have a right to allow ourselves to feel and learn from our anger." "You have to be willing to claim your right to uniqueness." Such rights, like "the right to enjoy the commonplace," have been liberated from meaning itself.

Works of pop psychology speak the same language and share a set of assumptions that, three or four decades ago when the rhetoric of rights was coming into force, must have seemed uncontroversial enough: for example, that people suffer from guilt and bear the effects of their upbringing into their adult years. Since then, styles and schools of pop psychology have distinguished themselves by the fantastic lengths to which they drive these axiomatic doctrines. That ours is a society of addicts, that a divine child resides within, that we live in a state of inner terror, that the world represents a conspiracy against our true self—conclusions like these seem incontestable to those who put credence in them because they derive from first principles. If in self-help literature all conclusions seem predetermined, it is because in fact they are.

Repeating the themes of his colleagues, one author writes,

> To continue growing, and living with ourselves, we realize we must liberate ourselves. It becomes time to stop allowing ourselves to be so controlled by others and their expectations and be true to ourselves. . . . We discover that who we are has always been good enough. It is who we were intended to be.

Were we intended before we existed? In pop psychology, everything seems to conform to some preexisting doctrine or model—evidence derives from theories, accounts of women who put themselves last echo "Cinderella," authors repeat themselves and one another, Phil McGraw tells the same story of himself that Charles Reich told a generation before (the story of people "wearing themselves out in pursuit of a self that is not their own"), twelve-step recovery programs play off that of Alcoholics Anonymous, and one's very life unfolds in accordance with a program devised by some vague higher power. By accepting the prescriptions of pop psychology, "we become in tune with the Plan for our life and our place in the Universe. And there is a Plan and a Place for us."

Pop psychology aspires to the universal. "I cannot fully describe the respect and reverence I have for every person who has contributed a story, for their willingness to share their inward struggles to live by universal and self-evident principles," says Stephen Covey, referring to the principles he lays down in *The 7 Habits of Highly Effective People*. For his maxims of success he claims the same grandeur as the principles of the Declaration of Independence. The drive for the universal, the tendency to expand, to overflow, to cross lines, to pass from the limited to the unlimited runs deep in a genre of writing that begins with personal problems and ends with vast, blurry spiritual intuitions. That is the course traced by *The Road Less Traveled*, whose first page observes that "Life is a series of problems" and whose last that "It is probable that the universe as we know it is but a single stepping-stone toward the entrance to the Kingdom of God." Charles Reich, celebrant of Consciousness III, concluded that "we must look forward to Consciousness IV, V, VI, and so forth," as if each stage of consciousness were but a stepping-stone to the next. Abraham Maslow predicted that humanistic, or Third Force, psychology would be succeeded by a more cosmic Fourth Psychology. After discovering seven principles of success, Stephen Covey recently discovered an eighth. The expansionary drive of pop psychology's rhetoric—its way of stretching both the language of rights and the definitions of abuse and addiction, for example—reflects a way of thinking that constantly acclaims "growth." It also reflects the expansion of clinical psychology, a field that dates to the Veterans Administration Act of 1946 but soon enough outgrew its original mandate of treating veterans, just as the PTSD population would grow to include potentially anyone.

Clearly, psychology is a growth market; and it was pop psychology that first seized the market's possibilities. The mighty opposites of pre-1960s psychology, psychoanalysis and behaviorism, were neither of them well suited to the marketplace or capable of real popularization. Freudianism was not only encumbered with esoteric machinery and language but conveyed an essentially discouraging message, ill adapted to American soil. (On the other hand, the airbrushed Freudianism of Transactional Analysis—"I'm OK—You're OK"—had great popular success.) Behaviorism might speak to a corps of psychological engineers but not to the wider public, and it was further disqualified in the 1960s by its now-Orwellian implications. Neither addressed people interested in self-help—that is, interested in curing their ills by themselves. Pop psychology does. Employing the language of positive thinking and the accusatory rhetoric of rights, drawing on the tradition of dissent while repudiating tradition, offering utopian promises in the manner of practical counsel ("Soon you have a whole new history"), pop psychology delivers a message appealing enough to have become a commercial force. It would not be so appealing if it did not borrow from, and dissolve the differences between, conflicting sources.

A commercial economy thrives on growth. Even before the full onset of the commercial revolution in eighteenth-century England, the satirical Bernard Mandeville perceived that no fixed line divided wants from needs, and that "if the wants of Men are innumerable, then what ought to supply them has no bounds." Translated into the language of pop psychology:

> The dividing line between a need and a want varies within each person. . . . You are the only one who can judge the relative strength of your needs and wants. If you feel that something you want is important for you, then it *is* important and you have a right to ask for it.

Marketing not material but psychological goods, and elevating those goods to the status of rights, self-help literature ministers to the expansion of what were once called imaginary needs. As the very proliferation of self-help manuals suggests, such needs have no limit. The pursuit of the authentic self, the self uncontaminated by the falsity of the world, is a quest without a grail. With its expansive definitions, exorbitant claims (as of an incest epidemic), and inflated statistics, pop psychology makes for an ironic gloss on the principle that what supplies our wants has no bounds. For every self-help book purporting to be the definitive system and the last word, like Phil McGraw's *Ultimate Weight Solution*, there is sure to be another.

In an essay entitled "Montana; or The End of Jean-Jacques Rousseau," Leslie Fiedler once argued that the American myth of innocence reached its limit in Montana, where reality exposed it as a lie. But in the land of dreams there are no limits, and shortly after Fiedler wrote, the psychological frontier was opened to all claimants—its exploration driven by a myth of innocence and a belief that with the abolition of morality and all that goes with it, people would behave morally at last. Pop psychology, with its fantasy of natural innocence and its figuration of innocence in the infant or the inner child, has not heard of the end of innocence. Fiedler spoke too soon. In the tradition of the human-potential enthusiasts at Esalen in the 1960s, pop psychologists preach living in the moment. Rousseau sought so fervently to live in the moment that he refused to recognize the children who sprang from his moments of love.

> He put his children in a public orphanage, but only because they were unwanted consequences of immediate pleasures savored in all innocence with Thérèse. He chose Thérèse to make her the servant of his immediate needs, telling her that he wished neither to abandon her nor to marry her, in other words that he wished to live with her in an eternal present, a series of moments without past or future. But nature here played a nasty trick on Jean-Jacques. The immediate pleasure of physical love creates a link to the future, a consequence: the child.

Living in the moment is not only not a new idea, it is an idea that has already been tested.

Rousseau became a therapist in his own right.

> He did his best to live up to the expectations of the countless readers who wrote because they had not found happiness in their lives. . . . Rousseau took on the role of master of happiness, healer of souls, and dispenser of useful remedies. To judge from his responses, this therapist's role did not displease him.

That Rousseau himself was a sufferer enhanced his charisma. "A healer who had been touched by an affliction himself was more apt to dispense a useful remedy than one who had never

suffered"—which helps explain the pop psychological convention of the therapist confessing his own troubles. And if pop
psychologists, following Rousseau, pose as masters of happiness, they also revive his fantasy that the world is united against
oneself. "If you feel as if you are being manipulated by forces
outside yourself, then you are a victim," declares Wayne Dyer,
speaking in effect for the entire self-help movement. Rousseau
returns, delusionally convinced that he is at the mercy of sinister forces. Such forces, according to Dyer, are "unquestionably
ubiquitous in our culture," meaning that everyone except the
reader (but including all other readers) belongs to the universal
conspiracy. The reader of *Pulling Your Own Strings* is envisioned as a well-intentioned person encircled by surly clerks,
petty tyrants of every description, "whiners, interrupters, arguers, braggarts, con artists, bores, [and] similar victimizers."
In the midst of this madness stands the purchaser of *Pulling
Your Own Strings*, "a worthy, important human being," like an
island utopia removed from the world, or, like Rousseau, "the
one exception from an otherwise universal malady." In pop
psychology, guilt is baseless—imaginary—but injuries to the patient or reader are always presumed real. In the land of the
morally impossible, one can receive injuries but not give them.

  Promising the moon, pop psychology addresses itself to human credulity. It rose to prominence around the time our public institutions suffered a loss of credibility in consequence of
Vietnam and Watergate, quite as if the polity's loss were its
gain. Portraying the government like everything else in the
world as an oppressive nuisance, *Your Erroneous Zones* appeared within two years of Richard Nixon's resignation. Wayne
Dyer was recently shown on television lecturing at length to a
rapt audience—an audience listening as it would never imagi-
nably listen to any other sort of orator, whether politician or

priest. The skepticism that normally greets rhetoric seems suspended in favor of those like Dyer who insist on addressing even readers directly, as though nothing as artificial as writing must be allowed to come between the audience and themselves.

Being rhetorical, pop psychology deals in commonplaces. When it was discovered that Martin Luther King had largely plagiarized his doctoral dissertation, there were those who said in his defense that in the oral culture of preaching, ideas are borrowed freely and used without attribution. In pop psychology too, ideas are borrowed, which is also to say that all its truths are presupposed. Looking back on *The Road Less Traveled* some years later, the author was impressed by its profundity but admitted, "I wasn't saying anything new. I was repeating things that Carl Jung and William James and others had said long before me." Pop psychology repeats pop psychology. The doctrine that our culture persecutes the self, for example, has been assumed and repeated like an axiom in self-help writings since the 1960s.

Pop psychology idealizes the self and disparages the world in the same measure. Such beatification of the self at the expense of the world reminds me of a comment made in 1985 on the cult of self fostered by "some humanistic and transpersonal psychologists."

> External authority, cultural tradition, and social institutions are all eschewed. The self in all its pristine purity is affirmed. . . . Such romantic individualism is remarkably thin when it comes to any but the vaguest prescriptions about how to live in an actual society.

That you possess unbounded power, that you can do whatever you want provided you are psychologically enlightened, that you should treat yourself at least as well as you treat others—such maxims do not seem designed for an actual world. They are all products of the spirit of antinomianism. A kind of secondary antinomianism is at work in pop psychology too—a belief that its message is of such importance that it transcends all else and excuses even self-contradiction. "You are always a worthy, important human being," Wayne Dyer proclaims, only to state a dozen lines later, "You are worthy not because others say so." The author of the most successful self-help work of our time later wrote, "Each one of us must make his own path through life. There are no self-help manuals." These are but variant illustrations of the besetting contradiction of pop psychology: that readers are constantly warned against dependence on anyone not themselves by someone who is not themselves, and constantly instructed that the way to self-determination is to follow the guidelines, exercises, urgings, and commands of this person.

A comprehensive survey of the Western utopian tradition published in 1979 concludes by pointing out an ironic

discordance between the expansion of revolutionary techniques in [sic] manipulating nature and the persistence of old-fashioned utopian wishes, holdovers from earlier agrarian or primitive nineteenth-century industrial societies. What distresses a critical historian today is the discrepancy between the piling up of technological and scientific instrumentalities for making all things possible, and the pitiable poverty of goals. We witness the multiplication of ways to get to space colonies, to manipulate the genetic bank of species man, and simultaneously the weakness of thought, fantasy, wish, utopia. . . . The social and psychological content of these fantasies . . . is generally threadbare.

I would characterize pop psychology, with its fantasy of re-engineering the self, in like terms. A holdover from the utopian movements of an earlier era (in this case the 1960s), it too is marked by poverty of thought and dullness of vision, by the copying of copies. By now the acceptance of limits and distinctions may be more authentic than the utopian defiance of the finite urged by pop psychology.

Of health benefits I can't speak, but certainly there are other gains to be reaped from the preservation of limits and distinctions, just as there are losses in their destruction. Only if we are willing to proclaim that everything is permitted should we submit to pop psychology's demand to defy any and every restriction on self. Only if we prefer to abolish standards of every kind, including those of competence, craftsmanship, and good practice, should we submit to its doctrine that standards represent an inhuman perfectionism and a crime against self, and that "the best we do is whatever we do." If a jury is to decide whether a sex ring operates as a day care center, it will have to bear in mind the difference between delusion and reality, despite the chapter in McGraw's *Life Strategies* entitled, "There Is No Reality; Only Perception." If I want to see things as they are, I will also have to distinguish between a fellow citizen and a prisoner of war, or a cult member, or a slave. As for the doctrine that everyone around me needs to be liberated, and that liberation means having old habits and attitudes erased and new ones installed—this I will have to abandon as a fantasy unsuited to a society of free persons.

Works of Self-help
Cited in the Text

Altea, Rosemary. *You Own the Power: Stories and Exercises to Inspire and Unleash the Force Within.* New York: HarperCollins, 2000.

Bass, Ellen, and Laura Davis. *The Courage to Heal: A Guide for Women Survivors of Child Sexual Abuse.* New York: Harper & Row, 1988.

Beattie, Melody. *Codependent No More: How to Stop Controlling Others and Start Caring for Yourself.* San Francisco: Harper & Row, 1987.

———. *The Language of Letting Go.* Center City, Minn.: Hazelden, 1990.

Borysenko, Joan, Ph.D. GUILT *Is the Teacher;* LOVE *Is the Lesson.* New York: Warner, 1990.

Buchholz, William M., M.D., and Susie Buchholz, Ph.D. *Live Longer, Live Larger: A Holistic Approach for Cancer Patients and Families.* Sebastopol, Calif.: O'Reilly, 2001.

Buscaglia, Leo, Ph.D. *Living, Loving & Learning.* New York: Fawcett Columbine, 1982.

Covey, Stephen. *Living the 7 Habits: The Courage to Change.* New York: Simon & Schuster, 2000.

Dyer, Wayne. *Pulling Your Own Strings*. New York: Crowell, 1978; reprint Avon, 2001.

———. *Your Erroneous Zones*. New York: Funk & Wagnalls, 1976.

Ferguson, Marilyn. *The Aquarian Conspiracy: Personal and Social Transformation in Our Time*. New York: Penguin Putnam, 1980.

Forward, Susan. *Toxic Parents: Overcoming Their Hurtful Legacy and Reclaiming Your Life*. New York: Bantam, 1989.

Gray, John, Ph.D. *How to Get What You Want and Want What You Have*. New York: HarperCollins, 1999.

Greenwald, Dr. Jerry. *Creative Intimacy: How to Break the Patterns That Poison Your Relationships*. New York: Simon & Schuster, 1975.

Harris, Thomas, M.D. *I'm OK—You're OK: A Practical Guide to Transactional Analysis*. New York: Harper & Row, 1967.

Kasl, Charlotte David, Ph.D. *Many Roads, One Journey: Moving Beyond the 12 Steps*. New York: HarperCollins, 1992.

Lew, Mike. *Victims No Longer: Men Recovering from Incest and Other Sexual Abuse*. New York: Perennial, 1990.

McGraw, Phillip C., Ph.D. *Life Strategies: Doing What Works, Doing What Matters*. New York: Hyperion, 1999.

———. *Self Matters: Creating Your Own Life from the Inside Out*. New York: Free Press, 2001.

McKay, Matthew, Ph.D., and Patrick Fanning. *Self-Esteem*. Oakland: New Harbinger, 1987.

McMahon, Susanna, Ph.D. *The Portable Therapist*. New York: Dell, 1994.

McWilliams, Peter. *You Can't Afford the Luxury of a Negative Thought*. Los Angeles: Prelude Press, 1995.

Miller, Stuart. *Hot Springs: The True Adventures of the First New York Jewish Literary Intellectual in the Human Potential Movement*. New York: Viking, 1971.

Newman, Mildred, and Bernard Berkowitz, with Jean Owen. *How to Be Your Own Best Friend*. New York: Random House, 1971.

Peck, M. Scott, M.D. *Further Along the Road Less Traveled*. New York: Simon & Schuster, 1993.

———. *The Road Less Traveled: A New Psychology of Love, Traditional Values and Spiritual Growth*. New York: Simon & Schuster, 2003; originally published 1978.

Pipher, Mary, Ph.D. *Reviving Ophelia: Saving the Selves of Adolescent Girls*. New York: Grosset/Putnam, 1994.

Potter-Efron, Ronald and Patricia. *Letting Go of Shame: Understanding How Shame Affects Your Life*. Center City, Minn.: Hazelden, 1989.

Reich, Charles. *The Greening of America*. New York: Random House, 1970.

Richardson, Cheryl. *Take Time for Your Life*. New York: Broadway, 1999.

Ringer, Robert J. *Looking Out for #1*. New York: Fawcett Crest, 1977.

Rubin, Theodore, M.D. *Compassion and Self-Hate*. New York: Simon & Schuster, 1998; originally published 1975.

Schaef, Anne Wilson. *Co-Dependence: Misunderstood—Mistreated*. San Francisco: Harper & Row, 1986.

——. *When Society Becomes an Addict*. New York: Harper & Row, 1988.

Schutz, William C. *Joy: Expanding Human Awareness*. New York: Grove, 1967.

Seligman, Martin E. P., Ph.D. *Authentic Happiness: Using the New Positive Psychology to Realize Your Potential for Lasting Fulfillment*. London: Nicholas Brealey, 2003.

Sheehy, Gail. *Passages: Predictable Crises of Adult Life*. New York: Bantam, 1977.

Sills, Judith, Ph.D. *Excess Baggage: Getting Out of Your Own Way*. Harmondsworth, England: Penguin, 1994.

Simon, Sidney B., and Sally Wendkos Olds, *Helping Your Child Learn Right from Wrong: A Guide to Values Clarification*. New York: Simon & Schuster, 1976.

Steinem, Gloria. *Revolution from Within: A Book of Self-Esteem*. Boston: Little, Brown, 1992.

Taubman, Stan, D.S.W. *Ending the Struggle Against Yourself: A Workbook for Developing Deep Confidence and Self-Acceptance*. New York: Penguin Putnam, 1994.

Notes

1. The Golden Path to Self-realizaton

p. 3, "equivalent of salvation, 'mental health'": Christopher Lasch, *The Culture of Narcissism: American Life in an Age of Diminishing Expectations* (New York: Warner, 1979), p. 42. Another robust critique of psychology's influence is Martin L. Gross, *The Psychological Society: A Critical Analysis of Psychiatry, Psychotherapy, Psychoanalysis and the Psychological Revolution* (New York: Random House, 1978).

p. 3, "how wondrous and interesting you can be": Taubman, *Ending the Struggle*, p. 139.

p. 4, honorable exceptions: Seligman, for one, does not go along with the vilification of morality in self-help literature.

p. 4, the absurd but academically fashionable doctrine that the laws of physics are socially constructed. See Alan Sokol and Jean Bricmont, *Fashionable Nonsense: Postmodern Intellectuals and the Abuse of Science* (New York: Picador, 1998).

p. 4, the sexual abuse of children. See Frederick Crews, *The Memory Wars: Freud's Legacy in Dispute* (New York: New York Review Book, 1995).

p. 4, "one can hardly imagine a time without it": Gertrude Himmelfarb, *The De-moralization of Society: From Victorian Virtues to Modern Values* (New York: Vintage, 1994), p. 12.

p. 5, "the same way that you fall in love with another": McMahon, *Portable Therapist*, p. 75.

231

p. 5, "Soon you have a whole new history": McGraw, *Self Matters,* p. 251.

p. 5, "I know how it all happened": McGraw, *Life Strategies,* p. 292.

p. 6, "the hands of trained experts": Charlotte Perkins Gilman, *Women and Economics* (New York: Harper & Row, 1966; orig. pub. 1898), p. 237.

p. 6, "to unskilled hands": Charlotte Perkins Gilman, *Herland* (New York: Pantheon, 1979), p. 83.

p. 6, on a desert island: Abraham Maslow, "Eupsychia—The Good Society," *Journal of Humanistic Psychology,* Fall 1961, p. 10.

p. 6, "external validation": Steven Starker, *Oracle at the Supermarket: The American Preoccupation with Self-Help Books* (New Brunswick, N.J.: Transaction, 1989), p. 160. This book renders a cautiously mixed verdict on pop psychology.

p. 7, "the secrets being sought": Starker, *Oracle,* p. 171.

p. 7, "you cease to be so": John Stuart Mill, *Autobiography* (Indianapolis: Library of Liberal Arts, 1957), p. 92.

p. 8, generic stories of psychological success. On Dickens and Smiles, see Jerome Meckier, *Dickens's* Great Expectations: *Misnar's Pavilion versus Cinderella* (Lexington: University of Kentucky Press, 2002).

p. 8, "assembled into widely-read anthologies": M. H. Abrams, *Natural Supernaturalism: Tradition and Revolution in Romantic Literature* (New York: Norton, 1971), p. 145.

p. 10, "this nature that he is afraid of expressing": Maslow, "Eupsychia," p. 8.

p. 10, "to disavow the very idea of the past": Leslie Fiedler, *A New Fiedler Reader* (Amherst, N.Y.: Prometheus, 1999), p. 193.

p. 10, "irrelevant history": McGraw, *Self Matters,* p. 252.

p. 10, "displacing Dick-Jane-Spot-Baby": Fiedler, *Fiedler Reader,* p. 204.

p. 11, "achievements, rewards, excellence": Reich, *Greening,* p. 85.

p. 11, "a self that is not their own": Reich, *Greening,* p. 278.

p. 11, "madness is health": Lionel Trilling, *Sincerity and Authenticity* (Cambridge, Mass.: Harvard University Press, 1971), p. 171.

p. 12, the new idiom of revolt: R. D. Rosen, *Psychobabble* (New York: Avon, 1975), p. 19.

p. 12, "Ethan looks as if he is beginning to feel frightened and guilty": Schutz, *Joy,* p. 12.

p. 12, "as the therapists and counselors of the next generation would do": Paul Jacobs and Saul Landau, eds., *The New Radicals: A Report with Documents* (New York: Vintage, 1966), p. 154.

p. 12, "a meaning in life that is personally authentic": Jacobs and Landau, *New Radicals,* p. 154.

p. 13, "your parents and your educators": cited in Buscaglia, *Living,* p. 98.

p. 13, "the whole of society": McGraw, *Self Matters*, p. 61. A sort of converse of this proposition is posed by *The Aquarian Conspiracy*, arguing as it does that the psychologically advanced constitute a conspiracy of the most beneficial kind.

p. 13, "the right to be who you are and how you are": McGraw, *Life Strategies*, p. 269.

p. 13, "the exhaustion of Utopias": Jacobs and Landau, *New Radicals*, p. 151.

p. 13, "before we can bring any decency into the world": Karl Popper, *The Open Society and Its Enemies*, Vol. I: *The Spell of Plato* (London: Routledge & Kegan Paul, 1952), p. 157.

p. 14, "putting . . . parents on trial": Peck, *Further Along*, p. 42.

p. 14, "how you took over and managed for yourself as best you could": Lionel Trilling, *The Last Decade: Essays and Reviews, 1965–75* (New York: Harcourt Brace Jovanovich, 1979), p. 175.

p. 14, "adopted out of history or tradition": McGraw, *Life Strategies*, p. 142.

p. 15, "the English language is rotten for good people": Abraham Maslow, *The Farther Reaches of Human Nature* (Harmondsworth, England: Penguin, 1976), p. 48n.

p. 15, "the best we do . . . is whatever we do": Rubin, *Compassion*, p. 190. Cf. McKay and Fanning, p. 134: "I invariably do the best I am capable of at the moment."

p. 15, "feels like a fight"; "competitive aggressivity": Trilling, *The Last Decade*, pp. 158, 156.

p. 16, "self-acceptance, love, and nurturing": Beattie, *Letting Go*, p. 158.

p. 16, "sum and substance of who you are": McGraw, *Self Matters*, p. 29.

p. 17, "the worst of your sins": Wendy Kaminer, *I'm Dysfunctional, You're Dysfunctional: The Recovery Movement and Other Self-Help Fashions* (New York: Vintage, 1993), p. 20.

p. 17, "The Healthiness of Depression": Peck, *Road*, pp. 69–72.

p. 18, "castigation for even a moment": Rubin, pp. 57–58.

p. 18, cured by action: Dyer, *Strings*, p. 242.

p. 18, dishonest, friendless, and insane: Maslow, *Farther Reaches*, ch. 16.

p. 18, "violation of any of its dictates and standards are revealed": Rubin, *Compassion*, p. 42.

p. 18, a Nazi guard: Rubin, *Compassion*, p. 139.

p. 18, "a cowardly, death-denying culture": Peck, *Further Along*, p. 52.

p. 18, "an addictive society": Schaef, *Co-Dependence*, p. 36.

p. 19, "sexism, capitalism, and lookism": Pipher, *Reviving Ophelia*, p. 23.

p. 19, "still mostly the product of the old ways": Richard Fairfield, ed., *Utopia U.S.A.* (San Francisco: Alternatives Foundation, 1972), p. 231.

p. 20, "Tomorrow I will like myself even more": McKay and Fanning, *Self-Esteem*, p. 133.

p. 20, Scott Peck's justification of exorcism in *People of the Lie*: M. Scott Peck, *People of the Lie* (New York: Simon & Schuster, 1983).

p. 20, "the most rapidly spreading social invention of the century, and probably the most potent": cited in Gross, *The Psychological Society*, p. 302.

p. 20, "simply 'Do'": Dyer, *Zones*, p. 127. The theme is standard.

2. Pop Psychology as a Utopian Enterprise

p. 21, "without blanching or passing moral judgment": Rochelle Gurstein, *The Repeal of Reticence* (New York: Hill & Wang, 1996), p. 131.

p. 22, from Lucky Strikes to racial equality. See Stewart Justman, *The Psychological Mystique* (Evanston: Northwestern University Press, 1998).

p. 22, has the status of a first principle in the pop psychology that fills sections of bookstores. Seligman's *Authentic Happiness*, informed by the doctrines of "Positive Psychology," stands out in *not* using words like "morality" as terms of reproach.

p. 22, "polluting flood of psychobabble": McGraw, *Life Strategies*, p. 23.

p. 22, "turn my head in shame": McGraw, *Life Strategies*, p. 294.

p. 23, "your own gifts, abilities, and dreams": McGraw, *Self Matters*, p. 302.

p. 23, "putting yourself in inferior positions": Dyer, *Strings*, p. 21.

p. 23, "no one else, just you": McGraw, *Self Matters*, p. 10.

p. 24, "a smorgasbord course in New Consciousness": cited in Lasch, *Narcissism*, p. 44.

p. 24, "incalculable harm": cited in Starker, *Oracle*, p. 55.

p. 25, "a very large erroneous zone": Dyer, *Zones*, p. 138.

p. 26, wiping the slate clean: McGraw, *Life Strategies*, p. 298.

p. 26, began to appear in our language: Peggy Rosenthal, *Words and Values: Some Leading Words and Where They Lead Us* (New York: Oxford, 1984), p. 11. See also the Arden edition of *Othello*, ed. E. A. J. Honigmann (Walton-on-Thames: Thomas Nelson, 1997), 2.3.198n and 3.3.203n.

p. 27, "armed with canes!": Michel de Montaigne, *The Essays: A Selection*, tr. M. A. Screech (Harmondsworth, England: Penguin, 1993), pp. 59–60.

p. 27, "through gentleness and freedom": Montaigne, *Essays*, pp. 69–70.

p. 27, "as if they were wilfully guilty": John Locke, *Some Thoughts Concerning Education* (Oxford: Clarendon, 1989), pp. 121–122.

p. 28, "restraining the destructive passions of men": Albert O. Hirschman, *The Passions and the Interests* (Princeton: Princeton University Press, 1977), pp. 14–15.

p. 29, "bring happiness to others": Ringer, *Looking Out*, p. 22.

p. 29, Eupsychia: Maslow, "Eupsychia," pp. 1–11.

p. 29, a small, closed community of noble souls: see Jean Starobinski, *Blessings in Disguise; or, The Morality of Evil*, tr. Arthur Goldhammer (Cambridge, Mass.: Harvard University Press, 1993), p. 120.

p. 30, "It offers us a recovery of self": Reich, *Greening*, p. 5.

p. 30, without citing the authority of Marx and Marcuse as Reich does: Reich, *Greening*, p. 81.

p. 30, "I'm glad I'm me": Reich, *Greening*, p. 219.

p. 31, "a state of unhealthy guilt": Borysenko, *GUILT*, p. 1.

p. 32, "even in our adult lives" : Taubman, *Ending the Struggle*, p. 15.

p. 32, "all nervously precautionary states of mind": William James, cited in Starker, *Oracle*, p. 23.

p. 32, "to promote a respect for 'respectability'": R. D. Laing, *The Politics of Experience* (New York: Pantheon, 1967), p. 41.

p. 33, "One must live completely at each moment": Reich, *Greening*, p. 225.

p. 33, "The present is all, and it is all-satisfying": Trilling, *The Last Decade*, p. 153.

p. 33, "to narrate everything about Utopia in the present tense": Robert M. Adams in Sir Thomas More, *Utopia*, tr. Adams (New York: Norton, 1975), p. 195.

p. 33, new drugs as they come onto the scene. Some, like Robin Norwood, author of the influential *Women Who Love Too Much*, follow trends that leave psychology itself behind. Turning her back on "all these people who thought I could fix their lives," she moved on to etheric bodies and soul evolution. *Macleans*, June 20, 1994, p. 28.

p. 34, "precisely how to restore them to your life": McGraw, *Self Matters*, p. 21.

p. 34, "I know a lot about what may be going on in your life": McGraw, *Self Matters*, p. 15.

p. 35, "when will there be a better time?": McGraw, *Self Matters*, p. 25.

p. 36, "we are extremely sensitive, vulnerable and impressionable": Rubin, *Compassion*, p. 135.

p. 36, "that serve the interest of actual self": Rubin, *Compassion*, p. 133.

p. 37, "to honor ourselves in spite of our fear or discomfort": Richardson, *Take Time*, p. 25.

p. 37, "putting [their] needs before others": Richardson, *Take Time*, pp. 6, 24.

p. 37, "selfish is a terrible concept": McMahon, *Portable Therapist*, p. 52.

p. 37, "sensitive," "patient," and "tolerant": Altea, *Power*, p. 103.

p. 38, "how things are progressing and what we need to change": Mc-Mahon, *Portable Therapist*, p. 25.

p. 38, "to face whatever life has in store for us": Rubin, *Compassion*, p. 218.

p. 38, "enjoying life's realistic good offerings": Rubin, *Compassion*, p. 75.

p. 38, "take responsibility for your emotions": McKay and Fanning, *Self-Esteem*, p. 167.

p. 38, "seeds of fear, obligation, or guilt": Forward, *Toxic Parents*, p. 5.

p. 39, is cited in pop psychology. For example, Borysenko, *GUILT*, p. 167.

p. 39, Alexander Pope and Edmund Spenser: See Altea, *Power*.

p. 39, "not marred or corrupted by technical discourse or scientific codes": Iris Murdoch, *Metaphysics as Guide to Morals* (Harmondsworth, England: Penguin, 1993), p. 164.

p. 40, "being all there, fully present": Taubman, *Ending the Struggle*, pp. xii, 3, 23.

p. 40, "Practice being spontaneous": Beattie, *Letting Go*, p. 164.

p. 40, "a world in which space, time, or number in the normal sense no longer exist": Isaiah Berlin, *Four Essays on Liberty* (Oxford: Oxford University Press, 1970), p. 70.

p. 41, only because of "the tyranny of shoulds" that people are "willing to die in wars": McKay and Fanning, *Self-Esteem*, p. 103.

p. 41, the Securities and Exchange Commission is "gestapo-like": Ringer, *Looking Out*, p. 242.

p. 41, "tyrannical concentration-camp form of living": Rubin, *Compassion*, pp. 35, 83.

p. 41, "building up a great race": Gilman, *Herland*, pp. 54, 95.

p. 41, a fine line if that. In Herland, medical or therapeutic categories have supplanted moral ones to this extent: such criminals as exist are treated, not punished. The pretense of treating offenders medically recalls the use of political psychiatry in the former Soviet Union.

p. 41, "With total discipline we can solve all problems": Peck, *Road*, p. 16.

p. 42, a mother bear who one day simply deserts her young forever: Dyer, *Zones*, pp. 189, 191.

p. 42, "how everyone else feels about their choices": Dyer, *Strings*, p. 4.

p. 43, "These *things* and *people* are not *me*!": Rubin, *Compassion*, p. 170.

p. 43, "we wash our hands of you": Hannah Arendt, *Between Past and Future* (Harmondsworth, England: Penguin, 1978), pp. 190–191.

p. 43, "how eagerly they sought to be instructed in Greek": More, *Utopia*, p. 62.

p. 44, "assumptions that underlie our present political State": Reich, *Greening*, p. 381.

p. 44, "an outlandish ability to delight in that reality": Dyer, *Zones*, p. 223.

p. 45, Rousseau was a "spiritual guide": Lynn Hunt, *Politics, Culture, and Class in the French Revolution* (Berkeley: University of California Press, 1984), p. 2.

p. 46, supervises his very thoughts. The tutor of Emile is given the name of Jean-Jacques; Fénelon served as tutor to the grandson of Louis XIV.

p. 46, "half-baked Rousseauism": Northrop Frye, *The Well-Tempered Critic* (Bloomington: Indiana University Press, 1963), p. 42.

p. 46, "of inner love, joy, peace, and confidence": Gray, *Get What You Want*, p. 50.

p. 46, "a nice girl or a nice boy": Robert Bly as cited in Borysenko, GUILT, p. 65.

p. 46, "prisoners of the urge to do what we 'should' do": Borysenko, GUILT, p. 1.

p. 46, "distort his naturalness": Greenwald, *Intimacy*, p. 36.

p. 47, cannot recover such innocence: Jean Starobinski, *Jean-Jacques Rousseau: Transparency and Obstruction*, tr. Arthur Goldhammer (Chicago: University of Chicago Press, 1988), p. 296.

p. 47, "the unsuspecting accomplice of their plot": Rousseau, *Confessions*, tr. J. M. Cohen (Harmondsworth, England: Penguin, 1953), p. 544.

p. 48, "unquestionably ubiquitous in our culture": Dyer, *Strings*, p. 2.

p. 48, "wipe the slate clean and start over in your thinking": McGraw, *Life Strategies*, p. 298.

p. 49, "some beginning strategies for wiping your guilt slate clean": Dyer, *Zones*, p. 102.

p. 49, proceed with "a clean slate": Ringer, *Looking Out*, p. 7.

p. 49, "See those labels on the blackboard and now see an eraser in your hand": McKay and Fanning, *Self-Esteem*, p. 203.

p. 49, "we are responsible for our own good time": Newman and Berkowitz, *Best Friend*, p. 7.

p. 49, "your authentic self, rather than your fictional self": McGraw, *Self Matters*, p. 63.

p. 50, "the greatest gift you can give to someone else": Richardson, *Take Time*, p. 26.

p. 50, "by being one's true self one offers others the most": Reich, *Greening*, p. 228.

p. 50, "from reconnecting with what I call your *authentic self*": McGraw, *Self Matters*, p. 9.

p. 50, "a powerful effect of authenticity and sincerity, of truth-telling": David Lodge, *The Art of Fiction* (London: Penguin, 1992), p. 18.

p. 51, the first prophet of Consciousness III: Reich, *Greening*, p. 392.

p. 51, "all the philosophies professed by the officially sanctioned sages were revealed as hollow": Michael André Bernstein, *Bitter Carnival: Ressentiment and the Abject Hero* (Princeton: Princeton University Press, 1992), p. 30.

p. 51, "have achieved far too inflated a status in our culture": Dyer, *Strings*, p. 21.

p. 52, "our vitality is low": Borysenko, GUILT, p. 86.

p. 52, "people who are victimized get blamed": Kasl, *Many Roads*, p. 312.

p. 52, "there are no accidents": McGraw, *Self Matters*, p. 58.

p. 52, "one of these young women bore a child": Gilman, *Herland*, p. 56.

p. 53, "Let us rejoice that we have got back to our childhood again": William Morris, *News from Nowhere* (London: Routledge & Kegan Paul, 1970), p. 87. Originally published in 1890.

p. 53, have tended toward authoritarianism. John Ruskin thought of setting up, in response to the ugliness and moral anarchy of the modern world, a "St. George's Guild." Of this ideal society he once said: "We will have no liberty upon it." John D. Rosenberg, ed., *The Genius of John Ruskin* (Boston: Houghton Mifflin, 1963), p. 373.

p. 53, "private world of Platonic essences": Maslow, *Farther Reaches*, p. xxi.

p. 54, "dystopian individuals who slip by the selection techniques": Maslow, *Farther Reaches*, p. 206.

p. 54, "Surrendering to a Power greater than ourselves is how we become empowered": Beattie, *Letting Go*, p. 66.

p. 54, "permanent, natural laws, like gravity": Covey, *7 Habits*, p. xviii.

p. 54, "You don't get a vote": McGraw, *Life Strategies*, p. 32.

p. 54, "you are likely to suffer severe penalties": McGraw, *Life Strategies*, p. 265.

p. 55, "When you come to the end of this sentence, put down this book": Taubman, *Ending the Struggle*, p. 138.

p. 55, "in fact I **insist** on it": Seligman, *Happiness*, p. 103. Bold in the original.

p. 55, "adopted out of history or tradition": McGraw, *Life Strategies*, p. 42.

p. 55, "an impossible cultural value system of which both we and our parents are victims": Rubin, *Compassion*, p. 30.

p. 55, "an implacable slave master": Rubin, *Compassion*, p. 83.

p. 56, "the three red flags": Simon Leys, *Chinese Shadows* (Harmondsworth, England: Penguin, 1978), p. 169.

p. 56, "dysfunctional culture": Pipher, *Reviving Ophelia*, pp. 12–13, 252.

p. 56, "The revolution must be cultural": Reich, *Greening*, p. 306.

p. 56, "the same ideological stew": Leys, *Chinese Shadows*, p. 167.

3. Blame

p. 59, "YOU ARE ACCEPTED, unconditionally": Harris, *I'm OK*, p. 227.

p. 59, "turn[ing] off the past": Harris, *I'm OK*, p. 243.

p. 59, "self-hating, overwhelming, castigating consciences": Rubin, *Compassion*, p. 128.

p. 60, "self-pity, confusion, and guilt": Gray, *Get What You Want*, p. 4.

p. 60, "All the great teachings and religions have led mankind to this point": Gray, *Get What You Want*, p. 11.

p. 60, "God wants you to have it all": *Get What You Want*, p. 92.

p. 60, "had to move through many blocks . . . you get what you want": Gray, *Get What You Want*, pp. 6, 43, 194, 172.

p. 61, "No matter who you might want to blame": McGraw, *Self Matters*, pp. 63-64.

p. 61, "There's a huge difference between blame and responsibility": McGraw, *Self Matters*, p. 64.

p. 61, "recognize that it is a new day?": McGraw, *Self Matters*, p. 298.

p. 62, "sometimes I forget what a wonderful person I am": Gray, *Get What You Want*, p. 190.

p. 63, "becomes an absurd activity": Berlin, *Four Essays*, p. 64.

p. 63, "lack of imagination": Berlin, *Four Essays*, p. 66.

p. 63, "justly, with detachment, on the evidence": Berlin, *Four Essays*, p. 67.

p. 64, "space, time, or number in the normal sense no longer exist": Berlin, *Four Essays*, p. 70.

p. 64, "it does not follow that it is never just": Berlin, *Four* Essays, p. 96.

p. 64, "without criticism, blame, guilt, or judgment": Taubman, *Ending the Struggle*, p. 139.

p. 64, "concepts like 'should' and 'must'": McGraw, *Self Matters*, p. 233.

p. 64, a concentration camp in our own minds: Rubin, *Compassion*, throughout.

p. 65, "our normal, scarcely noticed moral . . . attitudes": Berlin, *Four Essays*, p. 90.

p. 65, "a totalitarian slave master": Rubin, *Compassion*, p. 128.

p. 66, setting up a police-state in Jill's mind: Rubin, *Compassion*, pp. 26-27.

p. 66, "the demands and expectations of others": Taubman, *Ending the Struggle*, p. 7.

p. 66, "the evil is merely a pretext for the criticism": *Max Scheler on Feeling, Knowing, and Valuing* (Chicago: University of Chicago Press, 1992), p. 121.

p. 67, ends with "Reproach": Helen Vendler, *Poems, Poets, Poetry: An Introduction and Anthology* (Boston: Bedford/St. Martin's, 2002), pp. 114–115.

p. 67, a thought-experiment actually suggested by a therapist: McGraw, *Self Matters*, p. 28.

4. Guilt

p. 68, Woody Allen, *Without Feathers* (New York: Warner, 1976), p. 8.

p. 68, Norman Vincent Peale, *The Power of Positive Thinking* (New York: Fawcett, 1952), p. 124.

p. 68, "insuring the continuation of the self-hating process": Rubin, *Compassion*, p. 49.

p. 69, "exterminated, spray-cleaned and sterilized forever": Dyer, *Zones*, p. 90.

p. 69, "a state of mind you needn't endure": Ringer, *Looking Out*, p. 98.

p. 69, "don't feel guilty about looking out for Number One": Ringer, *Looking Out*, p. 101.

p. 69, "shoveling guilt by the trainload": Forward, *Toxic Parents*, p. 176.

p. 69, "taking healthy care of ourselves": Beattie, *Letting Go*, p. 12.

p. 69, "any behavior that keeps us from loving ourselves and others": Kasl, *Many Roads*, p. 345.

p. 70, "perpetuates the continuation of the 'bad' behavior": McMahon, *Portable Therapist*, pp. 25–26.

p. 70, "you'll never have to feel guilty again": McWilliams, *Negative Thought*, pp. 385–386.

p. 70, "we will continue to punish ourselves": Gray, *Get What You Want*, p. 122.

p. 70, "keeps you from feeling a healthy sense of worthiness and entitlement": Gray, *Get What You Want*, p. 259.

p. 71, "guilt is paralysis": McGraw, *Life Strategies*, p. 198.

p. 71, "There's nothing wrong with who you are": McGraw, *Life Strategies*, p. 272.

p. 71, "It is the fictional self that is grounded in guilt": McGraw, *Self Matters*, p. 177.

p. 71, "carrying the guilt of his brother's death": McGraw, *Self Matters*, pp. 272–273.

p. 71, "'I have to stop judging myself'": McGraw, *Self Matters*, pp. 263, 278.

p. 72, our own doing: see, e.g., Borysenko, *GUILT*, pp. 150–153.

p. 72, "not one tiny slice of that guilt will do anything to rectify past behavior": Dyer, *Zones*, p. 93.

p. 73, "a guilty state of mind will do nothing whatsoever to help the situation": Ringer, *Looking Out*, p. 99.

p. 73, "Then its purpose is finished": Beattie, *Letting Go*, p. 38.

p. 73, "We should tell her she is truly good, truly existent": Miller, *Hot Springs*, pp. 146–147.

p. 74, "you're supposed to feel guilty about it": Dyer, *Zones*, p. 93.

p. 74, "the qualifying act of moral adulthood": Leslie Fiedler, "Hiss, Chambers, and the Age of Innocence," in *An End to Innocence* (Boston: Beacon, 1955), p. 4.

p. 74, "when the Puritan heritage was *still* vitally felt in the respectable middle class": John Updike, *New York Review of Books*, November 18, 2004, p. 31; my emphasis. The Preface to *Is Sex Necessary?* cites the "sociologists, analysts, gynecologists, psychologists, and authors" who bring to the subject of sex "a good deal of scientific knowledge and an immense zeal. They joined forces and made the whole matter of sex complicated beyond the wildest dreams of our fathers." James Thurber and E. B. White, *Is Sex Necessary? or Why You Feel the Way You Do* (Garden City, N.Y.: Blue Ribbon Books, 1944; orig. pub. 1929), pp. xi–xii.

p. 75, "all guilt is harmful, unnecessary, and should be eradicated": "Plain Talk About Feelings of Guilt," DHEW Publication No. (ADM) 78-580, November 1977.

p. 75, "what are called people of fashion": Adam Smith, *The Wealth of Nations* (New York: Modern Library, 1937), p. 746.

p. 76, "a sixfold increase from 1960": Himmelfarb, *De-moralization of Society*, p. 223.

p. 76, "drinking himself into oblivion": McGraw, *Self Matters*, p. 264.

p. 77, "your innate ability to love yourself and forgive your mistakes": Gray, *Get What You Want*, p. 259.

p. 78, "and I've really acted different toward them": Wayne Booth, *The Company We Keep: An Ethics of Fiction* (Berkeley: University of California Press, 1988), p. 278.

p. 79, "servants and coolies I had hit with my fist in moments of rage": George Orwell, *The Road to Wigan Pier* (New York: Harcourt Brace Jovanovich, 1958), pp. 147–148.

p. 80, "a choice, something that you exercise control over": Dyer, *Zones*, p. 102.

p. 81, "you choose the physiology": McGraw, *Self Matters*, p. 68.

5. Obligation

p. 83, "like rhetoric itself": Erasmus, *The Praise of Folly*, tr. Robert M. Adams (New York: Norton, 1980), p. 34.

p. 83, "who will remind them of their greatness:" Richardson, *Take Time*, p. 2; cf. Altea, *Power*, p. 170.

p. 83, "you are worth it": McGraw, *Self Matters*, p. 25.

p. 83, "worthy of being known and accepted": Taubman, *Ending the Struggle*, p. 151.

p. 84, "most neglected responsibility: taking care of yourself": Beattie, *Codependent No More*, p. 6.

p. 84, "put your self-care above anything else": Richardson, *Take Time*, p. 6.

p. 84, "the bottom of the priority list": McGraw, *Self Matters*, p. 21.

p. 85, "You must decide which elements of your self-concept you value": McGraw, *Self Matters*, p. 253.

p. 85, "the stewardship of our own potential": Ferguson, *Conspiracy*, p. 391.

p. 85, give birth to themselves: Rubin, *Compassion*, p. 65.

p. 85, a book may be dedicated to its own author: Beattie, *Codependent No More*.

p. 85, "self-affirmation," "self-awareness," and "self-actualization": Taubman, *Ending the Struggle*, pp. 4–5.

p. 85, "then a pet will work as well": Gray, *Get What You Want*, p. 59.

p. 86, "a way to express your nurturing instincts": Gray, *Get What You Want*, p. 60.

p. 86, "a gift to yourself": McGraw, *Life Strategies*, pp. 205, 210.

p. 86, "or the following Monday night at 6:00": Taubman, *Ending the Struggle*, p. xxviii.

p. 87, "neither enforced by law nor by opinion": John Stuart Mill, *On Liberty* (New York: Norton, 1975), p. 95.

p. 88, "long train of abuses, prevarications, and artifices, all tending the same way": John Locke, *The Second Treatise of Government* (Indianapolis: Library of Liberal Arts, 1952), p. 126.

p. 88, "a place alongside the most valued documents of our founding fathers": Roger Shattuck, "De Gaulle and the Intellectuals," *Salmagundi*, Fall 1993, p. 18.

p. 88, "a person who believes he or she has a claim to be above the law": Shattuck, "De Gaulle," p. 24.

p. 88, "the real, true, genuine sum and substance of who you are": McGraw, *Self Matters*, p. 29. Robert McNamara, secretary of defense during the early years of the Vietnam War and the war's architect, has said that his heart was really with a man who burned himself to death in protest out-side the Pentagon.

p. 89, "rejects many of the laws, forms of authority, and assumptions that un-derlie our present political State": Reich, *Greening*, p. 381.

p. 89, "peership with God": Peck, *Road*, pp. 303–304, 305.

p. 89, administering high levels of (fictitious) electric shocks to a confederate: I discuss this experiment in *The Psychological Mystique*.

p. 90, post-traumatic stress disorder was made over to the presumed victims of sexual abuse: Frederick Crews, "The Trauma Trap," *New York Review of Books*, March 11, 2004.

p. 90, "sad, angry, hurt, vulnerable, betrayed, or frightened": Borysenko, GUILT, p. 77.

p. 91, "the most important person in the world, to whom you should be unswervingly loyal, is yourself": Dyer, *Strings*, pp. 167–168.

p. 91, "*you must prevail*": McGraw, *Self Matters*, p. 302. Italics in the original.

p. 91, "they block the joy of human *being*": Borysenko, GUILT, p. 40.

p. 91, "embarrassed or ashamed? confused? guilty?": Taubman, *Ending the Struggle*, pp. 62–63.

p. 93, "the family comes together and looks at each other's signs": Simon and Olds, *Helping Your Child*, pp. 119, 111.

p. 93, "a Tory or a dictator": Dyer, *Strings*, p. 158.

p. 93, "take precedence over all other human activities": Rubin, *Compassion*, p. 133.

p. 97, "*I will break free of the hold others, and their expectations, have on me*": Beattie, *Letting Go*, p. 324. Italics in original. Polonius's aphorism is also cited (erroneously) in Seligman, *Happiness*, p. 147.

p. 98, "its end is followed by the responsive utterances of others": M. M. Bakhtin, *Speech Genres and Other Late Essays* (Austin: University of Texas Press, 1986), p. 71.

p. 98, falling in love with myself : McMahon, *Portable Therapist*, p. 75.

p. 98, "The universal consciousness, or lifeforce, is present within each hu-man being as the Self": Borysenko, GUILT, p. 66.

p. 99, "Obsession shrinks reality to a single pattern": Iris Murdoch, *Existential-ists and Mystics* (Harmondsworth, England: Penguin, 1999), pp. 271, 455.

6. Patience

p. 100, the word "virtue" has itself dwindled to an archaism. Cf. Lionel Trilling's Introduction to Orwell's *Homage to Catalonia* (New York: Har-court Brace Jovanovich, 1952).

p. 101, patience, the endurance of injuries over time—that has got you, the reader, to the state you are in. Many a self-help book reads like something composed in haste. The very successful *Your Erroneous Zones* (1976), a work still echoing, is said to have been written in thirteen days. Rosen, *Psychobabble*, p. 41.

p. 101, "Applying one or two insights . . . can be put into practice immediately": Gray, *Get What You Want*, pp. 2, 81, 307.

p. 102, "you'll never have to feel guilty again": McWilliams, *Negative Thought*, p. 386.

p. 103, "There comes a time when the cup of endurance runs over": Martin Luther King, Jr., *Why We Can't Wait* (New York: Harper & Row, 1964). I forgo page references for the "Letter from Birmingham Jail."

p. 103, "She had decided it was time to be there for herself": McGraw, *Self Matters*, p. 287.

p. 103, "I cannot be owned by anyone else": Dyer, *Strings*, p. 5.

p. 103, sexism, poverty, and addiction in all its forms: Kasl, *Many Roads*, pp. xiv–xv.

p. 103, "outgrowths of an addictive society": Schaef, *Co-Dependence*, p. 36.

p. 104, "reign of terror": Rubin, *Compassion*, p. 54.

p. 104, "either internal or external in origin": Rubin, *Compassion*, p. 139. Emphasis in original.

p. 104, "our habits, customs, the expectations of others, rules, schedules, the state": Ferguson, *Conspiracy*, p. 193.

p. 104, "controlling because she has *no* self and is so dependent upon others": Schaef, *Co-dependence*, p. 35. My emphasis.

p. 105, "the key reality of twentieth-century existence": Reich, *Greening*, p. 354.

p. 105, "domination," "slaves," "being owned," "slavery": Dyer, *Strings*, p. 168.

p. 105, "when will there be a better time?": McGraw, *Self Matters*, p. 25.

p. 105, "The time is ripe . . . *Start now*": McGraw, *Life Strategies*, pp. 165, 175.

p. 106, "in favor of those you truly and actively choose": McGraw, *Self Matters*, p. 253.

p. 107, "you have a responsibility to do it": McGraw, *Self Matters*, p. 21.

p. 107, "you must prevail": McGraw, *Self Matters*, p. 302.

p. 107, "'It is my time, it is my turn; this is for me, and I claim it, here and now'": McGraw, *Life Strategies*, p. 225.

p. 108, "We find patience by surrendering to our feelings": Beattie, *Letting Go*, p. 95.

p. 108, if the disavowal of "the very idea of the past" had not been the talk of the sixties: Fiedler, *Fiedler Reader*, p. 193.

p. 109, "just like a prisoner of war or a cult member": McGraw, *Self Matters*, p. 187.

p. 109, "And I'm gonna take my sweet time about it, too!": Bass and Davis, *Courage*, p. 455.

p. 110, "you no-good, rat-bastard son of a bitch": McGraw, *Self Matters*, p. 281.

p. 110, becomes "Now-time": Michael Löwy, *Redemption and Utopia: Jewish Libertarian Thought in Central Europe* (Stanford: Stanford University Press, 1992), p. 207.

p. 110, "challenging and directing those very same forces. . . . Now is the time": McGraw, *Self Matters*, pp. 252–253.

p. 111, among "the most important ideologists of revolutionary messianism" in the twentieth century: Löwy, *Redemption and Utopia*, p. 18.

p. 112, "Probably not, because that isn't what he wanted": www .etstechnologies.com.

7. Choice

p. 114, "the right tactics for 'getting on'": Asa Briggs, *Victorian People* (Chicago: University of Chicago Press, 1972), p. 119.

p. 115, "without reference to the opinions of his predecessors": *Mill's Essays on Literature and Society*, ed. J. B. Schneewind (New York: Macmillan, 1965), p. 255.

p. 115, "what would you choose?": McGraw, *Self Matters*, p. 28.

p. 115, "to maximize your quality of life": McGraw, *Self Matters*, p. 253.

p. 116, "peership with God": Peck, *Road*, p. 305.

p. 116, "Progress depends on individuals who are innovators, who reject convention": Dyer, *Zones*, p. 152.

p. 116, "ought to be viewed as a victimizer": Dyer, *Strings*, p. xvii.

p. 117, "every part of human nature which stands out prominently": Mill, *On Liberty*, p. 65.

p. 117, "she needs a man to shelter and protect her": Pipher, *Reviving Ophelia*, p. 175.

p. 117, "to be handled within the family, usually at the father's discretion": Forward, *Toxic Parents*, p. 96.

p. 117, "a real obstacle to the fulfillment by the State of its duties": Mill, *On Liberty*, p. 97.

p. 118, "basis of [his] philosophy of life": Mill, *Autobiography*, p. 92.

p. 118, "He who does anything because it is the custom . . . has no need of any other faculty than . . . imitation": Mill, *On Liberty*, pp. 55–56.

p. 118, "convinced yourself that conforming was essential to your very survival": McGraw, *Self Matters*, p. 131.

p. 118, "the popular and tenacious forces of conformity": Rubin, *Compassion*, p. 246.

p. 119, "what you have been programmed to believe that you are 'supposed' to be and do": McGraw, *Self Matters*, p. 31.

p. 119, "doing as you're told, with no courage for your own life": Campbell as cited in Borysenko, *GUILT*, p. 157.

p. 119, "the tendency of the inward forces which make it a living thing": Mill, *On Liberty*, p. 56.

p. 119, we are not done developing after our emergence from childhood: Sheehy, *Passages*, p. 18.

p. 119, "without the constant attention of doctors, psychiatrists, and faith healers": Lasch, *Narcissism*, p. 359.

p. 120, This is the story McGraw tells ad infinitum: McGraw, *Self Matters*, pp. 64, 72, 119, 130, 132.

p. 120, "you are real. Let the world know it": McMahon, *Portable Therapist*, p. 139.

p. 120, "even sheep are not undistinguishably alike": Mill, *On Liberty*, p. 64.

p. 120, "except for what is customary": Mill, *On Liberty*, p. 58.

p. 120, "it is what I was doing yesterday?": McGraw, *Life Strategies*, p. 14.

p. 121, "everything in your life that you can identify as having been . . . adopted out of tradition or history": McGraw, *Life Strategies*, p. 42.

p. 121, "go through their sheep motions": *Zones*, pp. 152–153.

p. 122, "the factors that shaped us are moot": Kaminer, *Farther Reaches*, p. 14.

p. 123, "in which selves create, exercise choice, take responsibility, and develop unpredictably": Gary Saul Morson, "Prosaic Bakhtin," *Common Knowledge*, Spring 1993, p. 54.

p. 123, "if we do not have the necessary qualifications for making that choice": McMahon, *Portable Therapist*, p. 29.

p. 123, "the supreme act is the act of choice": Reich, *Greening*, p. 354.

p. 123, "you can walk away whenever you choose to let go": McMahon, *Portable Therapist*, p. 87.

p. 124, "The sense of being trapped is an illusion": Beattie, *Letting Go*, pp. 146–147.

p. 124, ten variants of "choose" and "choice": McGraw, *Self Matters*, p. 58.

p. 124, In a single paragraph of Rubin's *Self-Hate and Compassion*, I count fourteen: p. 179.

p. 124, "by choosing to make it a pleasant, exciting procedure": Dyer, *Zones*, p. 16.

p. 124, "people even choose things like tumors": Dyer, *Zones*, p. 19.

p. 124, "Just like Oprah, you have to help you": McGraw, *Self Matters*, pp. 9, 11. Sic.

p. 124, "put the whole thing out of [their] mind": Gilman, *Herland*, p. 71.

p. 125, "'few of us choose to listen to the call'": Peck, *Road*, p. 300.

p. 125, "to choose between an image of total freedom and an image of total determinism": Murdoch, *Existentialists and Mystics*, p. 328.

p. 125, "*your life is at stake*": Richardson, *Take Time*, p. 25. Emphasis in the original.

p. 125, "in the same automatic, choiceless way as the heart beats": Rubin, *Compassion*, p. 22.

p. 126, "complex enough to do justice to what we really are": Murdoch, *Existentialists and Mystics*, pp. 343–344.

p. 126, "You didn't choose to be born, but the reality is that you're here": Ringer, *Looking Out*, p. 15.

p. 126, "All of the choosing was done for you": McGraw, *Self Matters*, p. 93.

p. 127, "his own need to choose" a religion: Frank Kermode, *The Age of Shakespeare* (New York: Modern Library, 2004), p. 18.

p. 128, "you have to know what options are available, and you have to check them out": Simon and Olds, *Helping Your Child*, pp. 25–26.

p. 129, "without consideration of what you truly want": McGraw, *Self Matters*, p. 61.

p. 130, "acting a part they find neither humane nor wise": Sissela Bok, *Moral Choice in Public and Private Life* (New York: Vintage, 1978), p. 238.

p. 130, "for the great majority of patients . . . stringent adherence to honesty": Bok, *Moral Choice*, pp. 252, 254.

p. 132, "if we choose to have Self-Esteem, than [sic] we have control over ourselves" : McMahon, *Portable Therapist*, p. 49.

p. 132, "The highest forms of love are inevitably totally free choices and not acts of conformity": Peck, *Road*, p. 139.

p. 132, "We do not have to love. We choose to love": Peck, *Road*, p. 83.

8. Morality

p. 133, "the Judeo-Christian morality which up to now has characterized the history of Western civilization": Herbert Marcuse, *Five Lectures: Psychoanalysis, Politics, and Utopia* (Boston: Beacon, 1970), p. 65.

p. 134, "those needs which are a product of a person's authentic self, and those which are imposed from the outside by society": Reich, *Greening*, p. 81.

p. 134, "a fictional substitute that was defined from the outside in": McGraw, *Self Matters*, p. 7.

p. 135, "moral talker and moral experiencer": Laing, *Politics of Experience*, p. 37.

p. 136, "*Treat yourself at least as well as you treat other people!*": Rubin, *Compassion*, p. 140. Emphasis in original.

p. 136, "basic to . . . many religious and moral traditions": Bok, *Moral Choice*, pp. 98, 30–31.

p. 136, "polarizing issues into absolutely good and absolutely bad categories": Rubin, *Compassion*, p. 125.

p. 136, "suddenly realize that they have it in their power to do whatever they want": Peck, *Road*, p. 303.

p. 137, "because you want to, and for no other reason": Dyer, *Zones*, p. 120.

p. 137, "I can do anything I want, but what I want is determined by my awareness": McKay and Fanning, *Self-Esteem*, p. 134.

p. 137, "*ipso facto*, wrong": Joseph Epstein, *Envy* (New York: Oxford University Press, 2003), p. 4.

p. 137, "the best and wisest were ready to give help": Gilman, *Herland*, p. 115.

p. 137, shield the client or patient or reader from the world's cruelty. Many a self-help book reproduces in its own way the religion of Herland, with its nebulous concept of "an immense Loving Power working steadily out through [us], toward good." Gilman, *Herland*, p. 115.

p. 137, "Who tried to tell you what you should be thinking and feeling?": Taubman, *Ending the Struggle*, p. 49.

p. 138, "We waste a tremendous amount of our power judging others": Gray, *Get What You Want*, p. 235.

p. 138, "the boundaries of what you are willing to accept from life": McGraw, *Self Matters*, p. 233.

p. 138, "the folly of shoulds, musts, and oughts": Dyer, *Zones*, p. 148.

p. 139, "whether it is effective or ineffective in the pursuit of legitimate goals": Dyer, *Strings*, pp. 209–210.

p. 139, "Forget concepts of right and wrong": McKay and Fanning, *Self-Esteem*, p. 116.

p. 139, "We invariably relate better to other people when we relate better to ourselves": Rubin, *Compassion*, p. 17.

p. 139, "on your way to a deeply confident sense of self": Taubman, *Ending the Struggle*, p. 139.

p. 139, "how wondrous and interesting you can be": Ibid.

p. 140, "Thou shalt work in order to live happily": Morris, *News*, p. 68.

p. 140, a great "Clearing of Misery": Morris, *News*, p. 56.

p. 141, the mother who dare not tell Jill not to eat all the cherries: Rubin, *Compassion*, p. 27.

p. 141, "pediatricians—like myself": cited in Gross, *The Psychological Society*, pp. 268–269.

p. 141, "there is no reality; only perception": McGraw, *Life Strategies*, ch. 7.

p. 142, "The outrage is because I honor and value and love life": Bass and Davis, *Courage*, p. 455.

p. 142, "You are a good and nice person, but have a hard time saying no to others": Gray, *Get What You Want*, p. 259.

p. 142, "that will be quite good enough": Taubman, *Ending the Struggle*, p. 17.

p. 143, "every thing would appear to man as it is, infinite": cited in Borysenko, *GUILT*, p. 148; also in Ferguson, *Conspiracy*, p. 98.

p. 143, "as though they were commandments etched in stone": McGraw, *Life Strategies*, p. 163.

p. 144, "or break rules simply because you see fit to do so": Dyer, *Zones*, p. 139.

p. 144, "everything that up until now you may have treated with habitual and automatic resistance": McGraw, *Life Strategies*, p. 265. As is his manner, McGraw simply states in red a standard principle of pop psychology. Thirty years before, Charles Reich proclaimed that a person of advanced consciousness "should be constantly open to new experience, constantly ready to have his old ways of thinking changed" (*Greening*, p. 262).

p. 145, "such creativity that society would not know where to turn": Laing, *Politics of Experience*, pp. 45–46.

p. 145, "to suspend good judgment": McGraw, *Life Strategies*, p. 81.

p. 145, a self-murderer, a suicide": Trilling, *Sincerity and Authenticity*, p. 131. In Goethe's *The Sorrows of Young Werther*, suicide is indeed the preservation of authenticity. Both in art and in life this novel was imitated. Leslie Fiedler points out that the hero of the first novel written in the United States commits suicide "with that tearful story open on the table beside him." *End to Innocence*, p. 186.

p. 145, "not in a selfish way, but in a confident way": McGraw, *Self Matters*, p. 10.

p. 146, "'Could it get any better than this?'": McGraw, *Self Matters*, p. 36.

p. 147, "whenever we have feelings of self-contempt generally": Rubin, *Compassion*, p. 21.

p. 147, "the little murders we inflict on ourselves on a daily basis": Rubin, *Compassion*, p. 75.

p. 147, "the real, true, genuine sum and substance of who you are": McGraw, *Self Matters*, p. 29.

p. 148, "in order to acquire the purity of the victim": Starobinski, *Jean-Jacques Rousseau*, p. 250.

p. 148, "You have participated in a devastating conspiracy, with you as the unwitting fall guy": McGraw, *Self Matters*, p. 61.

p. 149, "everyone, every moral being, that is every human being": Murdoch, *Metaphysics*, p. 216.

p. 150, "we texture the detail of our moral surround and steer our life of action": Murdoch, *Metaphysics*, p. 260.

p. 150, "the various qualities and grades between good and bad, 'seep' through our moment-to-moment experiences": Murdoch, *Metaphysics*, p. 265.

p. 150, "the unique and profound presence and importance of a moral sense": Murdoch, *Metaphysics*, p. 297.

p. 150, "possibilities of fruitful and virtuous action": Murdoch, *Metaphysics*, p. 322. Dickens might well have agreed, his cast of characters including so many shackled with their own mind-forged manacles, as Miss Wade uses her imagination against herself.

p. 151, "the only kind of mature marriage that is healthy and not seriously destructive to the spiritual health and growth of the individual partners": Peck, *Road*, p. 93n.

9. Self-transformation

p. 152, sailors at sea engaged in the rebuilding of their own ship: Frederick Will, *Induction and Justification: An Investigation of Cartesian Procedure in the Philosophy of Knowledge* (Ithaca: Cornell University Press, 1974).

p. 153, "you are a different person now from the one who started this book": McGraw, *Self Matters*, p. 262.

p. 153, "fast, fast, fast": McGraw, *Life Strategies*, p. 23.

p. 153, "remaking ourselves from the inside out by some sort of therapeutic program": Stewart Justman, *Seeds of Mortality* (Chicago: Ivan R. Dee, 2003), p. 44.

p. 153, and post them on their refrigerator: Potter-Efron and Potter-Efron, *Shame*, p. 115.

p. 154, "radical new spheres of elected existence": Robert M. Adams, *The Roman Stamp: Frame and Façade in Some Forms of Neo-Classicism* (Berkeley: University of California Press, 1974), p. 7.

p. 155, "visible only to those he encounters": Hannah Arendt, *The Human Condition* (Chicago: University of Chicago Press, 1958), pp. 179–180.

p. 155, a generation was arriving at Consciousness III by conversion: Reich, *Greening*, p. 223.

p. 155, "design a new life": Richardson, *Take Time*, p. 2.

p. 155, "Has anybody noticed over the last fifty years that this crap doesn't work?": McGraw, *Life Strategies*, p. 290.

p. 156, "they have it in their power to do whatever they want": Peck, *Road*, p. 303.

p. 156, "the fact that life is difficult no longer matters": Peck, *Road*, p. 15.

p. 156, exorcisms where the devil is thrown out on the spot: reported in M. Scott Peck, *People of the Lie* (New York: Simon & Schuster, 1983).

p. 157, "as new modes of outlook and new desires come into being": Murdoch, *Metaphysics*, p. 330.

p. 158, "officially acknowledged the entire tradition of utopian thinking as its predecessor": Gary Saul Morson and Caryl Emerson, *Mikhail Bakhtin: Creation of a Prosaics* (Stanford: Stanford University Press, 1990), p. 398.

p. 158, the tension of a drawn bow: Erich Auerbach, *Mimesis*, tr. Willard Trask (Princeton: Princeton University Press, 1953), ch. 1.

p. 160, "the first of Shakespeare's great soliloquies": Kermode, *Age of Shakespeare*, p. 90.

p. 161, "Karenin 'would forget what he did not wish to remember'": Robert Alter, *Salmagundi*, Fall 1985–Winter 1986, p. 96.

10. Literature Rewritten

p. 163, "his own interests and his own self": Robert Garis, *The Dickens Theatre* (Oxford: Clarendon Press, 1965), pp. 211–212.

p. 164, "she drowns in a stream filled with flowers": Pipher, *Reviving Ophelia*, p. 20.

p. 165, "to learn that he had chosen to believe in himself": Sheldon Kopp, cited in Dyer, *Strings*, p. 18.

11. Constructing Stories

p. 170, "its marvelous inner growth as well as outer perfection": Gilman, *Herland*, p. 90.

p. 171, "so really awed": Gilman, *Herland*, p. 72.

p. 171, "how they applied the principles of *The 7 Habits of Highly Effective People* to these challenges, and the remarkable things that resulted": Covey, *7 Habits*, p. xvii.

p. 171, "I'm going to show you exactly, precisely why and how . . . have been robbed from you": McGraw, *Self Matters*, pp. 15, 21.

p. 172, "never tell anyone what has happened, or what is happening, to them": Forward, *Toxic Parents*, p. 147.

p. 172, "horrendous human acts are . . . always the outgrowths of self-hating, overwhelming, castigating consciences": Rubin, *Compassion*, p. 138.

p. 172, "the truth is that the average American citizen does not have a real friend in the world": Maslow, *Farther Reaches*, p. 219. Maslow was president of the American Psychological Association 1967–1968.

p. 173, Adolf Eichmann did what he did because his father wounded his self-esteem. See, e.g., Steinem, *Revolution*, p. 76.

p. 173, Assume parents "toxic": Forward, *Toxic Parents*.

p. 173, "filled with . . . creativity, wisdom, love, joy, enthusiasm, and contentment," which we proceed to forget: Borysenko, GUILT, p. 66.

p. 173, "She hears her mother's disdain. She feels defective": Potter-Efron and Potter-Efron, *Shame*, p. 9.

p. 174, "our duties, responsibilities, and roles too often assume control of us": Borysenko, GUILT, p. 1.

p. 175, "There had been more of what was good in life and more of life itself": translation by Louise and Aylmer Maude, revised by Michael Katz. See *Tolstoy's Short Fiction* (New York: Norton, 1991). For this and other works of literature, I omit page references.

p. 176, "the ordinary fundamental sense of contingency and accident which belongs with the concept of the individual": Murdoch, *Metaphysics*, p. 214.

p. 177, "Each event figures in many possible sequences even though only one sequence is realized": Gary Saul Morson, *Hidden in Plain View: Narrative and Creative Potentials in 'War and Peace'* (Stanford: Stanford University Press, 1987), p. 183.

p. 177, we each write the story of our life, right down to the bed we will die in, in early childhood: cited in Gross, *The Psychological Society*, p. 287.

p. 177, that conventional narrative closure "may falsify the truth": Frank Kermode, *Pieces of My Mind: Essays and Criticism, 1958–2002* (New York: Farrar, Straus & Giroux, 2003), p. 70.

p. 178, "drove carpools, and even practiced soccer with them": Buchholz and Buchholz, *Live Longer*, p. 289.

p. 178, "Today is my first priority": Buchholz and Buchholz, *Live Longer*, p. 292.

p. 179, "a forty-four-year-old man who, as it turned out, was terrified of growing old": Rubin, *Compassion*, p. 113.

p. 179, "became a magazine editor, and married a successful publisher": Peck, *Road*, pp. 35–36.

p. 180, "The doctors were unable to save her or our unborn child": Covey, *7 Habits*, p. 18.

p. 180, "You can't really argue against them": Covey, *7 Habits*, p. xviii.

p. 181, "Let go of all guilt—it is not yours": McMahon, *Portable Therapist*, p. 147.

p. 181, "suffocating, gagging": Bass and Davis, *Courage*, p. 447.

p. 182, "All we have to do is connect with it": Bass and Davis, *Courage*, p. 452.

p. 182, "It was the first book I'd ever read cover to cover. *The 7 Habits* was the second": Covey, *7 Habits*, p. 24.

p. 182, "universal, timeless, and self-evident principles": Covey, *7 Habits*, p. xviii.

p. 183, "priests, prophets, preachers, judges, leaders, patriarchal fathers, and so forth": Bakhtin, *Speech Genres*, p. 132.

p. 183, "The world has attacked your authenticity": McGraw, *Self Matters*, p. 210.

p. 183, "Seek help": McMahon, *Portable Therapist*, p. 121.

p. 184, "she had turned a hobby into a full-time fun job, and was making a very nice income": Dyer, *Strings*, p. 249.

p. 185, making it impossible for the reader to share the absoluteness of the author's judgment of this woman: see my discussion of this work in *Seeds of Mortality*.

p. 186, "practice of subtle, sensitive moral inference, the kind that most choices in daily life require of us": Booth, *The Company We Keep*, p. 287.

p. 186, the first step toward emancipation from the power of self-hatred: Rubin, *Compassion*, p. 141.

p. 188, "when she thought about his being happy in his new marriage, she felt resentful": Gray, *Get What You Want*, p. 248.

p. 188, intimate knowledge about their characters that both Tolstoy and James, among other authors, withhold out of respect for those characters: George Steiner, *On Difficulty and Other Essays* (New York: Oxford University Press, 1978), p. 133.

p. 190, "their parents continue to invade, manipulate, and frequently dominate their lives": Forward, *Toxic Parents*, p. 50.

p. 191, "Psychic and political health, it seems, could be achieved by breaking the pentameter": James Longenbach, *Modern Poetry After Modernism* (New York: Oxford University Press, 1997), p. 5.

p. 192, permanently cured of her promiscuity: Peck, *Road*, p. 171.

p. 192, "Once this woman reclaimed her authentic self, it was as if floodgates had opened": McGraw, *Self Matters*, p. 150.

p. 192, "exploded the cork and the repressed feelings flooded out": Schutz, *Joy*, p. 89. "Breaking Out": Schutz, *Joy*, p. 169.

12. Liberal Guilt

A version of this chapter appeared in *Salmagundi*, Summer 2004.

p. 194, guilt "can be thought of as an evil circle: a snake with its tail in its mouth": McMahon, *Portable Therapist*, p. 26.

p. 195, "a thing distinct from philanthropy, from affection for God or man, and from self-interest in this world or in the next": Mill in Schneewind, p. 262.

p. 196, "one of the commonest—yet most powerful—emotions that rule our lives": "Plain Talk About Feelings of Guilt."

p. 197, "I didn't whip those slaves into their compulsions": Donoghue, *Beauty*, p. 6.

p. 199, "lives on the potential and possible": Karl Mannheim, *Essays on Sociology and Social Psychology* (London: Routledge & Kegan Paul, 1953), p. 106.

p. 199, "the implicit dogma of American liberalism" was that a person of liberal views was incapable of being wrong: Fiedler, *An End to Innocence*, p. 8.

p. 200, "An evil conscience cannot flee from itself; it has no place to which it may go; it pursues itself": cited in Hannah Arendt, *Love and Saint Augustine* (Chicago: University of Chicago Press, 1996), p. 84.

p. 201, a passage that ends with an allusion to Macbeth's bloody hands. See Donoghue, *Beauty*, ch. 5.

p. 202, "treat the spasms like some irrational holdover from our childhood training": Charles Taylor, *Sources of the Self* (Cambridge, Mass.: Harvard University Press, 1989), p. 164.

p. 202, "so that they can be *worked on*": Taylor, *Sources of the Self*, p. 159.

p. 204, "the 'higher liberal,' that is, a liberal without goals, [is] possible only in Russia": *The Devils*, tr. Michael R. Katz (Oxford: Oxford University Press, 1992, p. 33.

p. 204, his only program being the lack of one. And his special treatment by the French authorities suggestive of the relationship that Stepan Trofimovich in *The Devils* has with his patroness.

p. 205, "the best course of morality that was ever written": Catalogue of the Library of Thomas Jefferson, Vol. IV (Washington: Library of Congress, 1955), p. 447.

p. 205, rings with echoes of *A Sentimental Journey*: Andrew Burstein, *The Inner Jefferson: Portrait of a Grieving Optimist* (Charlottesville: University of Virginia Press, 1995), p. 101.

p. 205, "acknowledging it's fault and making a just reparation.": Catalogue of the Library of Jefferson, Vol. IV, p, 447.

p. 206, "promote his own welfare and happiness": Anonymous, cited in R. S. Crane, "Suggestions toward a Genealogy of the 'Man of Feeling,'" ELH 1 (1934), p. 206.

p. 210, the transformation of a force that acts on the self as powerfully and intimately as guilt: cf. my discussion of guilt in ch. 3 of *Seeds of Mortality*.

p. 211, "adequate to deal with this pain and humiliation, curiosity about alternatives": Richard Rorty, *Contingency, Irony, and Solidarity* (Cambridge, England: Cambridge University Press, 1989), p. 198.

p. 212, a third party to human experience: See Stewart Justman, "Direct and Indirect Guilt in *Little Dorrit, Soundings*, Spring–Summer 2002.

p. 213, "they were sent into exile while he stayed on at Yasnaya Polyana [his estate]": Henry Troyat, *Tolstoy*, tr. Nancy Amphoux (Garden City, N.Y.: Doubleday, 1967), p. 647.

13. Epilogue: Distinctions and Boundaries

p. 215, "We are not second-class citizens," declares Melody Beattie in the name of her readers: Beattie, *Letting Go*, p. 155.

p. 216, "the commands of an implacable slave master": Rubin, *Compassion*, p. 83.

p. 216, "proposes to abolish . . . involuntary servitude": Reich, *Greening*, p. 356.

p. 216, "just as fully and really as a runaway slave might have in the pre–Civil War period": Ferguson, *Conspiracy*, pp. 103–104.

p. 216, "anything we feel we have to lie about": Schaef, *Co-Dependence*, p. 21.

p. 216, discovered seventy-three addictions: Buscaglia, *Living*, p. 98.

p. 216, 96 percent of the American population are co-dependents: Sharon Wegscheider-Cruse, cited in Schaef, *Co-Dependence*, p. 14. "I'm not OK" experiences: Gross, *The Psychological Society*, p. 287.

p. 217, "a manifestation of the disease process": Schaef, *Co-Dependence*, p. 21.

p. 217, "the sacred disease": Peck, *Further*, p. 150.

p. 217, science and religion are on the way to becoming the same thing: Peck, *Road*, pp. 227–228.

p. 217, "private holocaust": e.g., Forward, *Toxic Parents*, p. 121.

p. 217, most mental-health professionals are themselves untreated co-dependents: Schaef, *Co-Dependence*, e.g., p. 4.

p. 217, "accepted or rejected without recriminations of any kind": Rubin, *Compassion*, p. 154.

p. 218, "You have a right to become the person you were destined to become": David Viscott, *How to Live with Another Person* (1974), cited in Rosen, *Psychobabble*, p. 48.

p. 218, "If I'm not yet certain . . . right to allow ourselves to feel and learn from our anger": Beattie, *Letting Go*, pp. 62, 80, 202.

p. 218, "You have to be willing to claim your right to uniqueness": McGraw, *Life Strategies*, p. 269.

p. 218, "the right to enjoy the commonplace": Rubin, *Compassion,* p. 163.

p. 218, "It is who we were intended to be": Beattie, *Letting Go*, p. 286.

p. 219, "wearing themselves out in pursuit of a self that is not their own": Reich, *Greening*, p. 278.

p. 219, "And there is a Plan and a Place for us": Beattie, *Letting Go*, p. 66.

p. 219, "to live by universal and self-evident principles": Covey, *7 Habits*, p. xvii.

p. 219, "Life is a series of problems . . . a single stepping-stone toward the entrance to the Kingdom of God": Peck, *Road*, pp. 15, 311.

p. 219, "we must look forward to Consciousness IV, V, VI, and so forth": Reich, *Greening*, p. 363.

p. 220, a more cosmic Fourth Psychology: Gross, *The Psychological Society*, p. 310.

p. 221, "if the wants of Men are innumerable, then what ought to supply them has no bounds": Bernard Mandeville, *The Fable of the Bees* (Harmondsworth, England: Penguin, 1989), p. 137. Originally published in 1714.

p. 221, "then it *is* important and you have a right to ask for it": McKay and Fanning, *Self-Esteem*, p. 161.

p. 222, "a link to the future, a consequence: the child": Starobinski, *Jean-Jacques Rousseau*, pp. 231–232.

p. 223, "He did his best to live up to . . . one who had never suffered": Starobinski, *Blessings in Disguise*, p. 134.

p. 223, "If you feel as if you are being manipulated by forces outside yourself, then you are a victim": Dyer, *Strings*, p. 3.

p. 223, "unquestionably ubiquitous in our culture": Dyer, *Strings*, p. 2.

p. 223, "whiners, interrupters, arguers, braggarts, con artists, bores, [and] similar victimizers": Dyer, *Strings*, p. 164.

p. 223, "a worthy, important human being": Dyer, *Strings*, p. 31.

p. 223, "the one exception from an otherwise universal malady": Starobinski, *Blessings in Disguise*, p. 144.

p. 224, "I was repeating things that Carl Jung and William James and others had said long before me": Peck, *Further*, p. 175; cf. p. 155.

p. 224, "the vaguest prescriptions about how to live in an actual society": Robert Bellah, Richard Madsen, William Sullivan, Ann Swidler, and Steven Tipton, *Habits of the Heart: Individualism and Commitment in American Life* (Berkeley: University of California Press, 1985), p. 81.

p. 225, "You are always a worthy, important human being . . . You are worthy not because others say so": Dyer, *Strings*, pp. 31–32.

p. 225, "There are no self-help manuals": Peck, *Further*, p. 13.

p. 225, "is generally threadbare": Frank E. Manuel and Fritzie P. Manuel, *Utopian Thought in the Western World* (Cambridge, Mass: Harvard University Press, 1979), p. 811.

Index

A NOTE ON THE AUTHOR

Winner of the PEN Award for the Art of the Essay for his book *Seeds of Mortality*, Stewart Justman is professor of Liberal Studies at the University of Montana. Born in New York City, he studied at Columbia University and since the 1970s has lived in Missoula, Montana. He has also written *The Springs of Liberty* and *The Psychological Mystique*. He is married with two children.